Ordnance
The
Lake District
Landranger Guidebook

How to use this Guide

Pre-planning:
First look at the KEY MAP section – this shows the area covered, the towns and villages and the starting point for 12 Walks and 10 Tours. If you are unfamiliar with the area, look up some of the towns and villages in the PLACES OF INTEREST section. The WALKS or TOURS will provide further local information. The introductions will give you a feeling for the history, landscape and wildlife of the area.

On the Spot:
From your chosen base, explore the area by road or on foot. Stars after a place name indicate that it is featured in the PLACES OF INTEREST section (this is necessary as it is not possible to include every village and town because of space limitations). Some 28 places of interest are accompanied by maps to enable you to plan a short stroll. The scale of these is 2½ INCHES to 1 MILE (see CONVENTIONAL SIGNS for rights of way etc).

Landranger Maps:
These are the natural companion to the Guide. Places of interest are identified first with the number of the Landranger Map on which it appears (sometimes more than one). This is followed by two letters indicating the National Grid Square and by a 4-figure reference number. To locate any place or feature referred to on the relevant Landranger map, first read the two figures along the north or south edges of the map, then the two figures along the east or west edges. Trace the lines adjacent to each of the two sets of figures across the map face, and the point where they intersect will be the south-west corner of the grid square in which the place or feature lies.

Acknowledgements

We would like to thank those individuals and organisations who helped in the preparation of this book: Eddie Hibberd of the Ramblers' Association; Carol Ash at the National Park Office, Brockhole and Peter Battrick at the National Trust North-West Regional Office. Pat Morris wrote the Natural History section and Guil Winchester the all-important Gazetteer. Stan Morse provided the artwork; Elizabeth Battrick, the photograph of Beatrix Potter; The Wordsworth Trust, the portrait of the poet as a young man; The Sutcliffe Gallery, Whitby, the photograph of John Ruskin and Penguin Books the illustration of Jemima Puddleduck. The Forum provided the car for the tours.

Ordnance Survey   ISBN 0-319-00144-X
Jarrold Publishing ISBN 0-7117-0568-2

First published 1988 by Ordnance Survey and Jarrold Publishing
Reprinted 1991

Ordnance Survey   Jarrold Publishing
Romsey Road   Barrack Street
Maybush   Norwich NR3 1TR
Southampton SO9 4DH

Printed in Great Britain by Jarrold Printing, Norwich. 2/91

Contents

KEY MAP INDEX

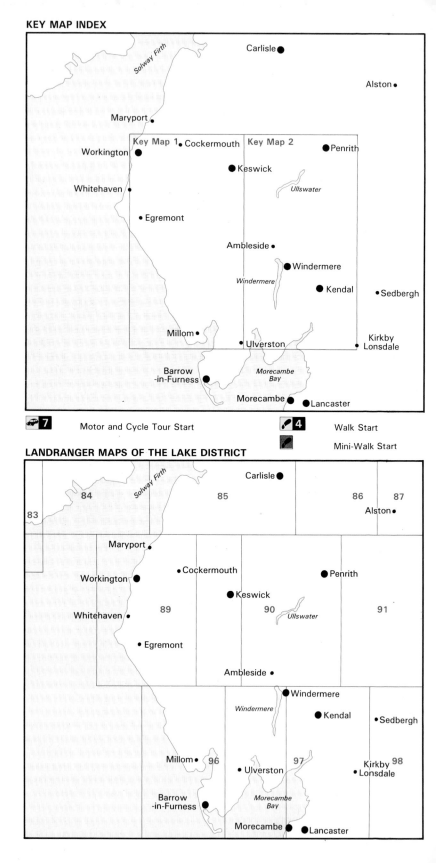

Solway Firth

Carlisle ●

Alston ●

Maryport ●

Key Map 1 ● Cockermouth

Key Map 2

Penrith ●

Workington ●

Keswick ●

Ullswater

Whitehaven ●

● Egremont

Ambleside ●

Windermere ●

Windermere

Kendal ●

● Sedbergh

Millom ●

Ulverston ●

Kirkby Lonsdale ●

Barrow -in-Furness ●

Morecambe Bay

Morecambe ●

Lancaster ●

🚗7   Motor and Cycle Tour Start   🥾4   Walk Start

👣   Mini-Walk Start

LANDRANGER MAPS OF THE LAKE DISTRICT

84

Solway Firth

Carlisle ●

85

86

87

Alston ●

83

Maryport ●

● Cockermouth

Penrith ●

Workington ●

Keswick ●

89

90

Ullswater

91

Whitehaven ●

● Egremont

Ambleside ●

Windermere ●

Windermere

Kendal ●

● Sedbergh

Millom ●

96

Ulverston ●

97

Kirkby 98 Lonsdale ●

Barrow -in-Furness ●

Morecambe Bay

Morecambe ●

Lancaster ●

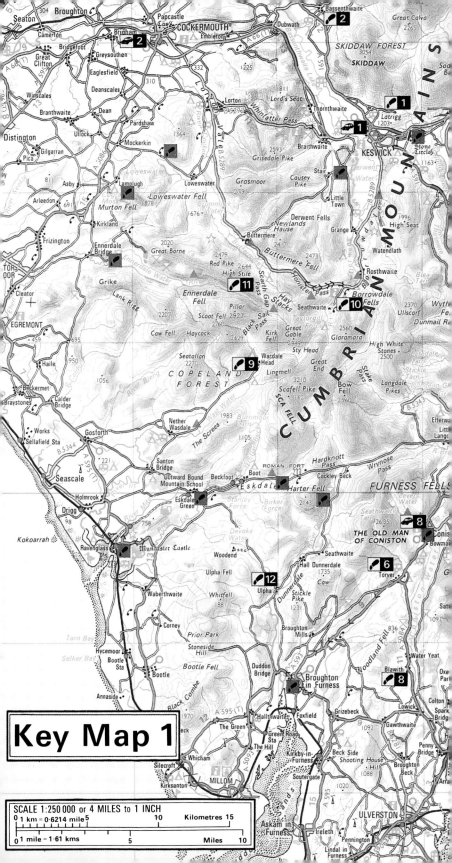

Key Map 1

SCALE 1:250 000 or 4 MILES TO 1 INCH

0 1 km = 0·6214 mile   5   10   Kilometres 15

0 1 mile = 1·61 kms   5   Miles   10

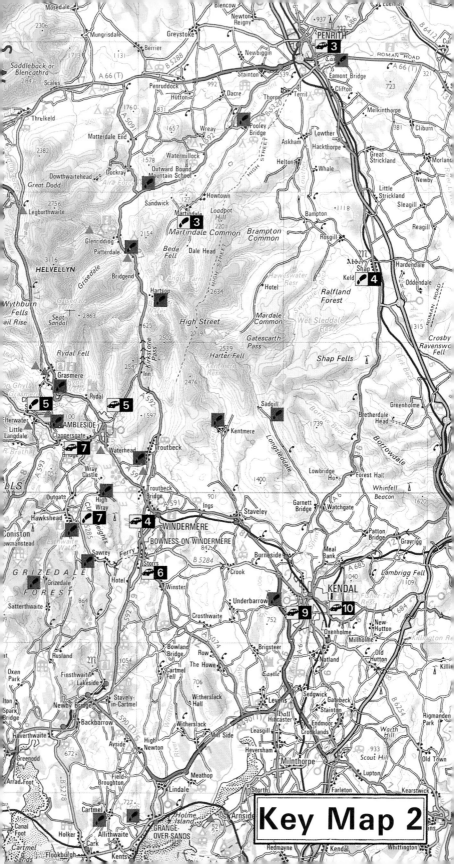

Key Map 2

Introduction
The Lakes

Generations of schoolchildren have looked at the images of Lakeland which decorate the boxes of pencils made at Keswick and escaped – in their imagination, and perhaps only fleetingly – from the confines of the classroom to the freedom of the Lakes. Four out of every five people in Britain live in towns, and more of them 'escape' to the Lake District than to any of the other National Parks.

What is special about the Lakes? William Wordsworth, who was born and lived in Lakeland, wrote in his 1822 Guide: 'I do not know any tract of country in which in so narrow a compass, may be found an equal variety in the influences of light and shadow upon the sublime or beautiful features of landscape....'
But what is it which gives the Lake District its unique scale and variety? The answer

Derwent Water

Wordsworth

'To me the meanest flower that blows can give
Thoughts that do often lie too deep for tears'.
William Wordsworth (1770-1850) was one of the greatest poets in the language. During his long life, he experienced every kind of change: the French Revolution, the Industrial Revolution and the Napoleonic Wars. It is possible to chart the change in Wordsworth during those years, from the fierce republican and innovative poet he was as a young man, to the elderly Poet Laureate who embraced orthodoxy in all things. It was a life with many tragedies in which he was always supported by his sister Dorothy:
　'She gave me eyes, she gave me ears;
　And tender cares, and delicate fears;
　A heart, the fountain of sweet tears;
　And love, and thought, and joy'.
It is a pity he tends to be remembered only for Daffodils – fine poem though it is – because there is so much more to his work. Born in the Lake District and spending much of his life there, the Lakes were both an inspiration

and a symbol for Wordsworth; the beauty and melancholy of the place were the man. In Intimations of Immortality *he wrote:*
'Though nothing can bring back the hour
Of splendour in the grass, of glory in the flower
We will grieve not, rather find Strength in what remains behind'.

Dunnerdale Forest

lies at its centre, just as graphite mined at Seathwaite lies at the centre of a Lakeland pencil. And the answer is also rock.

The beauty of a landscape – like the beauty of a human face – begins with the underlying structure. Three main types of basic rock go to make up the structure of Lakeland, with a fourth around the perimeter. To describe it in this way involves considerable simplification of the highly complex geology of the area, but three main types can be discerned, each creating its own distinct landscape. The oldest rocks are the Skiddaw slates, typical of the northern fells. These were formed between 500 and 600 million years ago from silt and mud deposited at the bottom of a vast ocean. These hard rocks, buckled by shifting continents and smoothed by water and ice, form the distinctive landscape of the northern fells like Saddleback and Skiddaw itself, from which they take their name.

The Skiddaw slates are some of the oldest rocks in Europe, but time has not mellowed them. The thin covering of soil – like skin stretched taut over an athlete's muscle – lends a quality of arrogant

Early Man

Back in time
200,000 years
(Palaeolithic)
Before the last ice age, Britain formed part of the European land mass. Neanderthal hunters probably penetrated as far north as the Lakes, though the most northerly recorded evidence is from North Wales. Traces of this earliest occupation could yet be found deep within the numerous caves found in the areas of carboniferous limestone fringing the Lake District.

24,000 – 13,000 years
The Lake District was again covered by glaciers, covering all but the highest peaks and extending to the adjacent plains. Except inside caves, all traces of earlier occupation will have been scoured away by the ice. Sea level dropped to at least 180 ft below its present height. Man was absent not only from Britain but all of northern Europe – this corresponds to the era of cave art in Southern France and explains its absence from northern regions.

13,000 - 10,000 years
The glaciers retreated and permanent ice disappeared from even the highest ground. Birch rapidly established itself as the dominant plant species and Man returned to the plains not far to the south. The Elk killed by hunters at Poulton-le-Fylde can be seen in the Harris Museum at Preston. From 11,000 to 10,000 years ago, a colder period set in and Man probably retreated southwards.

10,000 - 7,000 years
(End of Palaeolithic – Mesolithic)
The climate became slightly warmer than today and hunters returned to the Lake District valleys – flint implements from the Kirkhead Cave near Grange-over-Sands can be seen in Lancaster Museum. The sea rose rapidly to its present level by 8000 years ago, inundating most evidence for human occupation on the more fertile coastal plains. Submerged forests visible when there are exceptionally low tides are part of this vanished landscape.

Folly Bridge in Borrowdale

nudity to the northern fells. Skiddaw looms above Keswick like the menacing bicep of a buried Titan.

The dramatic scenery of central Lakeland is volcanic in origin. Over a period of some 100 million years molten lava forced its way up through the muds, and great volcanoes rose from the ocean floor. The rocks formed during this period proved resistant to erosion and are known as the Borrowdale volcanics. Not only Borrowdale, but also Sca Fell, the Langdale Pikes, the Old Man of Coniston, Helvellyn and all the soaring crags and ridges of central Lakeland had their origin during this period.

7000 - 5000 years
By 7000 years ago, hunters and fishers were established on the west coast of Cumbria, from Walney Island in the south to St Bees Head in the north. The concentration of food resources in places such as the estuary of the Esk at Ravenglass was an important factor in bringing about the transition from nomadic to settled communities.

5000 - 4000 years
(Neolithic)
The coastal plains and lowlands were gradually and permanently cleared of much of the forest by settled agricultural communities. The stone axe heads used for forest clearance (and now in many local museums) came from the central fells of the Lake District and were widely traded over northern England. The Henges at Mayburgh and King Arthur's Round Table, both south of Penrith, and the larger stone circles such as Swinside and Long Meg and Her Daughters are impressive monuments to the increasing social organisation of these peoples.

4000 - 3000 years
(Bronze Age)
The population continued to expand and by 3000 years ago pastoral communities – seasonally at least – had moved up onto the lower fells of the Lake District. Many cairns and enclosures found up to about 300 yds outer diameter are of this period, as are most of the smaller stone circles.

3000 - 2000 years
(Bronze Age/Iron Age)
The thousand years before the Roman Conquest saw a climatic deterioration and retreat from the uplands, which became reafforested until the late Roman period. In the lowlands a slightly rising sea level also caused abandonment of some low-lying areas, and trackways such as that at Stakes Moss in the Lyth Valley were built across wetter land. Around and within the Lake District, many enclosed settlements with hut circles probably date from this time.
(These dates are approximate and are generally in radiocarbon years, slightly longer than calendar years).

The Poets of Lakeland

Wordsworth acted like a magnet which attracted many of his leading literary contemporaries to the Lakes. Although his closest friends – Coleridge and Southey – became known with him as the 'Lakeland Poets', and all drew inspiration from the landscape, the only true 'poet of place' was Wordsworth.

Samuel Taylor Coleridge (1772-1834) was drawn to the Lakes by Wordsworth's friendship, a support he badly needed as brandy and opium took their toll on his powerful intellect. He wrote little poetry about the Lakes, perhaps the most important writing coming from his time there was his account of the ascent of Sca Fell – a classic of mountaineering literature. 'From whatever place I write you will expect that part of my travels will consist of excursions in my own mind.'

Robert Southey (1774-1843) was Coleridge's brother-in-law and Poet Laureate. Little read now (except unknowingly – he wrote 'The Three Bears') and lampooned at the time for abandoning his early beliefs for the sake of material success, he was less of a poet than Wordsworth and Coleridge, yet he loved the Lakes: 'Show me a man who cares no more for one place than another, and I will show you in that same person one who loves nothing but himself.'

Wast Water

The third basic rock type of the Lake District underlies the more gentle wooded landscape around Windermere and Coniston, which stretches east to Kendal and Kirkby Lonsdale. These rocks were formed beneath the sea during the Silurian period about 400 million years ago. Like the Skiddaw slates, the Silurian rocks were built up from deposits eroded from far-away mountains and carried into the sea by rivers.

Although it is possible, and convenient, to distinguish the three broad categories of rock and the present-day landscapes which they have created, it is important not to forget the immense physical changes which the rock strata have undergone since they were first laid down. Over aeons of time, the earth's crust has been buckled and sheared, ground and faulted. In its endless birth contortions the Lake District's belly has heaved up and sunk down again several times. At one point, molten granite filled-in underneath the heaving mountains; at another, sunk below a warm sea, marine organisms deposited their skeletal remains to form the limestone which now circles the Lake District and forms the Pennines further east. It was, finally, from a great, many-layered dome that the forces of erosion created the Lake District we know today.

Different writers have employed a variety of metaphors to explain the physical structure of Lakeland. Wordsworth's 'cartwheel' is still the best way to think of the lakes themselves: like spokes radiat-

The Ferry at Lakeside

ing from a hub. Norman Nicholson accounts for the rings of rock – older in the middle, newer around the edge – by describing the erosion of the original dome-shape, as 'slicing off the top of an onion'. But it is in his unforgettable description of the principal agent of erosion that Norman Nicholson shows himself to be one of the most powerful Lakeland writers since Wordsworth: 'It has been said that when God made England His finger touched but did not press, but that is not true of Cumberland and Westmorland. He pressed there all right. What is more, He used His nails. And the nails were ice.'

The Lake District as we know it today is the creation of the ice. Over a period of hundreds of thousands of years – sometimes receding, sometimes advancing – it was ice which carved Wordsworth's cartwheel of lakes. It was ice which engineered the spectacular waterfalls like Aira Force and Scale Force. It was ice which gouged out the basins which were to become the lakes – so efficient was this excavation that the bottom of Wast Water is some sixty feet lower than the level of the Irish Sea. Finally, it was ice which filled the lakes when it melted having choked the natural outlets with the rock debris it once carried.

A glacier moves across the landscape like a giant rasp: it carries with it splintered and broken rock which bites into the base rock like teeth under the immense weight of the ice. And when the temperature becomes warmer – as it did not later than 10,000 years ago – it drops all the rock it has carried with it. Some of these glacial erratics are immense – like the Bowder Stone in Borrowdale. But more typical is the Honister Pass connecting Buttermere and Borrowdale. This is a terrifying landscape which gives some idea of the destructive power of ice. It is as if the glacier has only just melted – which in geological terms, of course, it has – and rocks of every size are scattered everywhere in appalling chaos.

Since the passing of the ice, it has become again a landscape of stone and water: the sound of them together is Lakeland's pulse. Stone and water are at the heart of Lakeland's beauty; and to understand them, is to understand the place.

Unfortunately, the water we enjoy with launches and sailing boats in Windermere, and marvel at crashing on to the rocks at Aira Force; the water which turns the wheel of the bobbin mill and fills every secret valley with its own music, was once rain. It is an inescapable fact that moist air (cloud), blowing on to the land from the sea, is forced to rise over the fells of Lakeland. The higher the cloud climbs, the colder it becomes, and this drop in temperature reduces the capacity of the air to hold water. The resulting precipitation is uncomfortable and can be dangerous in certain conditions if proper protective clothing is not worn: even casual walkers should go prepared. The hardiest walker of them all, William Wordsworth, died after taking a chill because he went out in the rain without a hat.

The Lake District as a whole does not have significantly more rainy days than London. But there is considerable local variation, and when it does rain in the Lakes it tends to rain hard and long. To compensate for this there are the incomparable skies and sunsets of Lakeland, the beauties of its plant and animal life, as

Alfred, Lord Tennyson

At a time when mid and late Victorian art, architecture and literature are the subject of renewed interest, it is sad that Tennyson (1809-1892) the poet who dominated the age, has been rather neglected. As a result, it is still possible to find nicely-bound editions of his collected works at reasonable prices and anyone not acquainted with his poetry will not regret reading 'In Memoriam' or 'Idylls of the King'. Tennyson visited friends at Mirehouse, on Bassenthwaite, which is now open to the public. In the surrounding countryside he found the haunting imagery he needed for Morte d'Arthur:
... King Arthur's sword, Excalibur

Wrought by the lonely maiden of the Lake
Nine years she wrought it, sitting in the deeps,
Upon the hidden bases of the hills

well as the lakes and rivers themselves. Steaming anoraks and cold noses are soon forgotten at the sight of a rainbow vaulting across a leaden sky.

Water is the female principle in the eternal partnership that is Lakeland: rock is the male. A visitor with no knowledge of its history or geology cannot escape Man's use of his rich inheritance. Often a newly-surfaced road bringing tourists to the Lakes will be green with the crushed stone mined near Coniston where it has lain since it settled as dust from one of the great marine volcanoes. Travelling around Lakeland a kind of colour code emerges. In a rough and ready way this is true even of the towns: the predominant colour of Kendal is pale grey; Cockermouth, when not rendered, is dark grey; Penrith tends to be pink and Keswick green-grey.

St John's in the Vale, near Keswick

The earliest visible evidence of Man is also built in stone. The Lake District is rich in megaliths, but none can compare with Castlerigg above Keswick. Surrounded on all sides by mountains, it is as if each upright stone partakes of something of the distant peak behind it. Castlerigg is as moving as a cathedral at midday jostled by other tourists: solitary visitors, or those coming to it at sunset, may reconsider their scepticism concerning the beliefs of Early Man.

Successive peoples have worked Lakeland's most abundant raw material, leaving large and small stone relics of their tenancy: Bronze Age cairns at Devoke Water; the Roman Fort at Hardknott; the Norse crosses at Gosforth; the Norman castle at Kendal and the priory church at Cartmel; and all the houses – great and simple – in which Lakelanders have lived for the last thousand years.

The stone walls of the Lake District are the feature which first strikes many visitors to the area. Built during the eighteenth and nineteenth centuries, when labour was cheap, they have almost become part of the natural landscape – in doing so they make a very important point. Since the passing of the ice, Man has had more impact on the landscape of the Lakes than any other agent.

In understanding Man's impact on the Lake District many of the clues are, again, stone: it has been as important to the structure of human settlement in Lakeland as to the structure of the land itself. The stone walls date from the period

Coniston Water

The weir below Newby Bridge, south of Windermere

when farming the native Herdwick sheep was the dominant industry. Many of the walls enclose crazy, inaccessible pastures, but they are less indicative of megalomania than the increasing poverty of the land which drove the farmers higher and higher into the fells. Sheep lay the land bare to erosion and extract the life-giving minerals from the soil until only bracken can survive. Bracken is very beautiful, but it is not the natural covering of the fells: it is the spectacular winding sheet of dead land.

Man brought the sheep, and before that he cleared the forest which once covered the land. The stone axes which he used were worked from grey-green volcanic rock. So efficient were these tools that not

Kirkstone Pass

only was Lakeland stripped of its forests but as early as 5,000 years ago Neolithic entrepreneurs were exporting Lake District stone axes as far afield as Hamp-shire and Ireland. The most common place name-ending in the Lake District is 'thwaite' – it is not surprising that it means 'clearing'.

The early axe producers were the first to exploit the mineral wealth of the region, but many came after them. During the reign of Elizabeth I, German miners were brought to the Lake District to improve mining techniques. The pattern of human settlement in Lakeland was greatly influenced by the treasure buried in its tortured rock strata. Iron was first mined in the fells before richer deposits were found around Egremont and to the south at Millom. The coal deposits of the coast had been exploited for 2000 years and led to the heavy industrialisation of the eastern and southern fingers of the Lake District. No one has described these places better than the poet Norman Nicholson who was born, and lived all his life, in Millom.

Copper was mined around Coniston from the earliest times and the green slate associated with it is a prized building material. The granite of Shap and Threlkeld has long provided British cities with road surfacing and mottled red kerbstones. Eskdale granite comes in many different colours and was once transported on the narrow gauge 'Ratty Railway' which visitors can still enjoy.

The broad gauge railways of Lakeland followed the national pattern. Iron tendrils which pushed right into the heart of the Lakes at the height of Britain's industrialisation have now retracted or disappeared. Industrialisation created the

The Vikings

Spring came as a mixed blessing to the Anglo-Saxons and scattered Celtic communities who lived in Cumbria in the eighth and early ninth centuries. The warm weather and favourable winds brought shiploads of marauding pagan pirates across the North Sea. These were the Vikings – a name that in translation probably means 'frequenters of the sea-creeks and inlets'.

The Lake District was attacked by Viking ships from Norway who had sailed round the north of Scotland. For a time the rich summer plunder of Christian monasteries and productive Saxon farms and villages was enough. But gradually boats wintered, and sporadic raiding became an organised invasion and then settlement.

By the tenth century, Norse settlement in England was mainly confined to the north-west counties of Cumbria and Lancashire. Many villages in the area still bear their Scandinavian settlement names.

John Ruskin

John Ruskin (1819-1900) was a prophetic figure whose writings on artistic, moral and social matters deeply influenced the Victorians. In the volumes of Modern Painters *(1843-60) he championed the work of Turner, England's greatest painter of Romantic landscape, while* The Seven Lamps of Architecture *(1849) and* The Stones of Venice *(1851-3) gave impetus to the Neo-Gothic movement in architecture. It was also largely thanks to Ruskin that the Pre-Raphaelite painters became respectable, although – ironically – it was the Pre-Raphaelite John Millais who eloped with Ruskin's wife and became a party to the scandalous divorce case that ensued.*

Distressed by the ugliness and poverty created by nineteenth-century industrial society, Ruskin emerged in the 1860s as a trenchant social critic. In addition to his writings, many of them now directed at working-class readers, he launched several schemes of social improvement, most notoriously the Guild of St George, an unsuccessful utopian community. Ruskin spent most of his fortune on these and other philanthropic activities, including the revival of the hand-made linen industry in Langdale.

Long an admirer of the Lake District, he helped a needy friend in 1871 by purchasing a delapidated house on Coniston Water without even inspecting it beforehand. The house, Brantwood, became Ruskin's home for the rest of his life. Though his later years were clouded by intermittent attacks of insanity, he worked to the end, writing a classic autobiography, Praeterita. *His association with the Lakes is commemorated at Brantwood and also by the Ruskin Museum at Coniston.*

wealth and the iron (much of it Cumberland iron) for the railways: it also created a new class who used the railways to escape briefly from the new towns. The age of the tourist had come.

It must have seemed a terrible irony to Wordsworth that the railways which brought the invading tourists were constructed with minerals mined out of the bowels of Lakeland itself, and that he had written one of the most popular guides for tourists. Afterwards he was to write 'is there no nook of English ground secure from rash assault?'

It was a new age. Wordsworth and some of his more reactionary contemporaries can be forgiven for not understanding that all people – especially those living in industrialised towns – have a need to see and enjoy the natural landscape. They can be forgiven because, ultimately, the concerns of the nineteenth-century conservationists led to the creation of the National Parks which today help preserve the Lake District, and the other national parks, for everyone.

Crummock Water

The Character of the Lakes

Canon Rawnsley (left), Vicar of Crosthwaite, near Keswick, was instrumental in the preservation of the character of the Lake District. He was one of the founders of the National Trust, and Beatrix Potter (right), who lived at Near Sawrey, was one of the first to leave land to the Trust in her will. She and Canon Rawnsley are pictured with her father

Bassenthwaite Lake lies under the brooding bulk of Skiddaw. But it takes its personality from the trees, soft green pastures and low hills of its other banks, which make Bassenthwaite a peaceful, rather gentle place.

Buttermere and **Crummock Water** were once one large lake, separated over thousands of years by silt and rock debris. People have always compared the two lakes, they are so close, yet so different, like the two opposing brothers of so many ancient myths. Although the mountains surrounding Buttermere are mostly higher and include High Stile and Red Pike – down which tumbles Sour Milk Gill – its wooded slopes are more friendly and somehow more human in scale than its sibling. The lake was the setting of the all too human story of the *'Beauty of Buttermere'*.

Crummock Water is equally beautiful, but it is less welcoming and can be almost alien. Its steep-sided mountains fall sheer into the water under hump-backed Mellbreak. In winter Crummock can become like an enclosed, dark sea; the rain-carrying wind whipping the surface into short, spiteful waves.

Coniston can also have it savage moods, although it lies in the tamer country of southern Lakeland. Donald Campbell lost his life while attempting to break the world waterspeed record in 1967 as a result of one of Coniston's notorious changes of mood. The prosaic explanation for these sudden changes is its long thin shape and north-south orientation, which can exaggerate the effects of a shift in wind direction. All the lakes, not only Coniston, should be treated with respect by people sailing or swimming.

Derwent Water boasts one of the most famous views in Lakeland. Looking down the lake from Friar's Crag on the east shore, visitors can see the peaks of High Seat, the Borrowdale Fells and Sca Fell beyond. With its wooded islands and variety of natural features, Derwent Water is among the most beautiful of all the lakes.

Ennerdale Water is probably the least visited of all the lakes. But the peacefulness of this remote place has a special quality which has more to it than the absence of tourists. In the village churchyard Wordsworth was inspired to write: 'The thought of death sits easy on the man, Who has been born and dies among the Lakes'.

Ambleside

Haweswater is in fact a giant reservoir, with the drowned village of Mardale lost forever below the water. The scenery around Haweswater, particularly at the dale-head, is desolate and beautiful but the lake itself is unmistakably man-made.

Loweswater means 'leafy lake'. Only a mile long, Loweswater is both friendly and secluded, which makes it a favourite place for picnickers and lovers.

Rydal Water is the smallest of all the lakes. Its many beautiful features, it daffodils and bluebells in the spring, and its

Jemima Puddleduck, one of Beatrix Potter's memorable characters inspired by Lakeland

many connections with Wordsworth, make Rydal an essential part of any visit to the Lakes.

Thirlmere is certainly worth a detour when travelling on the A591 between Keswick and Grasmere. But although Thirlmere is carefully landscaped and manicured, it is a beautiful reservoir and not a lake.

Ullswater combines all the features which make Lakeland scenery beautiful. Its scale, the dramatic effects of light on the water, and the infinite variety of views from its shores and the fells around, make Ullswater the most 'complete' lake. Anyone unfortunate enough to be able to visit only one of the Lake District's lakes would do well to choose Ullswater, with its wonderful pattern of oak meadows, steep fells, dense woodland and rocky shores.

Wast Water is the deepest and most awesome of all the lakes. The rich hillocky country, set with ageing oaks, through which most travellers approach Wast Water does little to prepare them for its fierce beauty and desolation. If Milton's Satan had been able to choose his own landscape he would have chosen Wast Water.

Windermere is a place of steamers and pleasure boats. Man's hand is visible everywhere, but nothing detracts from the serenity of its soft wooded shores which remain beautiful throughout the seasons.

Natural History of the Lake District

The core of the Lake District is a dome of old hard rocks from which a number of valleys fan out in a radial pattern like the spokes of a wheel. During the Ice Ages an ice cap formed on the centre of the dome and glaciers radiated outwards down its flanks. They gouged out the valleys, giving them a U-shaped cross section, and frequently dumped moraines across the ends as they retreated. Many of these valleys then filled with water to generate the familiar Lakeland landscape of today: rounded hills with long narrow lakes in the valleys.

All the lakes are about the same age, roughly 10,000 years old (corresponding to the end of the last Ice Age) but this does not mean that they are all the same. Their present differences stem from details of their underwater topography and also from the surrounding human activity. In turn, the physical differences between the lakes govern many aspects of their wildlife interest.

The ten largest lakes range from Wast Water, which is cold and clear, and where the hard bare rocks plunge down to the edge of the water; to Esthwaite Water, which lies in a wide, green valley surrounded by fertile farmland, and whose relatively shallow water becomes quite warm in summer and full of algae. In two valleys a barrier has formed across the middle to create two lakes. Derwent Water and Bassenthwaite Lake drain north to the west of Skiddaw; while Buttermere and Crummock Water both lie in the next valley to the west and drain via the River Cocker to the River Derwent at Cockermouth.

The lakes vary greatly in area and depth: Windermere is the largest in area (6 sq. miles) but Wast Water is the deepest (maximum 260ft); Esthwaite and Buttermere are both less than half a square mile in area, but the former is only 51 ft deep at its deepest point whereas Buttermere goes down to 92 ft. The relationship of area to depth makes a considerable difference to the conditions in a lake. Shallow lakes of large area can be easily stirred up by the wind, but it takes a much stronger wind to mix the water of a deep lake right down to the bottom. Mixing is important because oxygen (which almost all living plants and animals need) can only enter the water from the air across the surface or from the activity of plants growing in the light near the surface of

Wast Water

the water. Mixing carries oxygen down to the lower layers of water and also brings up nutrients which the plants need from the bottom. Nutrients accumulate at the bottom of lakes as dead plants and animals decompose.

Cold water holds more oxygen than warm water. This means that deep lakes nearly always have some oxygen present in their bottom water, which remains cold throughout the year. In shallow lakes the bottom water may become quite warm in summer. This, combined with the fact that decomposition removes oxygen from the water more rapidly when it is warm, often results in a complete lack of oxygen at the bottom of the lake for part of the year. Mixing in the autumn gales is vital, as it replenishes the oxygen throughout the depth of the lake.

Because the rocks of the Lake District are very insoluble, the water entering the lakes contains very low concentrations of the chemicals which algae need to grow (unless they are artificially increased by sewage or fertiliser run off from farmland). So, compared with lakes in many other places, those of the Lake District are quite unproductive. But again, there is considerable variation between them. Professor Pearsall – who studied the Lake District lakes in the 1930s – recognised that the differences in productivity between the lakes were associated with the shape and fertility of the valley in which each lies. Professor Pearsall arranged the lakes in a series. This ranged from those with rocky shores and uncultivated catchments (such as Wast Water in which only 5% of the catchment area is suitable for

cultivation and 73% of the lake shore is rocky) to those with soft shores and a good deal of cultivation in the surrounding land (such as Esthwaite in whose catchment 45% of the land is suitable for agriculture and only 12% of whose shoreline is rocky).

Since the 1930s the differences between the lakes have been increased, because settlement, tourist development and agricultural improvement have proceeded apace. This is particularly true in the catchments with a higher proportion of flat, cultivable land. Development alongside the lakes inevitably results in pollution or nutrient enrichment, which alters the nature of the finely-balanced communities of plankton. This in turn affects the fish, birds and other wildlife.

Since 1935 scientific research on the lakes has been conducted by the Freshwater Biological Association whose world-famous laboratory is situated on the western shore of Windermere at the Ferry Landing. Windermere is the largest of the lakes. The dimensions of the lake basin and its catchment area disguise the fact that the long narrow lake actually lies in two basins. Windermere's basins are separated by a stretch of relatively shallow water less than 15 ft deep and by several islands, including Belle Isle near the ferry which crosses at the narrowest point. The north basin is 211 ft deep at the deepest point and – although the temperature of the surface water rises to 18-20°C in summer – the water at the bottom of the lake remains at 5-7°C all the year round. The lake only freezes over in exceptional years: there has been skating on Windermere in 1895, 1929 and 1963.

Windermere is among the more prod-uctive of the lakes. This is because its waters contain sufficient dissolved nutrients to support the growth of algae and plankton, and the complex food chains which they in turn support. It is fed at the north end by the Rivers Rothay and Brathay. The former has already passed through the smaller lakes of Grasmere and Rydal Water, both of which are relatively shallow and productive. Nevertheless, the natural concentrations of nitrogen and phosphorus in Windermere are low compared with those of some lakes in the British Isles despite the fact that they are augmented by the effluent of a sewage works which drains into the north basin. Nutrients are always present in sufficient quantity to support the growth of algae in the water. These are most abundant in the spring. In lakes such as Wast Water and Ennerdale Water – which have extremely low concentrations of nutrients – the water always looks clear. But even these lakes grow some algae in the spring and summer. In all the lakes, algae provide food for a great variety of small animals which in turn are the food for larger creatures, including fish.

Salmonid fish that are native to Britain, such as salmon and brown trout, prefer cold clean waters. Coarse fish, such as roach, are found in warmer, richer waters. The Lake District lakes span the range of these conditions, and most of them contain both sport (salmonid) fish and some coarse fish. Brown trout are the most common fish throughout the lakes and rivers of Lakeland. The deepest and coldest lakes – Wast Water and Ennerdale – have only trout and char; while Esthwaite Water, the most productive, also contains pike, perch, rudd and roach, but no char. A few salmon enter Lake District rivers to spawn and pass through the lakes en route, but they are less common than once they were.

Char are closely related to the salmon and trout, and like many species of that family there are both migratory and land-locked populations. They are very variable in form, but the species is distinguished by the brilliant white front edges of the fins. In the spawning season, the edges of the fins and the belly of the char turn blood red. Lake forms tend to be smaller than the migratory fish which feed in the sea. Populations of char are found in large, clear lakes all round the Northern Hemisphere as far south as the Alps. They occur in eight of the larger Lake District lakes, where they feed on small planktonic animals as well as insect larvae and molluscs. When large, char may be cannibalistic on their own young.

In Windermere there are two populations of char with different spawning times. One group spawn in shallow (3-15ft) water during November-December while the others spawn in much deeper water (45-65 ft) in the spring. The second type lay their eggs on a narrow tongue of gravel near the mouth of an inflowing stream, which presumably keeps it free of mud. In both cases the eggs are laid in a redd in the gravel and are covered over after fertilisation. There are small structural differences between the fish of the two populations and there has been some speculation over whether or not they constitute evidence that the one species might be evolving into two in the 10,000 years since the ice retreated and left lakes habitable for fish. However, artificial cross fertilisation still produces fertile progeny which shows that they are still technically the same species.

The char spend most of their time in deep water where fishermen catch them using a method known as 'plumbline' angling which is peculiar to the Lake District. A short stout rod with a bell on top is projected over each side of the boat. Each carries about 75 ft of line weighted at the bottom. To this main line, six side lines are attached at about 12 ft intervals. The hook on each line has a small shiny metal spinner which whirls in the water as the boat is rowed slowly along. When a fish is caught, the bell rings and the line is lifted in. The char used to be made into a paste and sold in shallow, round china pots with colourful pictures of the fish on the lid. These pots are now collectors items.

Fish also provide food for diving birds such as cormorants and goosanders. The shallow, productive lakes tend to have more ducks on them, especially around their margins. In the winter, visitors such as the goldeneye may be seen, but generally they do not breed here. The goosander has been gradually spreading south from Scotland, and first bred in the Lake District in the 1950s.

In addition to the ten large lakes, the Lake District contains innumerable small ones, called tarns. The most famous is Tarn Hows but there are hundreds of others. These too owe their existence to the action of ice. Many of them lie in corries at the heads of the valleys. Here the ice has gouged out a deep, bowl shaped hollow below towering walls of rock and in many cases deepened the water it can hold by depositing a moraine on the open side. Sometimes the outflow stream has cut down through the moraine and either drained the tarn completely or left it with only the depth accommodated by the rock basin. Other tarns have formed in dips and hollows scoured by the ice in otherwise flatter areas of rock. Many of these are quite shallow and rich in aquatic plants.

Plants grow most abundantly along

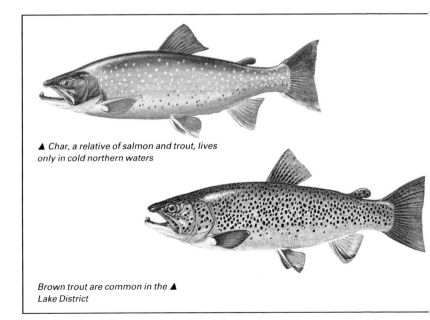

▲ Char, a relative of salmon and trout, lives only in cold northern waters

Brown trout are common in the ▲ Lake District

sheltered shores and bays, and they harbour a rich community of insects. Some of these insects, like water beetles and water boatmen, spend their entire lives in the water. Others, such as caddisflies and mayflies, are larvae which will leave the water as flying insects when they are mature. Many of these species form the familiar clouds of midges and mayflies that dance in the evening sunlight over the rocks and lakeside plants. Most of them do not bite humans; indeed many cannot feed at all and die within a day or two. They emerge from the water for one purpose only, to mate and lay eggs. The eggs are placed or fall back into the water and from them the next generation will develop. Dragonflies and their smaller cousins the damselflies are also conspicuous as adult insects, but the young stages of life history (called nymphs) live in water among plants. The beautiful Demoiselle Agrion damselfly – with bottle green body and dusky wings – reaches its northern limit of distribution here.

The high rainfall and hard rocks of the central fells ensure that innumerable streams tumble down the hills towards the valley floors. In the highest reaches of these streams the water moves so fast that it can carry with it all but the largest stones and boulders. This is a dangerous place for animals to live. They must either hide under the stones or cling closely to their surfaces. Although most of the water is moving very rapidly, just above

Dunnerdale Forest

the stones there is a thin layer of water – the boundary layer – which is moving much more slowly. Many stream insects, such as stoneflies, have flattened bodies which allow them to crouch within this layer.

Despite the difficulties of living in fast-flowing water, it does have several advantages for those able to do so. The water is cold, which enables it to hold a lot of oxygen, and it carries a continuous stream of particles which provides food for many stream dwellers. Blackfly larvae

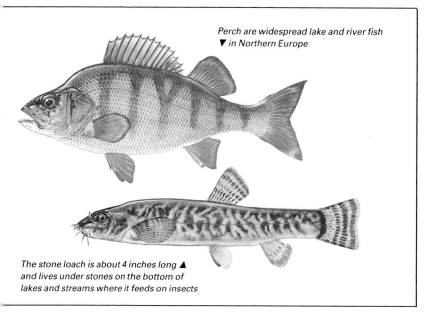

Perch are widespread lake and river fish
▼ in Northern Europe

The stone loach is about 4 inches long ▲
and lives under stones on the bottom of
lakes and streams where it feeds on insects

Sca Fell Pike above Wast Water

are typical inhabitants of such streams. They look like small caterpillars which are stuck end-on to the stones. In fact, they have hooks at one end which hold them in place as they raise their heads and extend their antennae out into the current. In this way they sieve the water for tiny crumbs of edible material.

Most of the particles suspended in the stream water are derived from material which has fallen into the stream from the surrounding vegetation, rather than from plants which have grown in the stream itself. Not many plants can keep a hold against the tug and turbulence of the water. Mosses and microscopic algae cling to the stones. But because the water does not contain many chemicals they cannot grow very abundantly, and the animals need material from outside the stream to supplement the available food. In turn, the insects of these mountain streams themselves provide food for carnivorous young trout. Adult trout move upstream from the lakes and rivers in the breeding season to lay their eggs on the stony bed of fast moving streams. When the young hatch they space themselves out in the current facing upstream, looking for food either drifting down with the water from further upstream, or scuttling incautiously among the stones. The insects also provide food for the dipper, that characteristic little bird of upland streams, who bobs up and down on a stone and then dives into the rushing

water to feed. Common sandpipers feed on the insect life of these stony streams and breed along their margins.

Lower down the hill the stream is joined by others and becomes wider and deeper. At the edges and on the bottom the current is reduced, which allows sand and silt to drop out of the water and settle on the bottom. This enables more plants to gain a foothold and different animals to take up residence – including those which burrow in the substrate. There is more food for fish, so other species join the trout and the total population increases.

Eventually the stream joins the river in the bottom of the valley and the water continues towards the sea. By driving over Hardknott Pass and turning down the Duddon Valley, one of the few in which there is no lake, you can follow the whole sequence from mountain beck, through lowland river to the estuary and the sea, all within a few miles.

East of the Duddon estuary lies Morecombe Bay which is internationally renowned for its bird populations. When the tide goes out, miles of mud and sand flats are revealed which provide feeding grounds for millions of birds, particularly waders and wildfowl which migrate to Britain for the winter. There are animals such as ragworms (which can reach densities of more than 4,000 per square yard) buried in the sand which can be found by birds such as curlews, godwits and others with long probing bills. Tiny gastropod molluscs (up to 30,000 per square yard) and the shrimps which get stranded as the tide retreats, have for centuries provided a crop for Man as well as the birds such as shelduck who live there all the year round.

Many birds come to Britain while their feeding grounds in Scandinavia are frozen solid during winter. Others, such as whimbrel and knot, stop off on migration to replenish their fat reserves for the long journey ahead. Many grey plover and knot remain here for the winter. Up to 50,000 knot have been recorded congregating in Morecombe Bay. As the tide rises these, and thousands of other birds, are pushed off the flats on to the sand banks and salt marshes around the perimeter of the Bay where they wait for the tide to go out and expose the mud again.

Further round to the west, the River Esk also drains a lakeless valley to the sea at Ravenglass. Here there are extensive sand dunes whose crests are covered in marram grass. The marram can withstand the constant wind and salt laden spray, and its rhizomes bind the sand and elongate as it accumulates. Further back from the sea the marram gives way to other grasses and a greater variety of flowering plants and mosses which could not withstand the conditions on the foredunes. When protected by the foredunes they gain a foothold and displace the pioneering marram grass. But if the marram is destroyed – as it all too often is by trampling feet – the wind gets in and blows the loose sand back onto the rear dunes thus burying their plant cover and the whole cycle of succession must start again.

The Ravenglass dunes are the summer nesting ground for an enormous colony of black-headed gulls and terns. Nesting on the dunes makes these birds and their offspring very vulnerable to predators such as foxes, and crows and birds of prey in the air. They gain a measure of safety from their number and it is advantageous to nest all at the same time. Those who start too early, or are delayed in their nesting, are much more likely to lose their eggs or chicks. At the height of the nesting season the air above the Ravenglass dunes is filled with swooping birds and the cries of the adults as they search for their mates or their chicks among the crowd.

Further north, in contrast to the low-lying sand dunes of Ravenglass, there are high sandstone cliffs at St Bees Head, near Whitehaven. Although just outside the area covered by this guide, it is a must for visitors whose particular interest is

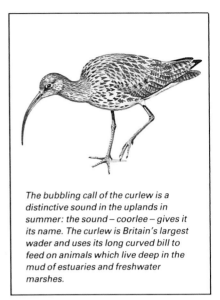

The bubbling call of the curlew is a distinctive sound in the uplands in summer: the sound – coorlee – gives it its name. The curlew is Britain's largest wader and uses its long curved bill to feed on animals which live deep in the mud of estuaries and freshwater marshes.

wildlife. Here there is an RSPB reserve protecting a spectacular colony of nesting sea birds, particularly auks such as guillemots, razorbills, puffins and the only English colony of black guillemots. There are also cliff-nesting birds such as kittiwakes and fulmars who, while they are less vulnerable to predators, look as if they are in constant danger of falling into the sea. Kittiwakes nest on seemingly impossible narrow ledges and their youngsters (usually two) face the cliff as they wait motionless for the parent to come and feed them. One false step would be disastrous until their wings are fully developed and the young kittiwakes can join the adults soaring on the updraughts.

In sheltered hedgerows all along the coastal fringe, visitors may see the hedge brown butterfly. This is a common species further south, but here is near its northern limit in Britain. Similarly the pale yellow brimstone is common here but rare further north. The yellow brimstone butterfly is associated with buckthorn, its larval food plant.

Immediately inland from the coast, the lakeland valleys are separated from each other by the rounded hills whose vegetation has been trimmed and detailed by the activities of Man and his grazing animals for the last 5,000 years or so. Once the ice had gone, the hilltops were almost entirely clothed with broadleaved forest. There is evidence of this in the tree stumps and branches buried beneath blanket peat on some of the highest fells.

A picnic site on the shore of Coniston Water

Today, even at lower altitudes, little of this deciduous forest remains and the hills are covered in grassland. Over the centuries sheep grazing has been the most constant enemy of forest regeneration and this remains so today. When Thirlmere was converted into a reservoir at the turn of the century, the land along its shores was fenced against people, sheep and deer. Within this fence, on the western side, birch, hazel and oak have regenerated in those areas that were not planted with conifers by the Water Authority. Protected from grazing they can grow in very steep and rocky places. It is ironic that a manmade lake has given us a reminder of what the natural forests of the area must once have looked like.

The history of the Lake District woods is recorded in the sediments on the bottom of the lakes and tarns. Pollen preserved in the mud can be identified when extracted from a core of sediment, the older layers lower down, the more recent towards the top. This shows how the tundra vegetation which followed the ice was replaced by deciduous trees and how these have now been largely replaced by grasses.

The woods of High Furness in the southern Lake District are now the largest

Ash trees are characteristic of damp, lime-rich soils. The Vikings made arrows and spears from ash, which has an important place in Norse mythology

Derwent Water in autumn

continuous area of semi-natural woodland in the North of England. The humid sessile oak woods are alive with songbirds in the spring. Pied flycatchers and redstarts are commonly seen. These woods are also home to some of the large species of woodland mammals, which were once much more widespread. They include red deer, roe deer, red squirrels, badgers and foxes. The rare pine marten, which had disappeared altogether, is now coming back in Grizedale forest.

Grizedale is the best place to see deer. The Forestry Commission have provided hides from which they can be watched by the general public. Many deer occur throughout the Furness woods and can be glimpsed, feeding in clearings or under the trees, by those who walk there early in the day. The red deer do not usually form large herds as they do in deer parks or on the Scottish moors but spread out in small groups. The highest numbers are seen near Graythwaite and on Claiffe Heights. There is also a herd on the open fell of Martindale but they are protected from disturbance by the public on a private estate. Rutting takes places in the autumn when the stags can be heard roaring their message of strength and virility across the valleys. The smaller roe deer are more common and widespread than the red deer, but they are much more difficult to see except just after dawn or at dusk when they sometimes emerge from the shelter of the woods to browse. They live singly or in small family groups.

The Lake District was of course the home of Beatrix Potter, the creator of Mrs. Tiggiwinkle the hedgehog and Jeremy Fisher the frog, whose boathouse can still be seen on the shore of Esthwaite Water. Her Squirrel Nutkin is a reminder that not so long ago the common (and only) English squirrel was the pretty red squirrel. Today the Lake District remains one of the strongholds of this species. It only occurs in a few isolated places elsewhere in England, to which the larger immigrant grey squirrel has not yet penetrated. The red squirrel is best adapted to pine forests but survived well in our deciduous woodland while there was no competition. They feed on buds, catkins and insects during the spring but in summer they are often short of food in deciduous woods, while they wait for the nuts and acorns to ripen. Their numbers fluctuate greatly from year to year.

Unfortunately grey squirrels are primarily adapted to living in deciduous

Canal Foot near Ulverston

Tarn Hows

trees and they do better than red squirrels in that habitat. Moreover they are much less reluctant to come down to the ground and exploit food available there. This also means they can survive in situations where the trees are too far apart for them to cross from one to the next through the branches. Red squirrels spend the great majority of their time up in the trees so they need quite extensive areas of continuous woodland to provide enough food to last them all year round. Consequently red squirrels live at lower densities, even in the best places. The

Red deer are twice the size of roe deer and have much larger antlers. Both are increasingly abundant

Dormice have similar requirements to those of the red squirrel and the Furness Woods contain what is probably the most northerly population of this species in Britain. They are strictly nocturnal and very tiny, so there is little hope of them being observed by the casual visitor.

Beyond this forested area, the Lake District hills are almost entirely bare of trees; open grassland, crossed by miles of dry stone walls and dotted with sheep, predominates. Overgrazing has almost completely eliminated heather moorland and the area of bracken, which sheep do not eat, is increasing. The dominant grass on the sheep walks is sheeps fescue but where the grazing is heavy it is sometimes replaced by the much less palatable mat-grass. This does at least provide food for the caterpillars of mountain ringlet, an alpine butterfly which is rare outside the Lake District (except in Scotland). Fortunately sheep also find wild daffodils unpalatable and each spring the lake shores and fields on the valley floors carry an enchanting display of dancing daffodils.

mixture of coniferous woodland planted by the Forestry Commission alongside the remaining deciduous forests in the southern Lake District supports a thriving population of red squirrels, and visitors stand a good chance of seeing this delightful animal if they walk through the woods and watch patiently.

The only really 'natural' vegetation is probably that found above the tree line and beyond the influence of sheep on the high stony ground. Here bilberry is common. Parsley fern and alpine lady's mantle are also characteristic of the Lake

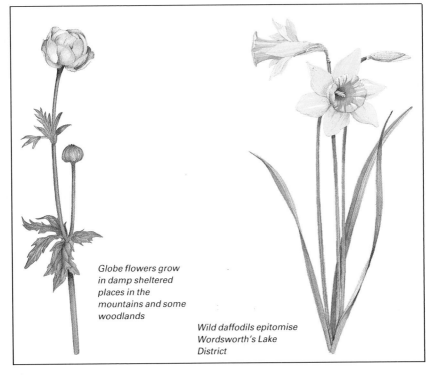

Globe flowers grow in damp sheltered places in the mountains and some woodlands

Wild daffodils epitomise Wordsworth's Lake District

Herdwick Sheep

Grasmere

District's mountain tops. Arctic species like mountain avens and cushions of moss campion do not compete well in places where other vegetation is established. They are found on the open stony areas where few other things can grow. Several mountain specialities are found on dry crags near the top of Helvellyn. Elsewhere, seepage of ground water offers opportunities for different plants, particularly mosses. The Skiddaw slates of the northern mountains yield almost no calcium and the water is acid. The wet patches there support different plant communities to those fed by the more calcareous waters oozing from the Borrowdale Volcanic rocks.

The lower fells are the realm of sheep. Beatrix Potter owned a farm at Far Sawrey (between Windermere and Esthwaite Water) where she kept and bred Herdwicks. Herdwicks are a particularly hardy breed and can remain out on the high hills all winter, protected by their straggly fleece (7 inches long in places). It is thought that they are derived from ancient hairy Norse sheep, a theory supported by genetic analysis which further indicates that they are different from all other British breeds of mountain sheep. The hairiness of the coat helps encourage rain to drip off instead of soaking into the fleece – a useful adaptation in these parts. However, that same feature means that the wool is very coarse for clothing. It also makes it difficult to dye the fleece, which is why it is normally used in its natural colour.

Herdwick lambs are dark. Although they have the run of the open hillsides, they spend their whole life rarely wandering far from their birthplace. This 'hefting instinct' is a valuable aid to survival because they are extremely familiar with their surroundings and always know where to find food, even when visibility is reduced to zero in fog and low cloud. This behaviour also helps the shepherd to find his sheep without having to search widely for them. However, other types of hill sheep offer a better economic return and pure Herdwicks are gradually becoming scarcer.

Beatrix Potter was very anxious that the breed should be preserved and they are in use on many of the farms belonging to the National Trust. The Trust was founded in the Lake District by Beatrix Potter and Canon Rawnsley and is now the largest landowner in the District. The Forestry Commission also owns a good deal of land but in 1935 agreed not to plant in the 300 square miles which constitute the heart of the Lake District.

Besides the sheep, the hilltops are home to many moorland birds. In the summer many species such as golden plover and curlew, which move to the coast and lowlands during winter, return to the hills to nest. The bubbling call of the curlew is one of the most character-

Peregrines are now increasing in numbers, although agricultural chemicals had reduced the total number to only 68 pairs in 1962. They nest on rocky hillsides, laying 3 or 4 eggs. A diving peregrine reaches speeds of 180 mph and is a marvellously efficient predator: its main food is rock doves and pigeons

istic sounds of the moorlands and epitomises the beauty of the wild uplands. Ravens nest on the crags and they too can be heard calling as they scout around for carrion with which to feed their chicks. Ravens are among the few birds that remain on the windswept hills all the year round. Most noteworthy of the Lake District birds is perhaps the Golden Eagle. Its huge size and broad, blunt wings are unmistakable. This magnificent bird became extinct as a breeding bird in England as a result of persecution by game keepers and egg collectors. Recently it has begun to breed again in the Lake District after a 200 year absence. The nesting site is closely-guarded and a well-kept secret.

The Lake District is also home to a wide variety of other birds of prey such as peregrines – now recovering from the devastating effects of pesticides – sparrow hawks and merlins.

West of the Lake District heartland, across the valley of the River Lune, through which the M6 runs, the radial pattern is lost and the hills begin to rise into the flanks of the Pennines. Shap Fell is the highest point on the railway line to Scotland and in the days of steam, two engines were needed to push and pull the trains over the summit 1000 ft above sea level. The arrival of the railway at Bowness-on-Windermere in the nineteenth century heralded the start of the tourist boom in the Lake District. Today the visitors come in their millions by road. The landscape and the wildlife of the Lake District were profoundly influenced by Man long before, but now there is a severe danger that the press of people will destroy the very thing they have come to see, the natural beauty of the region. It is the job of the National Park and other authorities to ensure that this does not happen.

Leisure activities

Useful Names and Addresses

TRANSPORT

Motoring
Automobile Association. Tel: (0228) 48484. Royal Automobile Club. Tel: (06993) 505. National Breakdown Recovery. Tel: (0274) 671299.

Bus, coach, etc.
National Express. Tel: (0228) 48484. Brown's Coaches, Market Place, Ambleside* (Local Tours). (05394) 32205. Silver Badge, Lake Rd, Bowness* (Local Tours) (09662) 3215. Duddon Valley Post Bus, Broughton in Furness* (06576) 220. Ribble Motor Services, Kendal*. Tel: (0539) 33221. Cumberland Motor Services, Tangier St, Whitehaven. Tel: (0946) 63222. Fellrunner Minibus Tours, Penrith* Bus Station (Local Tours). Tel: (0768) 67466. Martindale Post Bus, Crown Sq., Penrith* (0768) 62700. Mountain Goat Minibuses, Victoria St, Windermere* (Local Tours). Tel: (09662) 5161. Grizedale Post Bus, Head Post Office, Ulverston* (0229) 52011. Transport Enquiry Line, Preston. (0772) 263333.

Train
Furness Line: Preston; Lancaster; Carnforth; Silverdale; Arnside*; Grange-over-Sands*; Kents Bank; Cark and Cartmel; Ulverston*; Dalton; Roose; Barrow-in-Furness. Preston Station: (0772) 59439. Lancaster Station: (0524) 32333. Grange-over-Sands* Station: (04484) 2468. Ulverston Station*: (0229) 53219. Barrow-in-Furness Station: (0229) 20805. Lakes Line: Preston; Lancaster; Oxenholme; (Kendal*; Burneside; Staveley; Windermere*;) Penrith*; Carlisle. Oxenholme Station: (0539) 20397. Penrith* Station: (0768) 62466. Carlisle Station: (0228) 44711. West Cumbrian line: Barrow-in-Furness; Askam; Kirkby-in-Furness; Foxfield; Green Road; Millom; Silecroft; Bootle; Ravenglass; Drigg; Seascale; Sellafield; Braystones; Nethertown; St Bees; Corkickle; Whitehaven; Parton; Harrington; Workington; Flimby; Maryport; Aspatria; Wigton; Dalston; Carlisle. Workington Station. Tel: (0900) 2575 Whitehaven Station. Tel: (0946) 2414.

Steamers and Launches
Bowness* Bay Boating Co. Tel: (09662) 3360; (05394) 33187. Windermere* Iron Steamboat Co. Tel: (0448) 31539. Ullswater Navigation and Transit Co. Ltd Tel: (08532) 229; (0539) 21626. Derwentwater* Launch Co. Tel: (07687) 73013. Steam Yacht Gondola, Coniston* Pier. Tel: (0539. 2884).

Leisure Activities

Camping and Caravanning
There are several books listing caravan and camp sites in the UK. Details can be obtained from: The Camping and Caravanning Club, 11 Lower Grosvenor Place, London SW1W OEY. Tel: (01828) 1012. The Caravan Club, East Grinstead House, East Grinstead, West Sussex RH19 1UA. Tel: (0382) 26944.

Canoe hire
Bassenthwaite*: Mr Platt, Peil Wyke Harbour. Coniston*: Coniston Boat Centre Tel: (05394) 41366. Ullswater*: Royal Hotel, Dockray Tel: (08532) 356 Tindals, Glenridding Tel: (08532) 393. Motherby House Activities, Motherby, Penrith.; Tel: (08533) 368 Rookin House Farm, Troutbeck. Tel: (08533) 561.

Cycle hire
Askew Cycles, Kendal*. Tel: (0539) 28057. Harpers Cycles, Penrith*. Tel: (0768) 64475. Treetops, Pooley Bridge*. Tel: (08536) 267. Knotts Hill, Watermillock. Tel: (08536) 328. Windermere* Cycle Centre. Tel: (09662) 4479. The Cumbria Cycle Way is a 250-mile cycle route which avoids the high passes of the central fells. Copies can be obtained from local Information Centres. For further information contact the Cyclists Touring Club, 69 Meadrow, Godalming, Surrey GU7 3HS. Tel: (04868) 7217.

Fishing
North West Water Authority licences must be obtained: these are available from local fishing tackle shops and some Tourist Information Centres.

Most waters also need permits. The main exceptions are: Brothers Water; Coniston Water; Thirlmere; Ullswater; Windermere.

Detailed local information about the best waters for coarse and game fishing can be obtained from the various Angling Associations: Cockermouth Angling Association, 43 Oaktree Cres., Cockermouth* CA13 9HP. Tel: (0900) 826647. Kent (Westmorland) Angling Association, The Hyena, 9 Fountain Brow, Kendal* LA9 4NW. Tel: (0539) 23223. Keswick Angling Association, Springhaven, How Lane, Portinscale, Keswick* CA12 5RS. Tel: (07687) 72703. Windermere and

District Angling Association, 1, Cragwood Cottages, Windermere* LA23 1LQ. Tel: (09662) 5083.

Two books about fishing in the area which are currently available are: *Fishing in the North-West*, published by the North West Water Authority; *Lure of the Lakes* by A.W.C.Berry.

Golf
Cockermouth* Golf Club. Tel: (059681) 223. Grange Fell Golf Club. Tel: (04484) 3180. Kendal* Golf Club. Tel: (0539) 24079. Keswick* Golf Club. Tel: (07687) 72147. Seascale Golf Club. Tel: (0940) 28202. Windermere* Golf Club. Tel: (09662) 3123.

Horse Riding
Bigland Hall County Sports Ltd, Backbarrow*. Tel: (05395) 31361. F.Gilmore, Bassenthwaite*. Tel: (059681) 498. Robin Hood Centre, Bassenthwaite*. Tel: (059681) 296. A.R.Hogg, Greystoke*. Tel: (08533) 561. Holmescales, Kendal*. Tel: (0539) 29388. Keswick* Riding Centre. Tel: (0596) 73804. Trekkers, Milnthorpe. Tel: (04482) 2375. Side Farm, Patterdale*. Tel: (08532) 337. Rookin House Farm, Troutbeck. Tel: (08533) 561. Pennington School, Ulverston*. Tel: (0229) 56521. Claife & Grizedale, Sawrey*. Tel: (09662) 2105. M.J.Jagger, Windermere*. Tel: (09662) 3572. Limefitt Park, Windermere*. Tel: (05394) 32564. Wynlass Beck, Windermere*. Tel: (09662) 3811.

Motor and/or Rowing Boat Hire
Bassenthwaite*: Mr Platt, Peil Wyke Harbour (Rowing boats only). Butter-mere*: Mrs Richardson, Gatesgarth Farm (Rowing boats only). Coniston*: Coniston Boat Centre Tel: (05394) 41366. Crummock Water*: Mrs Beard, Rannerdale Farm (Rowing boats only). Derwent Water*: Keswick Launch Co. Tel: (0596) 72263. Esthwaite Water*: The Boat House, Esthwaite Trout Farm (Rowing boats only). Grasmere*: Mrs Allonby, The Boat House, Grasmere (Rowing boats only). Loweswater*: Scale Hill Hotel (Rowing boats only). Ullswater*: Tindals, Glenridding Tel: (08532) 393; Ullswater Marine Park, Watermillock Tel: (08536) 666. Windermere*: Bowness Bay Boating Tel: (09662) 3360 (Bowness) or (05394) 33187 (Waterhead); Fell Foot Country Park, Windermere (Rowing boats only) Tel: (05395) 31273.

Sailboarding
Performance Marine, Windermere* Marina Tel: (09662) 4232. Westmorland Water Sports, Beech Hill Hotel Tel: (09662) 5756. Glenridding* Sailboard School Tel: (08532) 575; (08534) 516. Bigland Hall County Sports Ltd, Backbarrow*. Tel: (05395) 31361. Ullswater* Marine Park, Watermillock, Tel: (08536) 666. Ullswater* Sailing School, Landends, Watermillock. Tel: (08536) 438.

Sailing Clubs, Schools and Dinghy Hire
Bassenthwaite* Sailing Club. Tel: (059681) 341. Coniston* Boat Centre. Tel: (05394) 41366. Coniston* Sailing Club. Tel: (0966) 41580. Glenridding Sailing School, The Spit, Glenridding*. Tel: (08532) 541; (08536) 601. Ullswater* Sailing School, Landends, Watermillock. Tel: (08536) 438/661. Performance Marine, Windermere* Marina. Tel: (09662) 4232. Windermere Lake Holidays Afloat, Bowness* (dinghies and yachts) Tel: (09662) 3415. Windermere* Yacht Club. Tel: (09662) 3106.

Sports Centres and Indoor Swimming
Cockermouth* Sports Centre. Tel: (0900) 823596. South Lakeland Leisure Centre, Kendal*. Tel: (0539) 29777. Keswick* Spa. Tel: (07687) 72760. Penrith* Swimming Pool. Tel: (0768) 63450. Troutbeck Bridge Pool. Tel: (09662) 3243. Ulverston* Pool. Tel: (0229) 54110.

Walking
The Lake District is unique in that there is free access to the open fell: this is not a legal right but a longstanding custom and should not be abused. In the valley bottom and on the lower slopes of the fells (wherever there are field enclosures) you should keep to the footpaths. Dogs MUST be kept under control.

Fell walking in the Lake District is superb, but the higher areas should be tackled only by fit and experienced walkers. Conditions on the fells should never be underestimated; they are often in sharp contrast to conditions in the valleys, and can quickly change. It is advisable to always take warm and waterproof clothing, a map and compass, sufficient nourishing food, a hot drink, first-aid kit, torch and whistle. Suitable footwear should be worn. Try to obtain a local weather forecast, plan your route carefully and give details of it to someone before leaving, allow plenty of time to finish the walk well before nightfall, and be prepared to modify the route if necessary.

Advice on fell walking can be obtained from the National Park Ranger Service at Brockhole, Windermere, LA23 1LJ (for details about the southern area) and at

Blencathra Centre, Threlkeld, Keswick, CA12 4SG (northern area). Details of guided walks can be obtained from the free newspaper, The Lake District Guardian, obtainable from Tourist Information Centres.

Details of guided walks can be obtained from the free newspaper, The Lake District Guardian, obtainable from Tourist Information Centres.

Water Skiing
Low Wood Ski Centre, Windermere*. Tel: (0966) 33338. Performance Marine, Windermere* Marina. Tel: (09662) 4232.

Youth Hostels
Ambleside* (90) (NY 37-03). Tel: (0966) 32304. Arnside* (97) (SD 45-78). Tel: (0524) 761701. Black Sail (89) NY 19-12). Buttermere* (89) (NY 17-16). Tel: (059685) 245. Cockermouth* (89) (NY 11-29). Tel: (0900) 822561. Coniston* (Coppermines) (96,97) (SD 28-98). Tel: (0966) 41261. Coniston* (Holly How) (96,97) (SD 30-98). Tel: (0966) (41323) Derwent Water* (89,90) (NY 26-20). Tel: (059684) 246. Elterwater* (90) (NY 32-04). Tel: (09667) 245. Ennerdale (89) (NY 14-14). Tel: (0946) 861237. Eskdale (89) (NY 19-01). Tel: (09403) 219. Grasmere* (Butharlyp How) (90) (NY 33-07). Tel: (09665) 316. Grasmere* (Thorney How) (90) (NY 33-08). Tel: (09665) 591. Hawkshead* (90) (SD 35-96). Tel: (09666) 293. Helvellyn* (90) (NY 36-17). Tel: (08532) 269. High Close (90) (NY 33-05). Tel: (09667) 212/313. Honister* (89,90) (NY 22-13). Tel: (059684) 267. Kendal* (97) (SD 51-91). Tel: (0539) 24066. Keswick* (89,90) (NY 26-23). Tel: (07687) 72484. Longthwaite (90) (NY 25-14). Tel: (059684) 257. Patterdale* (90) (NY 39-15). Tel: (08532) 441. Thirlmere* (90) (NY 31-19). Tel: (07687) 73224. Wast Water* (89) (NY 14-04). Tel: (09406) 222. Windermere* (90) (NY 40-01). Tel: (09662) 2301/ 3543.

PLACES TO VISIT

Abbeys
Cartmel* Priory (96,97) (SD 37-78) Shap Abbey* (90) (NY 54-15).

Amusement Parks
Holker Hall*. Tel: (044853) 328. Lowther* Park. Tel: (09312) 523.

Castles and Castle earthworks
Brougham Castle*. Tel: (0768) 62488. Egremont* Castle (89) (NY 01-11) Kendal* Castle (97) (SD 51-92) Penrith* Castle (90) (NY 51-29).

Cinemas, audiovisual shows, etc.
Zefferellis, Ambleside*. Tel: (05394) 33845. Royalty, Bowness*. Tel: (09662) 3364. Regal, Cleator Moor. Tel: (0946) 810230. Palladium, Kendal*. Tel: (0539) 22907. Alhambra, Keswick*. Tel: (0596) 72195. Palladium, Millom. Tel: (0657) 2441. Cosy Alhambra, Penrith*. Tel: (0768) 62400. Lakeland Experience Centre, Windermere*. Tel: (09662) 2223/4104. Ritz, Workington. (0900) 2505. Roxy, Ulverston*. (0229) 52340.

Factories, Mills, Power Stations, Quarries etc.
Heron Corn Mill, Beetham*. Tel: (0524) 734858. Weatheriggs Country Pottery, Clifton*. Tel: (0768) 62946. Wythop Mill (89) (NY 18-29). Tel: (059681) 394. Eskdale Corn Mill, Eskdale Green*. Tel: (09403) 335. Buttermere & Westmorland Green Slate Co., Honister Pass*. Tel: (059684) 230. Muncaster Mill*. Tel: (06577) 232. Sellafield Public Exhibition Centre (89) (NY 02-03). Tel: (0940) 28333. Kirkstone Slate Galleries, Skelwith Bridge*. Tel: (05394) 32553. Stott Park Bobbin Mill (96,97) (SD 37-88) Tel: (05395) 31087. Cumbria Crystal, Ulverston*. Tel: (0229) 54400. Furness Gallery, Ulverston*. Tel: (0229) 57657.

Forests and Forest Trails
Dodd Wood (89,90) (NY 23-28) Dunnerdale (96) (SD 23-99) Ennerdale (89) (NY 10-15) Grizedale* (96,97) (SD 33-94) Launchy Gill, Thirlmere* (90) (NY 30-15) Swirls, Thirlmere* (90) (NY 31-16) Whinlatter* (89,90) (NY 20-24).

Gardens
Graythwaite Hall*. Tel: (05395) 31248. Holehird* (0228) (23456) (County land agent) Holker Hall*. Tel: (044853) 328. Levens Hall*. Tel: (05395) 60321. Lingholm*. Tel: (07687) 72003. Mirehouse*. Tel: (07687) 72287. Muncaster Castle*. Tel: (06577) 614. Rydal Hall*. Tel: (05394) 32050. Sizergh Castle*. Tel: (05395) 60070. Stagshaw Gardens*. Tel: (05394) 32109.

Historic Houses
Belle Isle*. Tel: (09662) 3353. Brantwood*. Tel: (05394) 41396. Castle Dairy, Kendal*. Tel: (0539) 21170. Conishead Priory, Ulverston*. Tel: (0229) 54029. Dalemain*. Tel: (08536) 450. Dove Cottage*. Tel: (09665) 544. Courthouse, Hawkshead*. Hill Top*. Tel: (09666) 269. Holker Hall*. Tel: (044853) 328. Levens Hall*. (05395) 60321. Mirehouse*. (07687) 72287. Muncaster Castle*. Tel: (06577) 614. Old Windebrowe, Keswick*.

Tel: (07687) 72112. Rydal Mount*. Tel: (05394) 33002. Sizergh Castle*. Tel: (05395) 60070. Swarthmoor Hall, Ulverston*. Tel: (0229) 53204. Townend*. Tel: (05394) 32628. Wordsworth House, Cockermouth*. Tel: (0900) 824805.

Museums, Art Galleries, Exhibitions

Abbott Hall Art Gallery, Kendal*. Tel: (0539) 22464. Brewery Arts Centre, Kendal*. Tel: (0539) 25133. Cartmel* Priory Gatehouse. Tel: (05394) 33883. Cumberland Pencil Museum, Keswick*. Tel: (07687) 73626. Doll and Toy Museum, Cockermouth*. Tel: (0900) 85259. Grasmere and Wordsworth Museum, Grasmere*. Tel: (09665) 544/418. Grammar School, Hawkshead*. Grizedale* Visitor Centre. Tel: (022984) 373. Jack Hadwin Motorcycle Collection, Broughton in Furness*. Tel: (05394) 41494. Lakeland Country Base and Museum, Askham*. Tel: (09312) 418. Lakeland Motor Museum, Holker Hall*. Tel: (044853) 509. Laurel and Hardy Museum, Ulverston*. Tel: (0229) 52292. Lowes Court Gallery, Egremont*. Tel: (0946) 820693. Millom Folk Museum (96) (SD 17-80). Tel: (0657) 2555. Museum and Art Gallery, Keswick*. Tel: (07687) 73263. Museum of Archeology and Natural History, Kendal*. Tel: (0539) 21374. Museum of Lakeland Life and Industry, Kendal*. (0539) 22464. National Park Visitor Centre, Brockhole*. Tel: (09662) 6601. Railway Museum, Keswick*. Tel: (059682) 265. Railway Museum, Ravenglass*. Tel: (06577) 226. Ruskin Museum, Coniston*. Tel: (05394) 41541. Steam Museum, Penrith*. Tel: (0768) 62154. Whinlatter* Visitor Centre. Tel: (059682) 469. Windermere Aquarium, Bowness*. Tel: (09662) 4585/2294. Windermere Steamboat Museum, Bowness*. Tel: (09662) 5565.

Railways

Keswick* Railway Museum. Tel: (059682) 265. Lakeside & Haverthwaite Railway* Co. Ltd. Tel: (05395) 31594. Ravenglass & Eskdale Railway*. Tel: (06577) 226.

Theatres, Concerts, Talks etc.

National Park Visitor Centre, Brockhole*. Tel: (09662) 6601. Countryside Theatre, Bowness*. Tel: (09662) 2895. Theatre in the Forest, Grizedale*. Tel: (022984) 291. Brewery Arts Centre, Kendal*. (0539) 25133. South Lakeland Leisure Centre, Kendal*. Tel: (0539) 26702. Century Theatre, Keswick*. Tel: (07687) 74411.

Rosehill Theatre, Moresby, Nr Whitehaven. Tel: (0946) 2422. Renaissance Theatre Trust, Ulverston* (bookings only). Tel: (0229) 52299.

Waterfalls

Aira Force* (90) (NY 40-20) Colwith Force (90) (NY 32-03) Dungeon Ghyll (89,90) (NY 28-06) Launchy Ghyll Fall (90) (NY 30-15) Lodore Falls* (89,90) (NY 26-18) Scale Force, Crummock Water* (89) (NY 15-17) Skelwith Force, Skelwith Bridge* (90) (NY 34-03) Stanley Ghyll, Boot* (96) (SD 17-99) Stockghyll Force, Ambleside* (90) (NY 38-04) Taylorgill Force, Borrowdale* (89) (NY 22-10).

Tourist Information Centres

Ambleside*, Church St. Tel: (05394) 32582. Borrowdale, Seatoller* Barn. Tel: (059684) 294. Bowness-on-Windermere*, The Glebe. Tel: (09662) 2895. Cockermouth* Riverside Car Park, Market Place. Tel: (0900) 822634. Coniston*, 16 Yewdale Rd. Tel: (05394) 41533. Egremont*, Lowes Court Gallery. Tel: (0946) 820693. Glenridding*, Main Car Park. Tel: (08532) 414. Grange-over-Sands* Victoria Hall, Main St. Tel: (04484) 4026. Grasmere* Red Bank Rd. Tel: (09665) 245. Hawkshead* Brown Cow Laithe. Tel: (09666) 525. Kendal* Town Hall, Highgate. Tel: (0539) 25758. Keswick* Moot Hall, Market Square. Tel: (07687) 72645. Kirkby Lonsdale* 18 Main St. Tel: (0468) 7160. Millom, Millom Folk Museum, St George's Rd. Tel: (0657) 2555. Penrith*, Middlegate. Tel: (0768) 67466. Pooley Bridge*, The Square. Tel: (08536) 530. Ravenglass*, Ravenglass & Eskdale Railway Car Park. Tel: (06577) 278. Ulverston*, Coronation Hall, County Square. Tel: (0229) 57120. Waterhead*. (0966) 32729. Windermere*, Victoria St. Tel: (09662) 6499.

Other Useful Addresses and/or Telephone Numbers

Cumbria Tourist Board, Ashleigh, Holly Road, Windermere* LA23 2AQ. Lake District National Park Information Centre, Brockhole*, Windermere, LA23 1LJ. Tel: (09662) 6601. National Trust*, Rothay Holme, Rothay Road, Ambleside, LA22 0EJ. Tel: (05394) 33883. Forestry Commission, Peil Wyke, Cockermouth, CA13 9YQ. (059681) 616. Events Line. Tel: (09662) 6363. Weather Forecast (Fell Top conditions, updated twice daily). Tel: (09662) 5151. Windermere Lake Wardens. Tel: (09662) 2753.

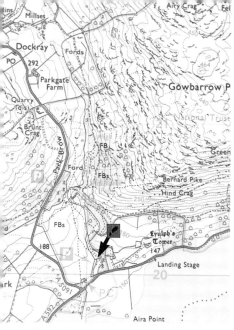

Ambleside

Places of Interest

Aira Force (90) (NY 40-20)
This famous waterfall is in Gowbarrow Park, on the west bank of Ullswater ★ , and is on **Tours 3** and **4**. There is a large car park on the A592 and the main falls are a few minutes walk (see map). The force falls 70 ft from beneath a stone footbridge, in one long and one short cascade: there are rapids above and below the main falls which are spectacular after rain.

Ambleside (90) (NY 37-04)
One mile north of Windermere ★ , and sheltered on the other three sides by fells, Ambleside lies on natural routes north and west. This strategic position gives the town a long history. The Romans built a fort at Waterhead ★ , one mile to the south, and drove a road west to the sea. Later on, the town was a crossing point for the old packhorse routes which dominated trade until the eighteenth century..

The present-day town is mainly Victorian. Although the railway stopped at Windermere, nineteenth-century tourists were not deterred. Some came by steam launch to Waterhead and then on by charabanc, while others came up the turnpike road. In 1855 the Ambleside Turnpike Trust recorded over 21,000 carriages across Troutbeck Bridge (between Windermere and Ambleside). Fifty years before a single carriage past Dove Cottage ★ merited an entry in Dorothy Wordworth's diary.

Traces of the older town can be found to the north, near the Kirkstone Road. Here there are narrow streets and cobbled alleyways. The streams which flow down from the fells were once used to power corn and bobbin mills and the water wheel where Stock Beck crosses North Road has recently been restored.

The Information Centre (1) is in Church Street, backing onto the small car park opposite the Library. This houses the Armitt collection of early books on the Lake District.

The National Trust have an information centre in Bridge House (2), a tiny two-room cottage built over a stone arch across Stock Beck. The building dates from the sixteenth century, when the land around was an orchard belonging to Ambleside Hall, and was originally a summerhouse and store for apples. It has been used at different times as a cottage (one family apparently brought up six children in it), a tearoom, a weaver's, a cobbler's and a gift shop. In 1926 local subscribers raised funds to buy the house for the National Trust, who opened it as their first information centre in 1956. Old House, on Smithy Brow, is on the former site of Ambleside Hall.

St Mary's Church (4) was completed in 1854. It was designed by Gilbert Scott and, unusually for the Lake District, has a 180ft spire. Wordsworth, who had an office in Ambleside in his capacity as Distributor of Stamps for Westmorland, took a great interest in the plans for a new church. He died before work started on the building but Mary Wordsworth, his widow, was present at the consecration and donated a bible and lectern. Wordsworth admirers have installed a memorial window at the east end of the north aisle, which has become known as the Wordsworth Chapel. Wordsworth's old office is next to the bakery on the corner of Church Street and Lake Road and is still called The Old Stamp House.

From the church there is a footpath across Rothay Park (3), bounded by Stock Ghyll and the River Rothay. To the east of the town, Stock Ghyll tumbles down from

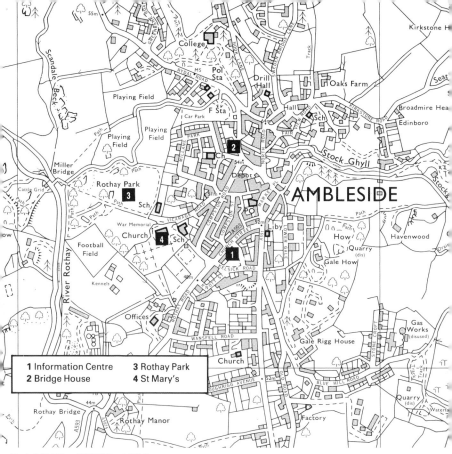

Scale 1:10 000 or 6 INCHES to 1 MILE

1 Information Centre   **3** Rothay Park
2 Bridge House   **4** St Mary's

the fells through a series of dramatic cascades. The best short walk in Ambleside is up Stock Ghyll Lane, which runs up beside the National Westminster Bank, and along the footpath beside the stream to Stock

Bridge House in Ambleside

Ghyll Force. This is one of the loveliest waterfalls in the Lakes, with the stream dividing to fall 90ft under a stone footbridge.

Tour 5 starts from Ambleside and **Tours 6,7 and 9** pass through it.

Arnside (97) (SD 45-78)
On the south side of the Kent Estuary opposite Grange-over-Sands ★ , this little fishing port is now a busy holiday resort. The town is built on a steep, wooded slope above the sandflats and is linked to Grange by a railway viaduct over the estuary. Much of this area is salt marsh, covered only by the spring and autumn equinoctial tides, and many rare shore birds have been observed. Guided walks across the sands to Grange can be arranged.
    Follow the signs from the promenade to reach Arnside Knott. This limestone outcrop gives an extraordinary view of the Lake District fells and the Pennines and there is a comprehensive view indicator at the top so that you can identify what you are looking at. The Knott was given to the National Trust in 1947 and there is a large car park and a nature trail. From the shilla (scree) slopes to the south there is a view of Arnside Tower, a ruined pele tower overlooking Morecambe Bay. Arnside is on **Tour 10**.

Ashness Bridge (see Watendlath)

Askham (90) (NY 51-23)
This charming limestone village lies just within the north-east boundary of the National Park and is on **Tours 3 and 4**. Mainly eighteenth-century, the houses and barns line a succession of village greens leading up from the River Lowther. Askham Hall, which stands above the river looking across at the shell of Lowther Castle ★ , is a typical semi-fortified house developed on the site of a fourteenth-century pele tower. It is the home of the Earl of Lonsdale.

St Peter's Church was rebuilt in 1832 by Robert Smirke, the designer of the British Museum, but contains remains of the original thirteenth-century church. The Lakeland Country Base and Museum, by the Queen's Head, is an offshoot of Lowther Outdoor Activities Centre and has displays relating to the geology, wildlife and industry of the area. The limestone fells around here have many stone circles and ancient settlements. One of the most attractive is on Askham Fell and is known locally as The Cockpit (NY 483-223).

Backbarrow (96,97) (SD 35-84)
The Leven valley, south of Windermere ★ , has a long history of industry, powered by water from the river. The charcoal came from Grizedale Forest ★ and was ferried down Windermere to Newby Bridge. This strategy was so successful that the Backbarrow iron furnace, which opened in 1711, only changed over from charcoal to coke in 1920 and was still producing iron in the 1960s. The Blue Works, which made industrial 'blue' for laundering, lasted until 1981. The dust from its tall chimney (now demolished) used to stain everything around blue, even the ducks in the river. The area has now been converted into a timeshare complex called The Lakeland Village and some of the industrial buildings have been preserved.

Bampton (90) (NY 52-18)
On the River Lowther, Bampton is the nearest village to Haweswater ★ , the
Bampton

reservoir which drowned the village of Mardale in 1937. There is a painting of Mardale church in the eighteenth-century church of St Patrick and two events formerly held at the famous Dun Bull Inn in Mardale are now held in Bampton. One is the Mardale Hunt and the other the annual Shepherds' Meet, which dates from the time when stray sheep were reclaimed. On the nearby moors there are the remains of a British settlement and numerous stone circles and earthworks, including a group of rocks known as the Giants Grave. Bampton is on **Tours 3 and 4.**

Bassenthwaite Lake (89,90) (NY 21-29)
The most northerly of the lakes, Bassenthwaite was probably once joined to Derwent Water ★ . It lacks a mountain dale head but compensates by lying beneath the western foot of Skiddaw ★ . There is a good view of the lake from the top of the Whinlatter Pass ★ , looking north.

The lake used to be owned by the Egremont Estates, but in 1979 went to the Lake District Special Planning Board ★ (LDSPB) to pay off death duties. In an attempt to preserve wildlife on the lake, motor boats are banned and there are no public launch sites for sailing boats although RYA members can use the Bassenthwaite Sailing Club in Dubwath. Rowing boats and canoes are permitted and can be hired nearby.

The west shore is marred by the A66 – a battle lost by the LDSPB – but there is access to the lake at Beck Wythop and Woodend. On the east shore there are some pleasant walks (see **Walk 2**). The Forestry Commission have several forest trails in Dodd Wood and the view from Dodd summit (1,612 ft) is magnificent. Mirehouse ★ is owned by the Spedding family, local landowners with a long history of literary connections, and has recently been opened to the public. Bassenthwaite Lake is on **Tour 2.**

Bassenthwaite village (89,90) (NY 23-32)
The village lies to the east of the A591, on the old coaching route from Keswick ★ to Carlisle. **Tour 2** passes through the village and **Walk 2** starts from here.

Bassenthwaite Church is 3 miles south of the village, in an isolated position near the lake shore. It is dedicated to St Bega and dates back to at least the tenth century (the saint landed at St Bee's Head in the seventh century). Its circular churchyard suggests that before this it may have been a Druid site.

Tennyson worked on his early poem *Morte d'Arthur* which he was to use in Idyls of the King while staying nearby at Mirehouse ★ and its setting is said to have been inspired by the church. The lines:
    I heard the ripple washing in the reeds,
    and the wild water lapping on the crag
were written while sitting at the lakeside.

Bassenthwaite

Belle Isle from Bowness

Beatrix Potter (see Hawkshead, High Wray, Hill Top, Lingholm Gardens, National Trust, Newlands Pass, Sawrey, Troutbeck)

Beetham (97) (SD 49-79)
This delightful village lies just outside the National Park, to the east of Arnside ★ . The Saxon church was badly damaged in the Civil War, when Parliamentary troops are said to have stabled their horses in it, but fragments of its fine glass windows remain and include a portrait of Henry IV. Beetham Hall is a former pele tower which is now a farm: its fourteenth-century Great Hall is in use as a barn.

Just outside the village, on the west bank of the river Bela, is the Heron Corn Mill. This restored water mill is in full working order (selling its own stone-ground flour) and has an exhibition about its history and the process of milling. It is a short riverside walk from the car park, reached by a footbridge behind the Henry Cooke Waterhouse Paper Mills.

On the right hand side of the road to Slackhead there is a sign to the Fairy Steps, a narrow cleft through a steep limestone crag. It is said locally that if you can get down the steps without touching the sides, your wishes will come true.

Belle Isle (96,97) (SD 39-96)
The largest and only inhabited island on Windermere ★ , Belle Isle lies just north of the Bowness ★ ferry crossing. The island has been owned by the Curwen family for over 220 years and has a unique Round House, built in 1774. It is apparently the only completely circular house in Britain and is now much admired: at the time it was described as a pepperpot! Wordsworth also disapproved, including Belle Isle in his *Guide to the Lakes* in a chapter subtitled 'Causes of False Taste in Grounds and Buildings', but relented when his son John married Isabella Curwen.

The Round House itself stands on the site of a Roman villa, with the original well still in existence underneath the house. The island was landscaped in the eight-

eenth century and there are formal gardens and woodland walks.

In 1988 the house was turned into a conference centre and is sadly no longer open to the public. Parties of twenty or more may visit the island by appointment with Mrs Curwen.

Birks Bridge (see Duddon River)

Black Combe (96) (SD 13-86)
This isolated outcrop of Skiddaw slate, in the south-west corner of the National Park, is one of the oldest hills in the world. It is apparently the most extensive viewpoint in Britain and from its summit (1,969 ft) it is possible on a clear day to see fourteen counties, as well as the Isle of Man and the Mountains of Mourne. North of Black Combe there is extensive evidence of Bronze Age settlement, with over 10,000 cairns. Swinside Stone Circle, on an eastern spur of Black Combe, is a cluster of fifty stones. It is on private land but can be viewed from a nearby footpath.

Blawith (96,97) (SD 28-88)
Blawith Common, which occupies 1,600 acres south-west of Coniston Water ★ , was acquired by the Lake District Special Planning Board ★ in 1971. On its northern boundary it joins onto the Torver ★ commons, already owned by the LDSPB.

Walk 8 starts in Blawith village (on **Tour 5)** and goes to the highest point of Blawith Fells, the Beacon. A bonfire lit on its summit used to serve as a warning of Scottish raids. At Brown Howe, to the north of the village, there is a car park and picnic area on the lake shore. It is possible to launch sailing dinghies and canoes from here.

Blea Tarn (see Great Langdale)

Boot (89,90) (NY 17-01)
Halfway up Eskdale is the tiny hamlet of Boot, tucked in under the fells. The cot-

tages are grouped around the Whillan Beck but the church lies beside the River Esk, ¼ mile to the south.

Eskdale Corn Mill, established in 1578, has been restored by Cumbria County Council and has exhibitions on milling and agriculture. It is reached by one of the two seventeenth-century packhorse bridges in Boot. The other is Doctor's Bridge which spans the river Esk about 2 miles upstream of the church. It was widened by a local doctor to get his horse and trap across.

In 1872 several veins of iron ore were discovered in the Eskdale granite near Boot, the most productive being the Nab Gill vein. It was decided to exploit the deposits, in spite of their remoteness, and in 1875 a railway line was laid to to Ravenglass ★ where it joined the main West Cumberland line. Mining only lasted eleven years but the Ravenglass and Eskdale Railway ★ remains, now converted to a 15 inch gauge. The ride up from Ravenglass to the Dalegarth terminus in Boot goes through the valleys of Miterdale and Eskdale and is a good way of avoiding the problems of parking in the village.

From the station it is a 2 mile walk to Stanley Ghyll Force, a romantic series of falls in a tree-lined gorge much appreciated by the Victorians. At the foot of the gorge is Dalegarth Hall, a fortified house with typical Lakeland round chimneys. Boot is on **Tours 1 and 7**.

Bootle (96) (SD) 10-88

On the western coast road between Millom ★ and Ravenglass ★ , this small ancient village lies on the lower slopes of Black Combe ★ . Two lanes lead down to the sea; one to Annaside, which lies at the mouth of the beck which flows through the village, and the other to Tarn Bay where there is a good beach.

The village has an entry in the Domesday book and a market charter dating from 1346. There was a Benedictine nunnery at Seaton, one mile north on the A595, and the church has a memorial to Sir Hugh Agnew who acquired the land after the Dissolution of the Monasteries. He was Henry VIII's cellarer.

Borrowdale (89,90) (NY 25-14)

From its source high up between the Langdale and Sca Fell Pikes ★ , the River Derwent flows north through what Wordsworth called the 'continuous Vale of Borrowdale, Keswick, and Bassenthwaite'. Borrowdale, the first of the three, runs from Seathwaite ★ to the head of Derwent Water ★ .

Driving up the valley, the road runs past the tiny hamlet of Grange ★ and then through a narrow pass between Grange Fell on the east and Scawdel to the west. These are the Jaws of Borrowdale. Below Grange Fell is the Bowder Stone, a huge and precarious-looking boulder

Borrowdale in autumn

Grange

abandoned by a retreating glacier during the last Ice Age. This exceptional glacial erratic is thought to weigh over 2,000 tons and can be climbed using a ladder.

The river here runs between steep wooded banks, backed by layers of fells and peaks. The trees are mostly broadleaf hardwoods, planted to replace the natural forests which were cleared to supply the iron ore furnaces. To the west is Castle Crag (980 ft), one of the best viewpoints in the Borrowdale area. The confederation of Celtic tribes known as the Brigantes – who held all the North of England before the arrival of the Romans – had a stone-walled stronghold on the top. It can be climbed from Rosthwaite and is also on **Walk 10** which starts in Seatoller ★ .

Just after Rosthwaite, the Langstrath valley comes down on the left. Ahead is the mass of the Borrowdale Fells. The main road bears right at Seatoller to cross the Honister Pass ★ to Buttermere ★ but a minor road continues on up Borrowdale to Seathwaite. Here the road stops. Ahead is Styhead Pass, an old packhorse way which runs east of Styhead Gill to Stockley Bridge and up round the east side of Great Gable to Wasdale Head ★ . From Stockley Bridge there is a view of Taylorgill Force, a magnificent 140ft cascade which many consider to be the Lake District's most spectacular waterfall.

The lower half of Borrowdale is on **Tour 1 and 2**.

Bowder Stone (see Borrowdale)

Bowness-on-Windermere (96,97) (SD 40-96)

The extension of the railway line to Windermere ★ station, one mile north of Bowness, transformed this small lakeshore village into a popular resort. Today it has a cheerful cosmopolitan character quite unlike any other town in the Lakes. This is partly because it is still the only central Lakeland town with a station, and so the only town accessible to day trippers, but also because the lake itself is wholeheartedly given up to boating, with the mountains at its head an incidental backdrop. Bowness is Arthur Ransome's Rio Grande, although sadly the Victorian boatsheds he described in Rio Bay were pulled down in 1973.

Even before the arrival of the railway, Bowness Bay had been discovered by Manchester businessmen. Poor Wordsworth lamented the coming of 'strangers not linked to the neighbourhood, but flitting to and fro between their fancy-villas and the homes where their wealth was accumulated...by trade and manufactures'. Some of these fancy-villas (along with their extensive lakeshore frontages) are still in private hands: most are now hotels or, like Brockhole ★ , owned by institutions.

There is a National Park Information

Scale 1:10 000 or 6 INCHES to 1 MILE

Centre **(4)** on the south side of Bowness Bay, in Glebe Road. The Countryside Theatre in the same building is used as a lecture hall. A second information centre, by the station, is shown on the Windermere ★ town map.

The boat line and cruise piers **(1)** are just to the north of the information centre. Two companies operate from here. The Windermere Iron Steamboat Company run a regular service up the lake to Waterhead ★ and down to Lakeside, using traditional Windermere steamers which take between 300 and 600 passengers. Tern, the oldest, was built in 1891. At Lakeside the boat connects with the Lakeside and Haverthwaite Railway ★ , which runs restored steam engines on a section of the old Furness branch line. There is also a mini-cruise, which is a round trip and takes about 45 minutes.

The Bowness Bay Boating Company operates launches and waterbuses and runs a variety of cruises, including trips round the islands and to the major National Park Centre at Brockhole. They also put on evening cruises and hire motor boats and rowing boats.

To the south, along Glebe Road, there are numerous boatsheds and the purposeful activity of a boating community. There is also an Aquarium, which has a display of fish native to the lakes and rivers of

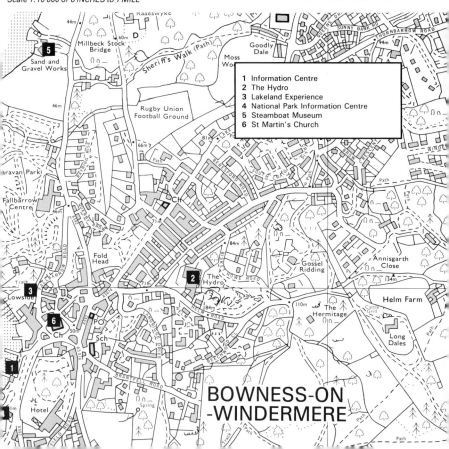

1 Information Centre
2 The Hydro
3 Lakeland Experience
4 National Park Information Centre
5 Steamboat Museum
6 St Martin's Church

BOWNESS-ON
-WINDERMERE

BRANDELHOW

Bowness from the other side of Windermere

The Steamboat Museum

Cumbria. These include the surprisingly large and aggressive char, a relic of the ice age found only in glacial lakes. It is related to the trout.

The Steamboat Museum **(5)** is to the north, on Rayrigg Road. Opened in 1977, it has a unique collection of restored boats, many of them raised by divers from the lake bottom. All the craft have some connection with the Lakes and they range in simplicity from Beatrix Potter's rowing boat and the Ferry Boat Ann (an example of the old wherries which used to ferry passengers and goods across Windermere) to the opulent steam launches in use when Windermere was the playground of the Lancashire rich. In fine weather visitors can take a cruise on S.L.Osprey, a classic Windermere steam launch which takes twelve passengers.

The craft with the oddest history must be the Esperance, built in 1869 for the Furness industrialist H.W.Schneider. He used it to commute each day to work; leaving his mansion in Bowness Bay (Belsfield, now a hotel) preceded by his butler carrying a silver tray; eating breakfast on board as Esperance steamed down Windermere to Lakeside; and finally taking a special train from Lakeside to Barrow. Later the boat was used by Arthur Ransome as the model

for Captain Flint's houseboat in *Swallows and Amazons*.

The parish church of St Martin **(6)** is in the centre of Bowness, on a site which has been occupied by a religious house for over 1,000 years. It was rebuilt in 1483, following a fire, and the present church is believed to have an old floor five feet below the nave. Some of the glass from the earlier church has been incorporated into the east window and the font bears the marks of the fire.

Like many other Lakeland churches, there are various painted texts and frescoes, including a Latin inscription (under one of the arches near the lectern) which gives thanks for deliverance from the Gunpowder Plot. The wooden statue of St Martin was carved by a local craftsman and is 300 years old.

The Lakeland Experience Centre **(3)** is an audiovisual display of the history of the Lake District. The Hydro **(2)** is a fine stucco building which opened in 1881 as the Windermere Hydropathic Establishment. It is now a hotel.

Tour 6 starts from Bowness and Windermere and the town is visited on **Tour 9**.

Brandelhow (90) (NY 25-20)
On the west shore of Derwent Water ★ , Brandelhow Woods were the first major property bought by the National Trust ★ . In 1902, when they acquired the land, the woods were considered as prime building land. The purchase was almost entirely due to campaigning by Canon Rawnsley, the vicar of Crosthwaite Church in Keswick ★ ; in 1922 the Trust bought Friars Crag, the magnificent viewpoint on the opposite side of the lake, as his memorial.

There is a very pleasant walk along here, starting either from the car park at the north end of Cat Bells (see map) or from one of Keswick Launch piers. High Brandelhow, Low Brandelhow and Hawse End are all on this part of the lakeshore and

The Ferry Drake

Brantwood is on **Tours 6 and 8**. There is a Ruskin Museum in nearby Coniston ★ .

Brockhole (90) (NY 39-00)
Formerly the country house of a Lancashire cotton magnate, Brockhole was converted in 1969 into the Lake District National Park Visitor Centre. It is one of the grandest of Windermere's Victorian villas, standing in large grounds which run down to the lake. The entrance is about 2 miles south of Ambleside ★ on the A591 and is on **Tour 6.**

The centre has a permanent 'Man in Lakeland' exhibition, covering 5,000 years of Lakeland life, and throughout the summer there are audiovisual shows twice daily and a variety of talks and special events. Local information centres have a What's On listing so that it is possible to check the day's programme in advance. There are walks and nature trails in the grounds and special activities laid on for children. Launches go from Bowness ★ or Waterhead ★ to the centre.

The Lake District National Park Visitor Centre

passengers can leave or join the launch at any of the stages. To the north of the car park a footpath leads to Lingholm Gardens ★ which are open to the public. They are at their best in late spring. Brandelhow is on **Tour 2.**

Brantwood (96,97) (SD 31-95)
This fine house on the east side of Coniston Water ★ was bought unseen by John Ruskin in 1872 (for £1,500) on the grounds that, 'Any place opposite Coniston Old Man *must* be beautiful.' It is now owned by the Brantwood Trust and open all the year round.

The house already contains- many of Ruskin's paintings and possessions, displayed as they were in his lifetime, and it is planned to return to Brantwood the extensive Ruskin collection now in the Isle of Wight. Largely forgotten now, Ruskin was an extraordinarily gifted man who influenced many of his contemporaries in his various roles as poet, artist, art critic and social reformer. These included such apparently diverse people as the pre-Raphaelite painters; Marcel Proust; Octavia Hill (one of the founders of the National Trust ★); and Leo Tolstoy, who wrote, 'Ruskin was one of the most remarkable of men, not only of England and our time, but of all countries and all times'. A later admirer of this rather tragic genius was Mahatma Gandhi.

One of the first alterations Ruskin made to the house was to build a six-sided turret onto his bedroom, overlooking the lake. This gives superb views in five directions. The old printing room in the grounds has an exhibition of original drawings by A.Wainwright, whose illustrated guides have influenced a generation of fell-walkers. There is a nature trail in the grounds.

Brothers Water (see Hartsop)

Brougham Castle (90) (NY 53-28)
South-east of Penrith ★ , this impressive thirteenth-century castle stands on a grassy mound beside the River Eamont. It is maintained by English Heritage and the entrance is from a minor road off the A66, on **Tour 3.**

The oldest part of the castle, the keep, was built at the beginning of the thirteenth century. Towards the end of the century it passed by marriage to Robert Lord Clifford, Edward I's right hand man, who added inner and outer gatehouses and made it the strongest fortress in the Eden valley. The castle later fell into disrepair (although James I and Charles I both stayed there) but was restored by Lady Anne Clifford after the Civil War. This formidable woman also restored the Clifford castles at Brough and Appleby and travelled between them with a small court, as if she was royalty. Cromwell apparently said, 'Let her build what she will, she shall

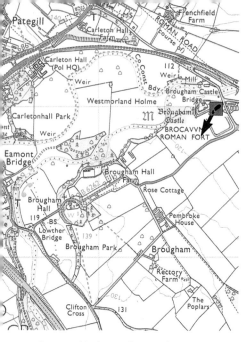

have no hindrance from me'.

South-east of the castle is the site of the Roman fort of Brocavum, built where the main road to Scotland crossed the road to York. Brocavum was linked to Galava, the fort at Waterhead ★ , by a road running along the top of the spectacular ridgeway known as High Street ★ . The fort is on private land and has not been excavated, but aerial photographs show that it was large and surrounded by a considerable civilian settlement.

There is a pleasant walk west along the banks of the river (see map). At Eamont Bridge there are two prehistoric earthworks, shown on the Penrith town map.

Broughton in Furness (96) (SD 21-87)
This attractive eighteenth-century market town lies just to the north of the Duddon Sands and is on **Tours 7 and 8**. The town is built on the side of a hill and the market square still has the old stone-slab stalls and 1766 clock. The church, at the top of the town, has a fine Norman arch. There are good views from the surrounding countryside over the Duddon Sands, a lonely stretch of mud flats once famous for its cockles.

The Old Town Hall now houses the Jack Hadwin Motor Cycle Collection. This is an enthusiast's private collection, with veteran and vintage machines all collected from within a radius of 50 miles. The oldest machine dates from 1899 and most are pre-1937.

Buttermere (89,90) (NY 18-15)
Approached over the Honister ★ or Newlands ★ Pass, Buttermere and Crummock Water ★ seem to lie together in an unbroken basin of high fells. In fact at the foot of this glacial valley there is another lake,

Loweswater ★ , hidden by the debris o rocks brought down by the glacier. Th three lakes were once one.

High Stile

Buttermere

The B5289 runs all along the east shore of Buttermere, with the peaks of High Crag, High Stile and Red Pike dominating the opposite side of the lake. At the foot of the lake there is a strip of flat fertile land, with Crummock Water beyond. Almost opposite is Sour Milk Gill, which spills out of an unseen tarn high up on Red Pike.

It is possible to walk all round the lake starting either from Buttermere ★ village or from Gatesgarth Farm which is at the head of the lake (see **Walk 11**). The farm has rowing boats for hire and there is good fishing. Buttermere is one of the Lake District lakes which contain char, a relative of the trout. No power boats are allowed in Buttermere.

Buttermere village (89,90) (NY 17-17)
This tiny hamlet lies beside Mill Beck, at the junction between Buttermere ★ and Crummock Water ★ . In the nineteenth century the Fish Hotel in Buttermere became famous when the landlord's daughter, Mary Robinson, married a man calling himself the Hon. Alexander Hope M.P. He turned out to be a bigamist wanted for forgery and was hanged a year later. The plight of the Beauty of Buttermere touched the hearts of the Victorians but in fact she married a local farmer and raised a large family so no great harm seems to have been done.

One of the most perfect Dale churches is in Buttermere, perched above the village on a shelf of rock. The wrought-iron gate into the porch shows a shepherd with his ewe and lamb. Buttermere is on **Tours 1 and 2**.

Cartmel (96,97) (SD 37-78)
This small village west of Grange-over-Sands is dominated by the magnificent church of St Mary and St Michael, once part of Cartmel Priory and the finest medieval building in the Lake District. The church managed to escape destruction during the Dissolution of the Monasteries because in 1188 the founder stipulated that there should be an altar with 'a priest for the people'. This meant that in 1537 the villagers could claim that the chapel of St Michael in the south aisle was a parish church.

The rest of the church was stripped of all valuables, including its lead roof, but eighty years later it was restored by George Preston of Holker Hall ★ who also gave the church an elaborate and beautiful oak screen. This was placed above the original choir stalls, which had survived their years of neglect. These have superbly carved misericords which include such medieval flights of fancy as The Pelican in Piety and The Mermaid with Two Tails. The whole church is spacious and impressive, with many interesting architectural features. There are two towers, one set diagonally on top of the other.

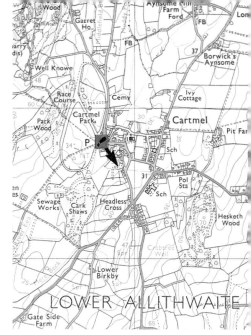

The main village is on the other side of a stream, centred around a square with a pump (see map). The houses are mostly seventeenth and eighteenth-century but the fourteenth-century Priory Gatehouse has also survived. It is owned by the National Trust and usually houses an exhibition of paintings by local artists during the summer. The Michael Gibbon Gallery, in a seventeenth-century cruck barn, has carved wood sculptures.

On the edge of the village is a racecourse, surrounded by parkland. It is the smallest National Hunt course and holds races only on the Spring and Late Summer Bank Holidays. Cartmel is on **Tour 10**.

Cartmel Fell (96,97) (SD 41-88)
The barn-like church of St Anthony was built by local farmers in 1504 to save themselves a seven-mile walk to Cartmel ★ Priory. It lies in the Winster valley, south-east of Windermere ★ , and can be reached by turning south off the unclassified road between Fell Foot and Crosthwaite (see **Tour 10**).

The church contains some fifteenth-century glass, including a charming picture of St Antony and his pig. There are some fine carved pews and a three-decker pulpit. A primitive pre-Reformation figure of Christ, the only example in England, is now in the Natural History and Archaeology Museum at Kendal ★ where it forms part of an exhibition on Christianity in Cumbria.

Castle Crag (see Borrowdale)

Castlerigg Stone Circle (89,90) (NY 29-23)
This prehistoric stone circle has an extraordinary setting, standing in a natural

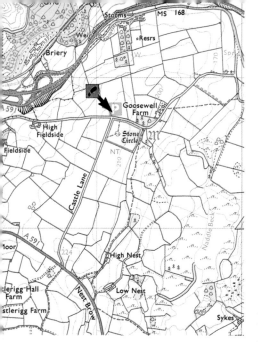

fight, taking their positions behind t
hedges and walls south of the village. T
Scots were driven from their positions, b
Cumberland's men were too exhausted
pursue them, so both sides could claim
victory.

The dead of both sides are buried in t
village, the Scots under an oak tree
Town End Farm, where there is a plaqu
and the English in the churchyard. T
Scots continued north, leaving a garris
in Carlisle which was retaken by the Du
on December 30th. His treatment of t
captured rebels earned him the title
Butcher Cumberland: heads of execut
prisoners impaled on the gates of Penr
were still there in 1766.

To the east of the village is Weatherig
Country Pottery, a nineteenth-century re
clay works which is now an industr
monument. Visitors can go round t
workshops and there is a museum d
playing old machines and tools. Potte
wheels are available for anyone who war
to try their own hand.

Castlerigg

amphitheatre surrounded by high fells. It is
between 3,000 and 4,000 years old (older
than Stonehenge) and contains thirty eight
stones, set in a slightly oval formation,
with a further ten stones in an internal
rectangle.

The circle is just to the east of Keswick ★
and is reached by a turning off the A591
south of the town (see map). In 1913 the
field it stands in was bought by Canon
Rawnsley, one of the founders of the
National Trust ★ , to prevent the stones
being damaged or exploited.

Claife Heights (see Windermere)

Clifton (90) (NY 53-26)
On December 18th, 1745, this little village
south of Penrith ★ was the site of the last
battle to be fought on English soil. One
month before, the Jacobite army had captured Carlisle and advanced as far south as
Derby. However at the beginning of
December they decided to retreat and were
pursued north by the Duke of Cumberland.
At Clifton the Scots were forced to turn and

Cockermouth (89) (NY 12-30)
The River Cocker flows north, carrying t
overflow from Buttermere ★ and Cru
mock Water ★ into the River Derwe
Cockermouth lies at the junction of t
two rivers, just outside the north-we
boundary of the National Park. In 1582
Elizabethan mapmaker described it as
populous and well trading Market Tov
neatly built but of low situation betwe
two hills'. This description could still a
ply: the town has an air of minding its ov
business, tolerating its tourists but n
overrating their importance.

The Information Centre **(1)** is in the rive
side car park, just to the south of t
Market Place. A stalled market is he
every week, preceded in the summer
the ringing of the Butter Bell, and there a
weekly cattle auctions. In the autumn the
are sheep sales.

Beside the market square is All Saint
Church, rebuilt in 1854 after a fire. Word
worth's father, John Wordsworth, is buri
in the churchyard. He died aged forty-tw
five years after Wordsworth's mother.
side the church there is a memorial wi
dow to the poet.

The Church Rooms south of the chur
stand on the site of the Old Gramm
School **(4)**. Fletcher Christian, the leader
the mutiny on the Bounty, was educate
there. So (briefly) was Wordsworth but
the death of his mother he was sent
school in Hawkshead ★ . On the north si
of the Market Place is the Doll and T
Museum **(2)** which has a collection
costume dolls and twentieth-century toys

North of Cocker Bridge, the River Cock
swings west to join the River Derwe
Cockermouth Castle stands in the ang
between the two rivers. The original cast
was built in the twelfth century but t
existing buildings are mostly thirteen

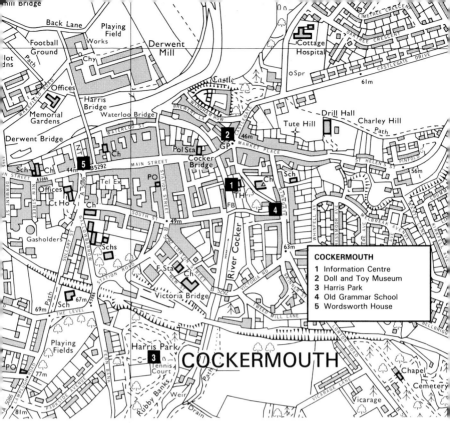

COCKERMOUTH

1 Information Centre
2 Doll and Toy Museum
3 Harris Park
4 Old Grammar School
5 Wordsworth House

Scale 1:10 000 or 6 INCHES to 1 MILE

and fourteenth-century. It is thought that much of the stone was looted from the Roman fort at Papcastle.

The castle has had a turbulent history; besieged by Scots in the fourteenth century, Yorkists in the Wars of the Roses and Royalists in the Civil War (Cockermouth being one of the few places in Cumberland and Westmorland held by Parliament). After the Civil War the castle was partly dismantled and fell into ruin. One wing was rebuilt in the last century and is used by the Egremont family; another houses the offices of the Egremont Estate Company. The castle is open to the public during the Cockermouth festival in August and the ruins contain good examples of underground 'oubliette' dungeons, so-called because they housed forgotten prisoners

The broad, tree-lined Main Street is to the west of the river Cocker. Many of the houses are colour-washed. The statue is of Earl Mayo, Viceroy of India, who was assassinated in the Andaman Islands by a convict.

Wordsworth House **(5)** is at the west end of Main Street and is the most imposing house in Cockermouth. It was owned by the wealthy Lowther family and went with John Wordsworth's job as estate and law agent for Sir James Lowther. All five Wordsworth children were born here, William being the second and Dorothy the third. There was a year between them. The house was bought by the National Trust in 1937 when the property was in danger of being demolished to make way for a bus station.

Wordsworth House

The Doll and Toy Museum

CONINGTON

Inside, nine rooms are furnished in eighteenth-century style and there is a tape-slide display in the old stables. There is a terrace walk at the foot of the walled garden, overlooking the river, which was remembered by both William and Dorothy with affection.

To the south of the town is Harris Park **(3)**. There is a pleasant walk along the river Cocker and a granite fountain with a statue of Dorothy Wordsworth as a child. **Tour 2** starts from Cockermouth.

Coniston

Coniston (96,97) (SD 30-97)

This grey slate village, on the north-west shore of Coniston Water ★ , owes its existence to the Old Man of Coniston (2,635 ft) which towers above the houses. Coniston was once one of Europe's most important copper mining areas and in the last century the copper mines employed 900 men and boys.

There is a large car park off the B5285, to the east of the church (see map). The Information Centre is near the post office, on the A593.

The Ruskin Museum is reached by a narrow lane on the opposite side of the road to the Information Centre. John Ruskin lived at Brantwood ★ (on the east side of the lake) and this tiny museum was opened by his admirers in 1901, the year after his death. It has some interesting pictures and photographs, as well as a slightly idiosyncratic collection reflecting Ruskin's interests in minerals, pressed flowers, and lace. There are also findings from local Neolithic burial mounds and an exhibit describing the attempts on the world water speed record by Malcolm and Donald Campbell, who between them held the record six times. Donald Campbell was

killed on Coniston Water in 1967 on a practice run: his body was never recovered and there is a seat commemorating his death on the village green opposite the car park.

Ruskin is buried in Coniston churchyard and has an elaborately carved tombstone, made from green Tilberthwaite slate. It was designed by his secretary W.G. Collingwood, who lived just north of Ruskin, at Lanehead. The Collingwood family later befriended Arthur Ransome and so form an odd link between the two men. Ransome wrote that the rest of his life was happier because of them.

Lake Road, just to the south of Church Beck, leads down to Coniston Pier (see map). The steam yacht Gondola is based here in the summer. This extraordinary craft was described when she was first launched in 1859 as 'A perfect combination of the Venetian Gondola and the English Steam Yacht, having the elegance, comfort and speed of the latter and the graceful lightness and quiet gliding motion of the former'. She takes 86 passengers and is a silent and luxurious way of seeing the lake. The Coniston Boating Centre, which hires out boats, is also based at the pier.

Coniston Hall, visible to the south from the pier, is the oldest building in Coniston. It is a magnificent fifteenth-century manor house, with massive round chimneystacks. By the beginning of the nineteenth century the building was largely in ruins, with the Great Hall being used to store corn, but it has recently been restored by the National Trust. The footpath along the west shore of the lake runs past the house.

A footpath also leads up Church Beck into Coppermines Valley, the site of most of the nineteenth-century copper mining. The Lake District National Park publish a walk in this area. Copper mining has a very long history in Coniston. The Romans probably mined for copper here, followed by the monks of Furness Abbey. In the sixteenth century German miners, based in Keswick ★ , were sent in and the ore carried north over Dunmail Raise ★ for smelting. Later it was shipped south to the port at Greenodd ★ and on to Wales. The Furness Railway extension to Coniston took over transport in the nineteenth century. The railway line was hotly opposed by Ruskin but was well camouflaged. Its closure in 1958 left the village isolated and managed to coincide with the opening of a comprehensive school in Coniston serving a wide area.

Tour 8 starts from Coniston and **Tours 5,6 and 7** go through the village.

Coniston Water (96,97) (SD 30-94)

The second largest of the southern lakes, Coniston Water runs from the dramatic volcanic rock of the Old Man of Coniston range into the Silurian slate and low, rounded hills of the south. At its foot the River Crake flows out into Morecambe Bay.

By car, Coniston Water is best seen from the east shore, where the road runs through woodlands close to the lake. There are Forestry Commission nature trails in the woods and good views of the Old Man of Coniston across the water. The best view of all is from Brantwood ★ , John Ruskin's house for the last thirty years of his life, which is open to the public. Ruskin described the mountain range opposite the house as 'the first great upthrust of mountain Britain'.

On the west shore there is now a path which starts just south of Coniston ★ village and runs almost the whole length of the lake. **Walk 6** starts at Torver ★ , 3 miles south of Coniston, and follows the lakeshore path for part of the way.

The two small islands are both owned by the National Trust and landing by boat is permitted. Peel Island, to the south, was the model for Wild Cat Island in the *Swallows and Amazons* books by Arthur Ransome. As a child, Ransome spent his holidays at High Nibthwaite (near the foot of the lake) and he was later befriended by the Collingwood family who lived north of Brantwood. The children in the books are partly based on the Collingwood grandchildren.

There is a speed limit of 10 mph on the lake. Public launching sites are at the Coniston Boating Centre at Coniston pier (which also hires out boats) and from the car parks at Brown Howe (south-west) and

Summer activity

Winter tranquility

Monk Coniston (north). Power boats can only be launched from Coniston pier. There is a sailing club at Coniston Hall which welcomes RYA members. The lake can also be seen from the Gondola, a luxurious nineteenth-century steam yacht which goes from Coniston pier to Parkamoor, on the south-east shore.

The steam yacht Gondola

Crook (97) (SD 46-95)

Tours 6 and 9 pass through the scattered village of Crook, which lies along the the B5284 from Kendal to Bowness. Crook Hall, south of the road, once belonged to the Royalist Philipson family who owned Belle Isle. During the Civil War, Robert Philipson (whose nickname was Robin the Devil) was beseiged on the island by Parliamentary forces led by a Colonel Briggs. The attackers had no artillery and after eight days the siege was lifted by Robin's brother, Colonel Huddleston Philipson. In revenge the two brothers rode on horseback into Kendal ★ church, where Colonel Briggs was at prayer, to try and kidnap him. The outraged congregation chased them out and managed to capture Robin's helmet. This is still displayed in Holy Trinity Church, Kendal.

Crosthwaite (see Keswick)

Crummock Water (89) (NY 15-18)
Crummock Water lies in the same glacial valley as Buttermere ★ and is separated from it by a narrow strip of flat land. For most of its length it runs between the massive fells of Grasmoor and Mellbreak, which tower above the driver (or walker) like a 'boot above a beetle', to quote the modern Lake poet Norman Nicholson.

The best views are from the north, looking up the lake. There is also a good view from Rannerdale Knott, which bulges out into the lake just north of Buttermere village ★. There is a tradition that the Norman army of William Rufus was massacred in the narrow cul de sac of the Rannerdale valley, falsely informed that it was a pass. It did not stop the Normans for long as all this land was ruled from Egremont ★.

Crummock Water

On the western shore there is a footpath which runs from Buttermere village to Loweswater ★ village, beneath the steep sides of Mellbreak. Looking across the lake, Grasmoor and Whiteless Pike provide a striking example of how different rock produces different scenery.

From this path, it is ¾ mile to Scale Force, hidden in a narrow gorge on the north shoulder of Red Pike. This is the highest waterfall in the Lakes, with a spectacular single fall of 172ft and two others of 20ft each. The falls are far less accessible now than they were when they formed part of the attractions on the 'Buttermere round'. This was a Victorian excursion from Keswick ★ which came down Borrowdale ★, over the Honister Pass ★ to Buttermere village, and back via the Newlands Pass ★. Visitors stopped at the Fish Hotel for lunch and could be rowed across Crummock Water to walk up a carefully maintained track. See **Tours 1 and 2**.

Dacre (90) (NY 45-26)
The ancient village of Dacre lies in the hills north of Ullswater. It is reached by a minor road connecting the A66 and the A592 and is on **Tour 3**.

The church is Norman but almost certainly stands on the site of a rare Anglo-Saxon monastery which was referred to by the Venerable Bede as early as the eighth century. Recent excavations discovered a Christian cemetery north of the church containing ninth-century coins, and an eighth-century stylus or pen in stone-lined drains to the south.

In the churchyard are fragments of two crosses. One is an eighth-century Anglian cross and the other is Viking and tenth-century. The Viking cross has carvings of Adam and Eve and the sacrifice of Isaac. There are also four stone bears, each 3ft high, which are a complete mystery. Very weathered, it has been suggested that they tell a story: the first asleep with his head on a pillar; the second attacked by a cat; the third shaking the cat off and the fourth eating the cat. The style of the carving is unique, making them impossible to date, but it seems likely that they came from the monastery and may perhaps have been guardians of the dead.

Dacre Castle, visible from the churchyard, is the best example of a pele tower in the Lake District. Built in the fourteenth century, during the savage Scottish raids which followed Bannockburn, the tower has walls 8ft thick with elaborate turrets and battlements. The house is owned privately and can be viewed by appointment.

Dalegarth (see Boot)

Dalemain (90) (NY 47-27)
South-west of Penrith, on the A592, the Georgian facade of Dalemain hides an Elizabethan manor house built on to a Norman pele tower. There have been no major changes since 1750 but the house remains 'a glorious confusion', to quote the publicity handout. The fifteenth-century hall has a fine fireplace and there is a Chinese drawing room (one of the Georgian improvements) which has the original hand-painted wallpaper and furniture. The Hasell family have owned the house for over 300 years and there are many family portraits. Sir Edward Hasell was the steward of Lady Anne Clifford, who restored Brougham Castle ★.

The pele tower houses the Westmorland and Cumberland Yeomanry Museum; there are also exhibitions of old farming and household implements and a Fell Pony Museum. The house stands back from the road and is surrounded by a large deer park. Dalemain is on **Tour 3**.

Derwent Water (89,90) (NY 25-21)
Lying between Bassenthwaite Lake ★ and Borrowdale ★, Derwent Water claims to be the Queen of the Lakes. It has a compact oval shape and wooded shores, backed by high fells. In summer the roads around the lake get very crowded but there are still

Derwent Water

some lovely walks. The best views are from Friars Crag, a short walk from Keswick ★ , and the road to Watendlath ★ .

The lake has four 'permanent' islands and a fifth which appears every three years or so and is actually a large clump of weeds, brought to the surface by marsh gas. It is known as the Floating Island but as Wordsworth pedantically points out 'with more propriety might be named the Buoyant Island'. It is in the south-west corner of the lake.

Of the others, Derwent Island was once used by the German miners imported by the Company of Mines Royal in the sixteenth century to mine the copper, lead and silver in the fells to the west of the lake. They used to grow vegetables on the island and brew beer. In the eighteenth century the island was bought by an eccentric offcomer (newcomer) called Joseph Pocklington who built a series of follies on it and staged mock sea battles.

St Herbert's Island is named after a hermit who lived there in the seventh century and was a disciple of St Cuthbert. In the fourteenth century an indulgence of forty days was granted to anyone who celebrated an annual mass on the island. It is said that pilgrims embarked from Friar's Crag but the name could also come from the monks of Furness Abbey who owned Derwent Water until the Dissolution of the Monasteries.

The best way to explore the lake is from one of the launches which start from Lake Shore, Keswick. They leave every half hour (more often in high season) and go alternately clockwise and anti-clockwise. The trip takes 50 minutes and stops at six piers around the lake: Ashness Bridge, Lodore Falls ★ , High Brandlehow, Low Brandlehow, Hawes End and Nicol End. There are good walks from all these and passengers can leave and rejoin the launch at any of the stages.

For drivers, the lake is best seen from the west side, where the road runs along above the lake. **Tour 2** follows this road and goes past Brandelhow ★ and Lingholm Gardens ★ . **Tour 1** follows the east side, passing the road to Watendlath ★ and Lodore Falls ★ .

Boats can be launched from the Keswick Launch Company piers at Lake Shore. There is a speed limit of 10 mph on the lake and the sailing is not good because of the surrounding fells.

Dodd Wood (see Bassenthwaite Lake)

Dove Cottage (90) (NY 34-07)
This small white cottage was Wordsworth's first home in Grasmere ★ . He moved in with his sister Dorothy in December 1799, when he was 29 and she a few days off 28. It was their first permanent home in the Lake District since their childhood and they were delighted with everything. Dorothy wrote, '..we were young and healthy and had attained an object long desired. We had returned to our native mountains there to live'. The cottage had earlier been an inn (The Dove and Olive-Bough) and was on the main road at that time.

Some of Wordsworth's finest poems were composed at Dove Cottage. Dorothy's journals in the first three years record the way in which the poetry was

Dove Cottage

slotted into the domestic routine. 'At Breakfast Wm wrote part of an ode. Mr Oliff sent the dung and Wm went to work in the garden.' Both spent a great deal of time in the garden, which slopes steeply up behind the house, and after his marriage to Mary Hutchinson (in 1802) Wordsworth increasingly took to writing out of doors. In 1808, with by then three children, the family reluctantly moved out. The bad weather in the previous summer may have been the last straw as Wordsworth was forced to work 'in that one room, common to all the family, to all visitors, and where the children frequently played beside him'.

The cottage is kept as it was when the Wordsworths lived there, with many of their belongings and some interesting portraits. As it is so small, visitors are taken on a guided tour in groups of not more than fifteen. The garden has been restored and the summerhouse rebuilt.

The Grasmere and Wordsworth Museum, in a converted stable block next door, has many original manuscripts by both William and Dorothy. The display is in chronological order and is an excellent introduction to Wordsworth's life.

Duddon River (96) (SD 23-99)
One of the most beautiful stretches of this river, thought by Wordsworth to be the

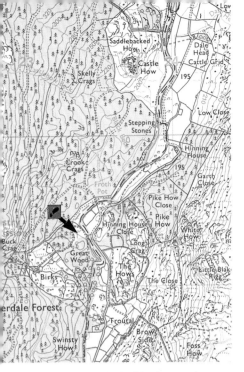

Dunmail Raise was formerly on the boundary between Westmorland and Cumberland and there was a good xenophobic saying in Westmorland that 'Nothing good cums ferm ower't Raise'.

Eamont Bridge (see Penrith)

Egremont (89) (NY 01-10)
This small market town lies outside the western boundary of the National Park, between the fells and the sea. As its name suggests, Egremont was a Norman town, planned and laid out in the twelfth century by William de Meschines, then Lord of Copeland. The ruins of the red sandstone castle still stand above the river.

From the castle can be seen the ruins of Egremont's more recent past, the spoil heaps and worked-out mines of the nineteenth-century mining boom. The town lies at the heart of a rich iron-ore field which made it a centre for mining as early as the twelfth century. In the middle of the nineteenth century this ore acquired a new value with the discovery of the Bessemer process for making steel. The process needed phosphorus-free iron and Cumberland suddenly found itself in a monopoly position, with the only major deposit in the country. In forty years the number of miners rose from sixty to over six thousand.

In the wide Main Street, still used to hold a weekly street market, is Lowes Court Gallery. This sixteenth-century building now houses an information centre and an art gallery which shows the work of local artists. Egremont's annual Crab Fair, first held in 1287, is famous for its gurning competition. Contestants put their head through a horse collar and pull faces: the worst wins.

Elter Water (90) (NY 33-04)
Lying at the foot of the two Langdale valleys, Elter Water is an oddly-shaped

The Langdale Pikes from Elter Water

loveliest in the Lake District, can be seen by parking in the Forestry Commission Froth Pot car park near the head of Dunnerdale (see map). This is on **Tour 8**. Cross the bridge and follow the footpath south to Birks Bridge, a famous packhorse bridge over a narrow, deep, gorge. After rain the water can rise right up to the parapet and there are flow-through holes to prevent the bridge being damaged by flooding.

For a longer walk the river can be followed downstream. South of here it runs through the steep sides of Wallabarrow Gorge to the hamlet of Seathwaite ★. To the east is a less familiar view of the Coniston range, with the smooth face of Dow Crag. To the west is Harter Fell (2,140 ft). One of the routes to the summit begins at Birks Bridge and goes up through Dunnerdale Forest. This plantation dates from the 1930s. At one time the Forestry Commission had designs on the whole of Upper Eskdale and Dunnerdale but the public outcry halted planting and most of the land was eventually sold to the National Trust.

Dunmail Raise (90) (NY 32-11)
The traditional dividing line between north and south Lakeland, Dunmail Raise lies on the main pass that runs north from Ambleside ★ through the Thirlmere ★ trough. In AD 943 it was the site of a battle between the Norse King Dunmail, of Cumbria, and the Anglo-Saxon King Edmund, of Northumbria. The battle was won by Edmund, who then gave the north-western part of Cumbria to Malcolm of Scotland in return for a promise of future help. The site of the battle is marked by a cairn which is now between the two carriageways of the A591 and is on **Tour 1**.

ake which is sometimes downgraded into a tarn. It is privately owned but there is a footpath along the eastern shore which gives a magnificent view of the Langdale Pikes to the west. Park in the car park on the B5343, just west of Skelwith Bridge ★ , and go through the wood on the other side of the road to reach the River Brathay. The footpath runs north to the lake. To the south is Skelwith Force, worth a brief detour. The bed of the river suddenly drops 16 ft and the water pours over the edge in a solid mass.

The footpath past the lake leads on into Elterwater village. This attractive hamlet is centred round a small green and is separated from the B5343 by a large, open common. Elterwater is on **Tours 6 and 8**. **Walk 5** starts from the village and goes up into the valley of Great Langdale ★ .

Ennerdale Water (89) (NY 10-14)

The most westerly of all the lakes, Ennerdale Water is also the most remote. It is served by only two roads, one running to a point halfway up the north shore and the other stopping short of the western end of the lake (see map). The view from the western shore, looking towards Pillar (2,927 ft), is one of the finest in the Lake District.

In 1980 Ennerdale Water was the subject of a remarkable battle. The North West Water Authority applied for planning permission to raise the level by a further 4ft, which amongst other things required embankments up to 10ft high. The proposal was fought by the Lake District Special Planning Board, all the District Councils involved, the Countryside Commission, the Friends of the Lake District – and the National Trust, who owned a small piece of farmland which would have been largely submerged if the plan had gone ahead (see

Ennerdale Water

map). The National Trust gave notice that, if the Planning Enquiry went against them, they would invoke their inalienable right to the land – a right which could be over-turned only by Parliament. The Enquiry decided that 'in view of the possible delays entailed in Parliamentary procedure' an alternative source outside the National Park, on land not owned by the National Trust, should be found. This was the first time the unique rights of National Trust land had been tested and the precedent is encouraging for all lovers of the Lakes.

It is possible to walk all round the lake, starting either from the west end or at the Forestry Commission car park at Bowness Knott. At Anglers Crag, on the south-east shore, the high path round the crag is easier and gives dramatic views up the valley. The Forestry Commission have produced three different trails starting from Bowness Knott which may help to reconcile walkers to the spruce plantations which blanket the upper part of the valley. These were planted in 1925 and the subsequent outcry led to an agreement that the Commission should leave the central 300 square miles of the National Park alone. At the head of the valley, where Scarth Gap Pass leads north into Buttermere ★ and Black Sail Pass leads south into Wasdale ★, the plantations give way to the open fells. Ennerdale Water is one mile east of Ennerdale Bridge and is on **Tour 1**.

Eskdale Corn Mill (see Boot)

Eskdale Green (89) (NY 14-00)

This small village lies where the single road west across Hardknott Pass ★ branches out to run down into the valleys of Wasdale, Miterdale and Eskdale. Yet another road turns south-east to cross over Birker Fell and come down into Dunner-dale at Ulpha ★ . This is driven on **Tour 7**.

Eskdale Green is a good base for exploring the lower half of Eskdale, which runs south-west from here to the sea. This wide fertile valley is almost deserted below here as the main road crosses over into Miterdale. Alternatively, there is a good view from Muncaster Fell, the granite ridge to the west of the village. Take the path that skirts Rabbit How to the south (see map). The upper half of Eskdale, which runs up through wild, dramatic scenery to the highest peaks in England, can be seen from Hardknott Pass.

It is also possible to take the miniature Ravenglass and Eskdale Railway ★ to Eskdale Green (or Irton Road) and walk back along the river Esk. The river winds through woods and pasture to emerge into the sand dunes at Newbeggin.

Esthwaite Water (96,97) (SD 36-96)
Lying between Hawkshead ★ and Sawrey ★ , this small lake is surrounded by fields and low wooded hills. The lake is privately owned but a road runs all the way round it and there a car park at the south-west end which gives access to the shore. The best view of the lake is from the Nab, a small promontory at the northern end, which can be reached by a footpath from Hawkshead. This is all Beatrix Potter country, and very pretty.

Esthwaite Hall, on the western shore, is the birthplace of Archbishop Sandys, who founded Hawkshead Grammar School in 1585. The Sandys family still own the lake but they now live at Graythwaite Hall ★ , 2 miles south of here. Esthwaite Water is on **Tour 6**.

Far Sawrey (see Sawrey)

Fell Foot Park (see Windermere)

Flookburgh (96,97) (SD 36-75)
This small village on the Cartmel peninsula is a mile from the sea but has always earned its living by fishing. Its name comes from the flukes (flounders) which are found on the sandflats. Flukes are still caught here, using stake-nets, but today Morecambe Bay shrimps are the most important industry. The shrimps are caught in purse-nets which are dragged over the sands using tractors and trailers. At the mouth of the trawl are two beams, a foot apart. As the lower beam reaches them, the shrimps jump upwards and fall into the net. There are also cockle beds, but cockling is no longer a major industry.

Glenridding (90) (NY 38-17)
On the west side of Ullswater ★ , this small mining village is now a centre for climbing and boating. There is an information centre in the large car park.

The Ullswater steamers operate from Glenridding pier. Non-powered craft can be launched by the Willow Trees (north of the steamer pier) and on the beach. The

The steamer pier in Glenridding

Glenridding Sailing School and the Ullswater Sailing School operate from here; boats and sailboards can be hired.

Inland, the Glenridding valley runs up to the Greenside lead mine, once one of the most profitable lead mines in the country. In 1875 it produced lead and silver ore worth more than £1 million. The mine closed in 1962. The problem was always transport: when the mine was first opened the ore was carried over the Helvellyn ridge (via Sticks Pass) to be smelted in the Newlands ★ valley. Later the Penrith-Keswick railway line (now closed) made it possible to transport the ore to Newcastle.

The Lake District Ski Club has a ski-tow and hut above Glenridding and some of the Helvellyn slopes are excellent for skiing. Glenridding is on **Tour 4**.

Gosforth (89) (NY 06-03)
St Mary's Church in Gosforth has some remarkable relics of the early Viking set

tlers. The most extraordinary is a tenth-century cross in the churchyard which shows how the Norsemen simply added the Christian religion which they found on their arrival to the old Norse religion which they brought with them. The wheel cross is at the top of a tall pillar which is carved with bark at the base and represents the sacred ash tree. On one side is the crucifixion, with a soldier piercing the side of Christ with a sword, and on the other are scenes from Norse mythology − Vidar fighting the double-headed dragon-wolf and Heimdal guarding with his horn the rainbow bridge which leads to the realm of the gods. ·

Inside the church are other Norse carvings, including the Fishing Stone which shows Thor trying to catch the Midgard Serpent: similar stones have been found in Sweden and Denmark. There are also two good examples of Norse hog-back tombstones, one carved with two groups of men armed with spears and round shields.

Gosforth is on the western boundary of the National Park and is just off **Tour 1**.

Gowbarrow Park (see Ullswater)

Grange (89,90) (NY 25-17)
This small hamlet on the river Derwent is one of the prettiest villages in the Lake District. It is reached by a narrow double bridge off the B5289 and is on **Tour 2** and **Walk 10**. Peace How, the knoll to the west of the village, was given to the National Trust in 1917 by Canon Rawnsley. There are magnificent views from the top.

In 1209 most of Borrowdale ★ was bought by Furness Abbey, which at one time was the second richest Cistercian monastery in England. They also owned Derwent Water ★. Grange, which lies between the two, became their home farm.

Grange-over-Sands (96,97) (SD 40-77)
Just outside the southern boundary of the National Park, Grange-over-Sands looks out over the sands of Morecambe Bay. The town is a Victorian seaside resort, created by the coming of the Furness railway in 1857, and claims the mildest climate in the Lake District (its winter temperatures are comparable with the south of England). There are ornamental gardens, a bandstand, and a mile-long promenade between the railway line and the beach. The currents make swimming in the sea dangerous but there is an excellent salt-water swimming pool at the west end of the promenade.

The town's name reflects its earlier history, both as a granary for nearby Cartmel ★ Priory and as a landmark on the route across the sands of Morecambe Bay. Before the coming of the railway, the sands were the main road from Lancaster. The medieval packhorse trains crossed

from Hest Bank, above Morecambe, to Kents Bank, to the west of the town − a distance of 8 miles. In the eighteenth century the approach across Morecambe Bay was a popular part of the Lakes Tour and the stage coach from Lancaster continued until the middle of the nineteenth century.

Guided walks across the sands still take place and details can be obtained from the information centre in Main Street. The sands should not be attempted without a guide: they are criss-crossed with deep channels which are impossible to see when the tide rises − and an inch is enough to cover the plain of flat wet sand and leave the walker a mile out at sea.

Behind the wooded slopes of the town is a dramatic limestone escarpment (see map). At the summit is Hampsfell Hospice, a limestone building erected by a former vicar of Cartmel for the 'shelter and entertainment' of wanderers. There is a direction finder on the roof and an astonishing view in every direction. Grange-over-Sands is on **Tour 10**.

Grasmere (90) (NY 33-66)
The classic view of this lovely circular lake is from Loughrigg Terrace, looking north to the high fells which close in at Dunmail Raise ★. In the foreground is Grasmere village ★ and behind it Helm Crag, said to look like a lion lying down by a lamb. Park at White Moss Common and follow the circular walk through the woods and back along the River Rothay (see map).

Grasmere is a glacial lake, hollowed out by ice. The single central island, formed from the debris left behind by the glacier, was a favourite excursion for the Wordsworths. They used to row across, taking a picnic. There is an extraordinary descrip-

Grasmere village (90) (NY 33-07)

Just south of Dunmail Raise ★ , the traditional dividing point between north and south Lakeland, Grasmere is on **Tours 1,5 and 6**. The village grew out of a string of hamlets on what was once the old packhorse route across White Moss Common. Dove Cottage ★ , Wordsworth's first home, was in Town End. In the fifteenth and sixteenth centuries Grasmere was a flourishing centre of the fulling industry, which cleaned and thickened the locally woven cloth, but by the time the Wordsworths arrived there were no mills left. The Grasmere and Wordsworth Museum, next to Dove Cottage, has two rooms devoted to local history.

There is a National Park Information Centre near the Garden Centre in Red Bank Road (see map) and a National Trust Information Centre in Church Stile, opposite the churchyard. Church Stile is sixteenth-century and was formerly an inn, one of the many in the district that had a cockpit. Samuel Taylor Coleridge and Wordsworth stayed here on their walking holiday in 1799 and Wordsworth wrote to his sister that he had found 'a small house in Grasmere empty which perhaps we will take'.

In the churchyard are the Wordsworth graves. William, Dorothy and Mary are buried close to Mary's sister Sarah Hutchinson, who died fifteen years before any of the others. A single stone first records her death – the mourners expressing 'an earnest wish that their own remains may be laid by her side' – and later reports that they 'are now gathered near her'. The headstone to William Wordsworth is to his son, another William. Two of Wordsworth's other children died while the family were living at Grasmere Rectory opposite the church; one aged six and the other four. The family moved to Rydal Mount ★ to get away.

St Oswald's church is thirteenth century, with massive pillars and exposed rafters. The north aisle was added in the sixteenth century and accounts for the odd construction of the roof. Wordsworth's description in *The Excursion* is as good as any:
'Not raised in nice proportions was the pile,
But large and massy; for duration built..'
There is a marble memorial to Wordsworth with an inscription written by the Oxford theologian John Keble.

In August each year the church holds a traditional Rushbearing Ceremony, dating from the time when the church floor was covered in rushes. Afterwards the village children parade round the village and are rewarded with Grasmere gingerbread, stamped with the name of St Oswald. The gingerbread shop by the church used to be the village school in Wordsworth's time.

The third Wordsworth home in Grasmere is Allan Bank, where the family lived for three years after they left Dove Cottage and before they moved to the Rectory. It lies to the west of the village and is

tion in Wordsworth's *Guide to the Lakes* of an optical illusion when he and Dorothy saw a 'newly created island'; the second one larger, higher and clearer than the first. After some time the island faded and then turned upside down and disappeared, leaving behind a clear area of ice of the same size. Dorothy and her brother William decided that it had been an inverted reflection of Silver How, probably caused because the ice was thinly covered with water.

The lake belongs to the National Trust and power boats are banned. Boats can be launched (and hired) from Pavement End, Grasmere village, and fishing permits can be obtained from the Information Centre. In summer the 'beach' under Loughrigg Terrace gets very crowded but there is always the island. Wordsworth thought the view from a boat on 'the bosom of the Lake' the best of all.

Grasmere

reached by a lane leading out of the main square, to the right of the Red Lion. The house has a magnificent view, looking across to Seat Sandal and Fairfield, but the chimneys smoked and Wordsworth quarrelled with his landlord. Allan Bank is owned by the National Trust.

Graythwaite Hall (97) (SD 36-91)
West of Windermere ★ , Graythwaite Hall is owned by the Sandys family who hold much of the land round here, including Esthwaite Water ★ . The gardens are open to the public in April, May and June, when they are at their best. They were landscaped by Thomas Mawson, a Victorian who wrote a book called 'The Life and Work of an English Landscape Architect', and are 'natural' gardens with a mass of rhododendrons and azaleas. The steepsided ghyll, overlooked by the Hall, is particularly beautiful.

Great Langdale (90) (NY 32-04)
The valley of Great Langdale, which runs west from Elter Water ★ , is one of the most dramatic in the Lake District. To the north the Langdale Pikes rise almost sheer from the valley bottom. This jagged volcanic range has five peaks, the two highest being the twin mountains of Harrison Stickle (2,415 ft) and Pike o' Stickle (2,323 ft). Neolithic stone-axe factories have been discovered on Pike o' Stickle, over 5,000 years old. The axes were made from tuffs (extremely hard rock formed from volcanic dust) and were roughed out with granite hammers before being taken to the coast. There they were polished with sandstone before being exported.

The head of the valley is closed in by a wall of high mountains, with Bow Fell (2,960 ft) straight ahead and Crinkle Crags (2,816 ft) and Pike of Blisco to the south. The old packhorse route to Wasdale ★ went to the north of Bowfell and ran up Rossett Gill and past Angle Tarn and Sprinkling Tarn to Sty Head Pass, between Borrowdale ★ and Wasdale. On a map of 1777 this was marked as a major road!

Blea Tarn

The modern road turns south past Side Pike and crosses over into Little Langdale ★ , which runs parallel to Great Langdale to the south. The narrow road climbs steeply and then runs through a lovely hanging valley, with Blea Tarn in its centre. There is a car park at the top of the pass and it is possible to walk all round the tarn. Great Langdale is on **Tours 6 and 8**.

Greenodd (96,97) (SD 31-82)
Formerly an important port, Greenodd lies at the mouth of the river Crake, where it flows into the tidal waters of the river Leven. Copper ore and slate were brought down the Crake from Coniston Water ★ to be shipped out from here, and cotton for the cotton mill at Backbarrow ★ was shipped in.

Some of the old staithes remain and there are some pleasant buildings. The A590 cut through the centre of the town and at one time ran along the old quay. However there is now a bypass to the south with a picnic area overlooking the Leven estuary.

Greystoke (90) (NY 44-30)
The church of St Andrew in Greystoke is one of the largest and most beautiful in Cumbria. It dates from the thirteenth century and until the Reformation was a collegiate church, with six chaplains. The spacious interior has massive pillars and arches, and a lovely east window, which includes fragments of thirteenth-century glass. The oak stalls used by the college canons still exist and have carved misericords.

Greystoke suffered heavily from the plague, as did Penrith ★ , and there is a plague stone outside the church where coins were purified in vinegar before changing hands. The hollowed-out stone is set in the ground about a hundred yards along the footpath which runs north from the church. There is also an old sanctuary stone on the road leading to the church. This used to stand in the middle of the road, to mark the boundary beyond which fugitives from justice could claim sanctuary, but is now behind a grille in the wall of the swimming pool.

On the opposite side of the village is Greystoke Castle, built in the fourteenth century. The castle was acquired by Thomas Howard, Duke of Norfolk, during the reign of Queen Elizabeth and is still in the Howard family. There are several other large houses around the village and Sir Gordon Richards had his racing stables here.

Greystoke is 4 miles west of Penrith, on the B5288. It is on the old Roman road that ran south-west from the fort at Voreda or Old Penrith (NY 49-38) to a temporary camp at Troutbeck (NY 38-27). Many people believe that the road must have gone on through Keswick to join the

GUMMERS HOW

Roman road running over Whinlatter Pass ★ but the missing section has yet to be traced.

Grizedale Forest (96,97) (SD 33-94)
Between Coniston Water ★ and Windermere ★ is the large forest of Grizedale. The original mixed oak forest was ruthlessly exploited as a source of charcoal for iron smelting, first by the monks of Furness Abbey and later by the ironmasters. By the eighteenth century the woods could no longer support the industry (each of the large furnaces used 200 acres of coppice annually) and the ironmasters started to move away; although the largest furnace of all (at Backbarrow ★) went on using charcoal until 1920.

In the eighteenth century the Grizedale Estate started to plant conifers (mainly for pit props) and the Forestry Commission, who took over in 1937, have continued this policy. Broadleaf trees remain in some areas however and those surrounding the clearing in the valley bottom are particularly beautiful (see map). They were planted as ornamental trees around Grizedale Hall: the house has now been pulled down but the Forestry Commission still have their administrative centre here.

There is also an information centre with a wildlife exhibition and deer museum. The commission take wildlife conservation in the forest seriously and there are hides and forest trails. A large barn on the site has been converted into the Theatre in the Forest, which puts on plays and concerts in the summer. Grizedale Forest is on **Tours 8 and 9**.

Gummers How (96,97) (SD 39-88)
At the south-east end of Windermere ★ , this small knoll gives a tremendous view

Gummers How

up the lake, with the high fells beyond. There is a footpath to the summit from the car park above Fell Foot, about a mile up the unclassified road to Bowland Bridge (see **Tour 10**). Even the view across the road from the car park is worth stopping for.

Hardknott Pass (89) (NY 23-01)
This is the second highest pass in the Lake District (1,291 ft), and the most dramatic – with gradients of 1-in-3 in some places and hairpin bends. The Romans were the first to drive a road through here but their road was further to the south – and much straighter.

Near the summit there is a small parking place and to the west a birdseye view of the Roman fort which guards the pass, perched on a shelf of rocky fell 400ft below (see map on this page). From above, the outlines of the buildings can be clearly seen. The fort is square, with towers at each corner and a gate in the middle of each wall – even on the north-west, where the ground falls sheer away. Inside, two roads run at rightangles, gate to gate. The road from the main gate (which faces the road) goes to the headquarters

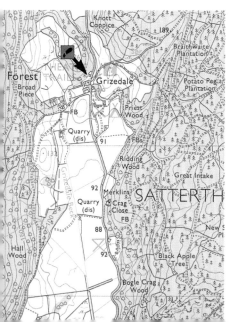

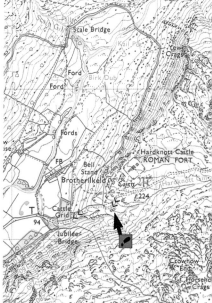

The Roman fort

Hardknott Pass

building. To its right is the granary, the strongest building in the fort, and to the left the commandant's house. The 500-strong garrison lived in wooden huts.

Between the fort and the road is the bathhouse, fed by a local beck but equipped with underfloor heating in two of the four rooms. The round building close by was the equivalent of a sauna. To the north-east the parade ground can still be seen, three acres of levelled ground. Even, or perhaps especially, in this wild place the troops must be kept busy. Coins and pottery suggest that the fort was occupied between AD 120–138 and AD 160–197. It was called Mediobogdum and the troops based here were Dalmatian: they would have marched here from their native land (now Yugloslavia).

A short walk from the car park will bring you to one of the most extraordinary views in the Lakes. Walk east along the road and then north through the gap between Border End and Hardknott. Ahead of you are the Lakeland giants of Sca Fell, Sca Fell Pike ★ and Bowfell, with the river Esk far below. Dorothy Wordsworth called it a 'glittering serpent stream'.

Hardknott Pass (and Wrynose Pass ★) are on the only road west from the central Lake District and are on **Tours 1 and 7.**

Hartsop (90) (NY 41-13)

This fellside hamlet lies to the east of Kirkstone Pass ★ and is on **Tour 4**. It has a magnificent position, backed by high fells, and is the best starting point for High Street ★ . The road stops just beyond the village and there is a small car park.

Many of the farm buildings in the village are seventeenth-century and some cot-tages have the old spinning galleries. All the land around here was once a Norman hunting forest and Wordsworth spells the village name as Hartshope. The arms of the Hartsop family, who built Hartsop Hall, carried three harts' heads. The hall dates from the fourteenth century and is south-west of Brothers Water (see map). This large tarn was given to the Treasury in 1947 by the Earl of Lonsdale, in lieu of death duties, and passed on by them to the National Trust. It was the first time that the Treasury had handed over property to the Trust as an unconditional gift. There is a footpath along the south shore of the tarn: it is little visited, with Ullswater ★ so close, and is a good place for birdwatchers.

Haweswater (90) (NY 48-44)

The largest reservoir in the North-West, Haweswater was once a small lake set in a green fertile dale. Wordsworth described it as 'a lesser Ullswater'. In 1940 the Man-chester Water Authority built a 120ft dam across the foot of the lake and raised the water level by a staggering 96ft. The entire

The reservoir of Haweswater

valley was flooded and the village of Mardale – together with several farms which formerly supplied butter and milk to Manchester – completely submerged.

A road now runs up the south-east bank of the reservoir and there is a car park at the head of the valley. Access to the water-line is impossible from the road but there is a footpath down the north-west bank. The concrete rim surrounding the water is discouraging. The valley head however is magnificent, with the dramatic High Street ★ range to the west and Harter Fell to the south. Two passes run up from here: Gate Scarth Pass to the east of Harter Fell leads through into Longsleddale ★ ; and Nan Bield Pass, to the west, runs past Small Water and down into the Kentmere ★ valley.

Haweswater is in the north-east of the National Park and can be reached from Bampton ★ (on **Tours 3 and 4**). The policy of the LDSPB and the North West Water Authority is to keep Haweswater as near-wilderness and its silence and isolation have their admirers, especially among fell-walkers who see it from above. Others see it as a dead valley with no village, and no farms, and the fells, in the graphic words of Norman Nicholson, 'plunged up to the waist in cold water'.

Hawkshead (96,97) (SD 35-98)
Set in lovely rolling hills near the head of Esthwaite Water ★ , Hawkshead is the most picturesque of the Lake District's villages. It was a medieval wool town and is still an attractive muddle of squares and courtyards, many linked by narrow arch-ways. Most of the houses are seventeenth-century and some still have outside stone staircases. The town once boasted seven inns and still has four.

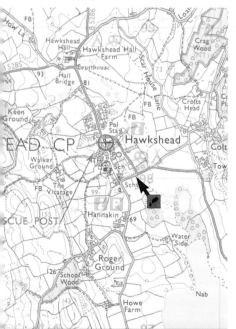

Hawkshead village

The fifteenth-century Courthouse

Only residents' cars are allowed in the village centre and there is a large, rather ugly, car park at the edge of the village. The National Park Authority have an Information Centre in the car park and there is another, National Trust, Information Centre in Main Street (see map). This is housed in Thimble Hall next to the 'Bump and Bend' cottage, so called because of the difficulty lorries and buses once had in getting past the overhanging upper storey.

Thimble Hall is next to the former offices of Heelis Solicitors. William Heelis was the husband of Beatrix Potter, who lived near-by in Sawrey ★ , and there is a Beatrix Potter exhibition in the building. On display is the collection of original drawings which were shown at Hill Top ★ until 1981.

Hawkshead Grammar School, opposite the car park, is now a museum. Words-worth was sent to school here after the death of his mother. He was eight years old and stayed until he left to go up to St John's College, Cambridge. The school was a good one, founded in 1585 by Arch-bishop Sandys, and Wordsworth's first

St Michael's Church

recorded poem was in honour of its bicentenary. Less precociously, he carved his initials on his desk: they are now covered with glass for posterity. The main room downstairs is set out as an eighteenth-century schoolroom, with long wooden benches, and there is an exhibition and library upstairs.

A path leads round the back of the school into the village centre. The Main Square is dominated by the seventeenth-century Shambles, which had butchers' stalls on the ground floor and other shops above.

St Michael's church, which stands over the village, dates from the fifteenth century. In Wordsworth's day it was white-washed but its rough-cast was removed in 1875 and it is now Silurian stone, with red sandstone around the doors and windows. Inside, the bulky columns and arches are decorated with coloured dogtooth patterns and there are the painted texts so typical of Lakeland churches. Near the north door is an interesting record of a Burial in Woollen. To conform with a 1666 Act of Parliament, to protect the wool trade, the certificate registers that 'the corps was nott put in wrapt or wound up or buried in any shirt, shift, sheet or shroud made or mingled with flax hempe silke haire gold or silver or other than what is made of sheeps wool onely'.

There are several pleasant walks around Hawkshead (see map). To the north of the village is the fifteenth-century Courthouse which is all that is left of Hawkshead manor, held by the monks of Furness Abbey for 300 years. The building is owned by the National Trust and a key can be obtained from the Information Centre. The courthouse is on **Walk 7**, which starts in Hawkshead.

To the east is Colthouse, the hamlet where Wordsworth lodged while he was at school, and to the south is Esthwaite Water. The lake is owned by the Sandys family, who are still the local landowners, but there is a public footpath across the fields to the Nab, a promontory which gives a good view of the lake. Hawkshead is on **Tours 5 and 9**.

Helvellyn (90) (NY 34-15)
At 3,118ft, Helvellyn is the third highest peak in the Lake District and the most climbed. It stands in a long range of fells between Thirlmere ★ and Ullswater ★ and can be approached from either valley. To the west the range slopes smoothly down to the lake, but to the east the ice has scooped out a series of corries, leaving only narrow ridges between them. The most famous example holds Red Tarn and is bounded by Swirral Edge to the north and Striding Edge to the south.

Routes to the top go in and out of fashion. Wordsworth recommends in his guide the route from Wythburn, at the head of Thirlmere. In 1805 he climbed Helvellyn from here with Walter Scott and the scientist Humphrey Davy. Nowadays the most popular routes are from the east, starting from Glenridding ★ or Patterdale ★ .

High Street (90) (NY 44-11)
This magnificent ridgeway runs north-south between Ullswater ★ and Haweswater ★ . It is 11 miles long and well over 2,000ft for most of its length. Its name comes from the Roman road which ran along the top and connected the fort near Brougham Castle ★ to the Galava fort at Waterhead ★ . It is thought the Romans probably improved an existing British road.

The ridge is narrow in some places (especially at the Straits of Riggindale, to the east of Hartsop ★), but the summit is a broad plateau. At one time an annual fair was held here at which horses were raced.

High Wray (96,97) (SD 37-99)
From the car park at Red Nab, east of High Wray, there is a pleasant walk along the west shore of Windermere ★ to Wray Crag (see map). Wray Castle, a castellated Victorian folly built in the 1840s, is worth a detour. Turn inland at High Wray Bay and right along the road past the church.

Beatrix Potter spent a series of happy summers in Wray Castle, rented by her family as a holiday house. It was here that the family became friends with Canon Rawnsley, one of the founders of the National Trust ★ , who was then the vicar of Wray. This forceful and sympathetic character was a great influence on Beatrix

Potter and it was he who suggested that she submit 'The Tale of Peter Rabbit' to Frederick Warne & Co., who eventually published all her books.

High Wray is reached by a minor road off the B5286 between Ambleside ★ and Hawkshead ★ and is on **Tour 5**.

Hill Top (96,97) (SD 37-95)

In 1905 Beatrix Potter bought this small farm in Sawrey ★ as an 'investment'. She was thirty nine at the time and still lived at home with her wealthy parents. But she had already published five of her 'little books' and in the same year she became engaged (against her parent's wishes) to Norman Warne, the son of her publisher. Within a few months he was dead and Hill Top became for her a 'fresh beginning'.

She never lived there, keeping on the previous tenant John Cannon as a farm manager, but for the next eight years she used it as a retreat; somewhere to write and draw and garden. In the summers, when her parents used to rent a large house in the Lake District for three months, she would come over four days in the week.

The seventeenth-century farmhouse and its surroundings became the raw material for her books. She once wrote to a friend, 'I can't invent. I only copy'. The interior of the house appears in both '*Tom Kitten*' and '*The Roly Poly Pudding*', which was inspired by the rats which overran the house when she first bought it. 'Mrs Cannon has seen a rat sitting up eating its dinner under the kitchen table in the middle of the afternoon'. '*Jemima Puddleduck*' shows the outside of the farm, with the Cannons themselves making an appearance. '*Pigling Bland*' comes from a venture into pig farming. 'I spent a very wet hour inside the pig-sty drawing the pig. It tries to nibble my boots, which is interrupting.'

In 1909 Beatrix Potter bought another, larger, farm in Sawrey and in 1913 she married the local solicitor, William Heelis, and moved into the farm cottage. As Mrs Heelis she became a notable farmer, respected for her flocks of Herdwick sheep. Increasingly she used her money to buy up land, seeing ownership as the only way to protect the Lake District from the perils of outside developers. All her estates (over 4,000 acres) came to the National Trust ★ on her death.

For Hill Top, she retained a special affection, keeping it throughout her life as a retreat. She left instructions in her will that it was not to be lived in and that nothing was to be altered. In 1946, two and a half years after Beatrix Potter's death, the National Trust opened Hill Top to the public. They have followed her wish to keep the house as it was and there is a limit on the numbers admitted at any one time. To keep the overall number of visitors down, the house is shut on Fridays.

Hill Top is on **Tour 6**. The National Trust

has opened a Beatrix Potter museum in William Heelis's old offices in Hawkshead and on display are the original watercolours for the books.

Holehird (90) (SD 40-00)

Two of the loveliest and least known gardens in the Lake District are in the grounds of the Holehird Cheshire Home, east of Windermere ★ . The entrance is on the east side of the A592, about ¾ mile north of the mini-roundabout on the A591.

Follow the drive up the hill, with the lawns of the Cheshire Home on your left, until you reach a large car park. Ahead of you is a walled garden and behind and above it an alpine garden. Both are run by the Lakeland Horticultural Society and have an large collection of plants in a superb setting. From the alpine garden there are magnificent views to the west, especially at sunset. The gardens are free but donations are welcome.

Holker Hall (96,97) (SD 35-77)

Owned by the Cavendish family, Holker Hall itself is rather overpowered by the extras which it uses to attract visitors. Various events are staged in the large deer park that surrounds the house, including hot air ballooning, horse trials and model aircraft rallies. There is also a Craft and Countryside Museum, a Baby Animal House and part of the Zanussi Collection of Victorian, Edwardian and wartime kitchens. The Lakeland Motor Museum (with a separate entrance fee) has a display of vintage cars and motor cycles and a replica of Donald Campbell's Bluebird, which sank on Coniston Water ★ .

Holker Hall dates from the sixteenth century but the only part of the house which is open to the public is the nineteenth-century mansion which was built to replace the old west wing, burnt down in 1871. The older part of the house is lived in by the Cavendish family, who have owned the estate since 1756. The Victorian building was built on the grand scale by a firm of Lancaster architects and has an impos-

Holker Hall

ing cantilever staircase and extensive panelling. The gardens are the best feature. They were designed by Joseph Paxton and are beautifully maintained. Holker Hall is on **Tour 10.**

Honister Pass (89,90) (NY 22-13)

The Honister Pass (1,176ft) runs from Borrowdale ★ to Buttermere ★ and is on **Tours 1 and 2.** It is a narrow twisting road with 1-in-4 gradients and is best driven from east to west, when the valley of Buttermere opens up before you. Great Gable (2,949 ft) dominates the view to the south and on the Buttermere side the road runs down beside Gatesgarth Beck, backed by Honister Crag. The National Trust own the land on either side of the pass and have resisted attempts to widen the road, feeling that this would destroy its character.

The Honister green slate quarries at the top of the pass are still working and can be visited by arrangement. The slate is dressed and polished here and there are workshops and galleries.

Honister Pass

Howtown (90) (NY 44-19)

On the east shore of Ullswater ★ , the bay at Howtown is a popular centre for boating. There is a public launching point for all craft (up to 20 ft) and the Ullswater Yacht Club is based at Thwaithill Bay, 1 ½ miles to the north.

The Ullswater steamers stop at Howtown and one of the best ways to see the lake is to take the steamer from Glenridding ★ to Howtown and walk back along the east shore. Beyond Sandwick there is

no road and the path goes through wild and unspoilt scenery, with lovely views across the lake. **Tour 3** goes through Howtown and follows the road south as far as Martindale Hause, the start of **Walk 4.**

Ings (97) (SD 44-98)

The hamlet of Ings boasts an eighteenth-century church in the Renaissance style which would look more at home in the City of London. It was founded by a local man, Robert Bateman, who had made a fortune overseas. The floor is Italian marble and was much admired by Wordsworth who visited the church when he was at school in Hawkshead ★ . He also found the story of the founder romantic and wrote an epitaph which is now engraved on a brass plate in the church.

'He was a parish boy – at the church door

They made a gathering for him ...;

This got Bateman to London apparently and he was then sent

'Beyond the seas, where he grew wondrous rich

And left estates and monies to the poor'.

The almshouses beside the church were also built with Bateman's money.

Ings is on **Tours 4,6 and 9**. The church is on the old main road which here runs to the south of the A591.

Irton (89) (NY 09-00)

The isolated church at Irton, just inside the western boundary of the National Park, has a ninth-century Anglian cross which is thought to have been erected for an Anglo-Saxon thegn or his wife. 'Tun' means farmstead and the name Irton indicates an Anglian settlement here during the brief period between the Celts and the Norsemen. The church can be reached from Santon Bridge ★ (on **Tours 1 and 7**) by taking the road to Gubbergill and then turning north down a lane which leads to the church.

The red sandstone cross is on the far side of the graveyard, surrounded by gravestones, and is in an excellent state of preservation. It is elaborately carved with knotwork and has graceful, curving arms. On the west side the runes read 'Pray for..'.

Keld (90) (NY 55-14)

This small hamlet of old stone cottages is just to the west of Shap ★ , which is on **Tours 3 and 4.** It is thought to have been used by the monks of Shap Abbey to house their tenants. The small chapel in the village was probably also built by the abbey. It is a simple stone building which has been used as a cottage at some time and still has a partition wall with a fireplace. Five of the windows are in perfect condition and the east window is contemporary with the east window in the belfrey of Shap Abbey. In 1918 the chapel was given to the National Trust and the key can be obtained from the house opposite.

Walk 4 starts from Keld and visits Shap Abbey.

Kendal (97) (SD 51-92)

Known as the Auld Grey Town, Kendal is the largest town in Cumbria apart from Carlisle. The motto on the town's arms is Pannus mihi panis (Wool is my Bread) and the town's prosperity dates from the fourteenth century, when Kendal pioneered the woollen industry in Britain. The famous Kendal Green was a coarse cloth worn by bowmen, the green colour achieved by dyeing the cloth first yellow with dyer's broom (which still grows wild in the Kent valley) and then blue with woad.

The layout of the town reflects its history. The main street runs between the river Kent and Kendal Fell, changing its name from Kirkland to Highgate to Stricklandgate as it goes north. The Information Centre **(1)** is next to the Town Hall, in Stricklandgate. Just north of here, between the Market Place and Finkle Street, are the Shambles **(11)**. These are the butchers' shops, built when the original meat market was abandoned because the slope did not give sufficient drainage. The Old Shambles are on the opposite side of the road, behind the Fleece Inn.

Walking south down Highgate, you will see the old gateway to Sandes Hospital **(10)**. In 1659 a cotton manufacturer called Thomas Sandes built almshouses on this site for eight widows, who were to work at carding and spinning. The present buildings are nineteenth-century but the original gateway, with the arms and initials of Thomas Sandes, survives. Also in Highgate is the Brewery Arts Centre **(3)**, a converted brewery which has a theatre, gallery and restaurant. The Centre holds annual Folk and Jazz festivals.

Holy Trinity

Kendal lies on the River Kent

The Kendal yards lie to the west of Highgate. As the cloth trade expanded, the crofts behind the houses were filled in to form narrow alleyways running at right-angles to the main street. In Kendal's heyday the fells behind would have been covered with tenter-frames for stretching the cloth, giving the steep slopes the look of a Mediterranean vineyard.

Castle Howe, the mound to the west of the yards, is the site of an eleventh-century Norman motte and bailey castle built by the de Lancasters. On the top is a monument to William of Orange **(8)**, commemorating the Glorious Revolution of 1688. The ruins of the later, thirteenth-century, castle can be seen on the other side of the river, on Castle Hill **(5)**. This belonged at one time to the Parr family and Catherine Parr, the last wife of Henry VIII, was born here. On her marriage she gave her husband a coat of Kendal cloth.

Walking south into Kirkland brings you to the parish church of Holy Trinity **(6)**. This thirteenth-century gothic church is the second and widest in England, with five aisles and a forest of pillars and arches. There are chapels dedicated to the Parrs of Kendal Castle and the Stricklands of Sizergh Castle ★ and several fine brasses to the Bellinghams, another landowning family. The helmet left behind by Robin the Devil (see Crook ★) is on display.

Behind the church is Abbot Hall **(2)**, a

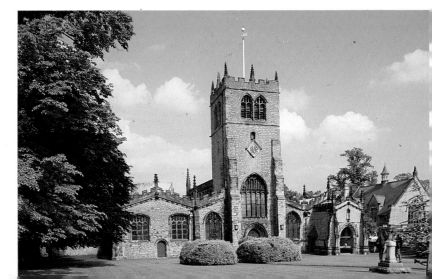

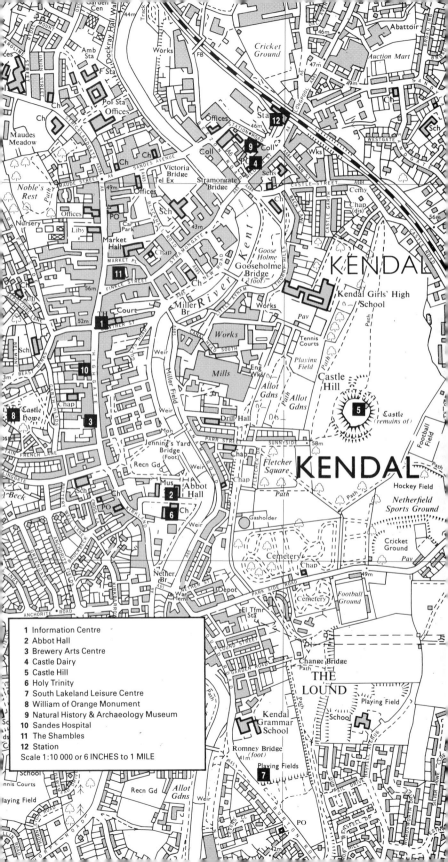

KENDAL

1 Information Centre
2 Abbot Hall
3 Brewery Arts Centre
4 Castle Dairy
5 Castle Hill
6 Holy Trinity
7 South Lakeland Leisure Centre
8 William of Orange Monument
9 Natural History & Archaeology Museum
10 Sandes Hospital
11 The Shambles
12 Station
Scale 1:10 000 or 6 INCHES to 1 MILE

Abbot Hall Art Gallery

Kentmere (90) (NY 45-04)

The narrow valley of Kentmere runs up into the High Street ★ range, with the parallel valleys of Troutbeck ★ and Longsleddale ★ on either side. Where the valley widens out (see map) there was once a lake. The earth here contains silicon from the diatoms which lived in the water and is quarried for industrial purposes. A Viking spearhead has been found and a medieval canoe.

At the head of the valley is the church of St Cuthbert, built on the site of a church in which St Cuthbert's body rested on its way to Durham. There is a small car park, which gets very crowded in summer. Kentmere Hall, on the west side of the valley, is a farmhouse built onto the side of a fourteenth-century pele tower. Bernard Gilpin, a leader of the Reformation who was known as the Apostle of the North was born here. There is a bronze memorial to him in the church.

There is a pleasant walk around Kentmere Tarn, all that remains of the lake. To the north, a footpath leads to the Nan Bield Pass (2,000 ft), the route to Haweswater ★ or the High Street range. The footpath to the west is the Garburn road, an old packhorse way that leads to Troutbeck, and there is also a path east to Sadgill.

well-proportioned Georgian mansion standing in a small park. The house is now used as an art gallery, with eighteenth-century furniture and paintings downstairs and more modern work upstairs. Some of the period furniture was made by the local cabinet-makers Gillows of Lancaster and there is a large collection of paintings by George Romney, a Lancashire lad who eloped with a servant girl from Kendal. She and the children remained in Kendal while he made his name as a portrait painter in London, returning at the age of sixty five to be nursed by her until her death.

Next door to Abbot Hall is the Museum of Lakeland Life and Industry, housed partly in the stable block and partly in the Jacobean Grammar School. This excellent museum won the first Museum of the Year Award, in 1973. There are fascinating reconstructions of workshops, showing how the original tools were used, and rooms furnished with the dark oak furniture typical of the Lake District.

From Abbot Hall Park, you can cross the river by a footbridge. To reach Castle Hill and the ruins of Kendal Castle (5), turn right and then left along Parr Street. There is a fine view of Kendal from the top of the hill. The former Castle Dairy (4) is to the north, in Wildman Street.

Nearby, in Station Road, is the Natural History and Archeology Museum (9). This is one of the earliest museums in the country, originating from the private collection of a Mr Todhunter who set up an exhibition of 'curiosities' in 1796. In the 1830s the Kendal Literary and Scientific Society, whose members included John Dalton, Richard Owen and William Wordsworth, acquired the collection and opened a museum. There are three galleries: the Kendal and Westmorland Gallery traces the history of Man in the Lakes from the Stone Age onwards and show the development of Kendal in the Middle Ages as a wool town; the Lake District Natural History Gallery shows the natural history of Lakeland; and the World Wildlife Gallery shows animals from all over the world, with the emphasis on conservation of rare species.

On the A65 going south is the South Lakeland Leisure Centre (7), which offers various sports facilities. **Tours 9 and 10** both start from Kendal.

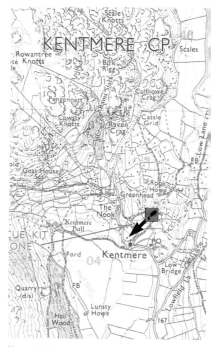

Keswick (89,90) (NY 26-23)

Once a mining town, Keswick expanded into a tourist centre with the coming of the railway in the nineteenth century. It has the most magnificent position of any of the Lake District towns, sandwiched between Skiddaw ★ and Derwent Water ★ .

	Key		
1	Information Centre	6	Keswick Spa
2	Boat Landings	7	Museum & Art Gallery
3	Century Theatre	8	National Trust Information
4	St Kentigern	9	Pencil Museum
5	Friar's Crag	10	Railway Museum

Scale 1:10 000 or 6 INCHES to 1 Mile

Derwent Water and Keswick from Hawes End

The Information Centre **(1)** is in the Moot Hall in the Town Square. The original Moot Hall was built in the sixteenth century, when Elizabeth I brought prosperity to the 'lytle, poore market town' by importing German miners to exploit the copper, lead and silver in the surrounding fells. The hall has been a prison, a town hall and a market. The present building is nineteenth-century and has a curious one-handed clock. Upstairs is a small gallery.

Walking west along the Main Street brings you to the Railway Museum **(10)**, above the Natwest Bank. The railway line to Keswick no longer exists and the museum has a collection of photographs and relics, including working signals. There are working models and a continuous film show.

Farther along the road on the right is Keswick School, with Greta Hall visible on the hill behind. Samuel Taylor Coleridge lived here for four years and Robert Southey for forty. Their wives were sisters. Coleridge wrote, 'I question if there be a room in England which commands a view of mountains and lakes and woods superior to that in which I am now sitting'. The house is now part of the school.

On the right just before you cross Greta Bridge is the Cumberland Pencil Factory, which has a unique Pencil Museum **(9)**. The first pencils in the world were made in Keswick by this company, using graphite mined from the Blacklead or Wadd mines in Borrowdale ★. The museum traces the development of the pencil from the original strips of graphite encased in wood to the present day. Early restored machinery is on display and various unusual pencils, including a wartime pencil which contains a map of Germany and a compass.

The road continues towards Portinscale. Just after High Hill, turn right along Church Lane, signposted to Crosthwaite. The name means 'Clearing of the cross' and it is thought that St Kentigern, bishop of Glasgow, set up his cross here on his flight from Scotland to Wales and preached to about six hundred people. This was in the sixth century. The present church of St Kentigern **(4)** dates from the fifteenth century and has many connections with Coleridge, Southey and the Wordsworths. Southey's grave is on the south side of the church, close to a viewfinder for the Borrowdale and Derwent Fells. The church has a magnificent position, with Skiddaw almost in the churchyard. Inside the church there is an effigy of Southey with an inscription and memorial verses written by Wordsworth. Canon Rawnsley, a lifelong campaigner for the preservation of the Lake District and one of the founders of the National Trust ★, was vicar of Crosthwaite for thirty four years.

North of the Information Centre, the Keswick Museum and Art Gallery **(7)** in Station Road has a collection of original manuscripts by literary figures associated with the Lakes. Horace Walpole and John Ruskin are represented, as well as Southey, Wordsworth and Coleridge. There is a large collection of minerals, including musical stones on which enterprising visitors can play tunes. They were played to Queen Victoria. Also in Station Road is the Keswick Spa **(6)**, a new swimming pool with 'sub-tropical flora and real waves'.

Derwent Water lies south of Keswick, at the end of Lake Road. In the car park in Lake Road is the Century Theatre **(3)**. For nearly twenty years this was a pioneering touring company, carrying its theatre with it in the form of ex-army trailers which folded out into an auditorium seating over two hundred people. In the seventies the theatre was grounded, by a combination of rust and the cost of transport, but there is now a resident company which puts on three plays in rotation during the summer months.

The National Trust Information Centre
(?) is opposite the boat landings (2). This is
(?e starting point for the Keswick Launch,
(though passengers can join or leave the
(aunch at any of the other six stages. The
rcuit of the lake takes about 50 minutes
(nd it is possible to go either clockwise and
(nti-clockwise.

From here it is a short walk to Friars Crag
(?). This famous viewpoint looks across
(erwent Water and down into Borrow-
(ale ★ . On the top there is a monument to
(uskin, who thought the view one of the
(ree most beautiful in Europe. It was
(pparently his earliest memory. More
(ecently Norman Nicholson, the Lake poet
(ho died in 1987, wrote, 'One crag opens
(ehind another, unfurling like a metal
(ose'.

Old Windbrowe, the house where Wil-
(am and Dorothy Wordsworth lived for a
(hort time before they moved to Dove
(ottage, is in a suburb of Keswick to the
(orth-east of the town centre. The house
(vas lent to them and was their first home
(a the Lake District since their childhood.
(he ground floor rooms are furnished in
(he style of the period and can be visited by
(ppointment. Castlerigg Stone Circle ★ is

cale 1:10 000 or 6 INCHES to 1 MILE

just to the east of Keswick.

Tour 1 starts from Keswick and **Tour 2**
passes through the town.

Kirkby Lonsdale (97) (SD 61-78)
Situated in the south-east corner of
Cumbria, Kirkby Lonsdale stands on a high
bank overlooking the river Lune. Built of
yellow limestone, the town belongs more
to the Pennines than to the Lake District,
but its solid eighteenth-century houses
and cobbled streets make it a pleasure to
explore. It has been the market town for
the Lune valley since as early as the thirteenth century and is almost completely
unspoiled.

The Information Centre **(1)** is in Main
Street, south of the Market Square **(3)**. The
square was built in 1822 and contains the
only ugly thing in the town, a covered
market cross which doubles as a bus
shelter. Before the square was built,
markets were held in the streets around
the church: Fairbank, Horsemarket, Swinemarket and Market Street.

To the north, St Mary's church **(8)** dates
from the twelfth century and probably
stands on the site of a Saxon church which
was given to York Abbey in 1093 by Ivo de
Tailbois 'for the good of his soul, and that
of Lucy his Wife'. The abbey seems to have

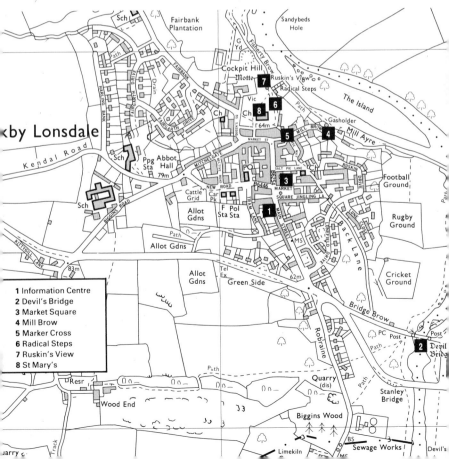

1 Information Centre
2 Devil's Bridge
3 Market Square
4 Mill Brow
5 Marker Cross
6 Radical Steps
7 Ruskin's View
8 St Mary's

responded by building a new church. The west end has a fine Norman archway beneath the tower and inside there are three Norman ribbed arches.

Follow the footpath to the north of the church to the Gazebo and then walk along the Brow to Ruskin's View **(7)**, marked by a plaque in the wall. He considered it '...one of the loveliest scenes in England, therefore in the world. Whatever moorland hill, and sweet river, and English forest foliage can be at their best is gathered here...'.

Returning to the churchyard, the Radical steps **(6)** lead down to the river. At the bottom there is a footpath running south along the river bank to the Devil's Bridge **(2)**. The bridge has three graceful arches and used to carry the old turnpike road from Kendal to Keighley; its age is uncertain. 200 yards further downstream is the Devil's Neck Collar, a circular hole in a large block of limestone that sticks out into the river.

To return from the Gazebo to the centre of town, take the left hand path through the churchyard and walk through a narrow alleyway into the cobbled Swinemarket. The old market cross **(5)** stands in front of Abbott's Hall: it was moved here in 1819 from Market Street because of the traffic. Mill Brow **(4)**, which runs steeply down to the river, once had seven waterwheels powered by a stream which is now channelled underground. The mills made snuff, calico and horseblankets.

Kirkby Lonsdale is on **Tour 10**.

Kirkstone Pass (90) (NY 40-09)
This dramatic pass runs from Ullswater ★ in the north to Windermere ★ in the south and is on **Tour 4**. It is the highest road in the Lake District (1,489ft) and usually the first to get snow. There is good skiing on the slopes near the Kirkstone Pass Inn.

It is not a difficult road to drive and is one of the few passes that was open to coaches in the nineteenth century. At that time the road went south to Ambleside ★ , down a narrow twisting road known as the Struggle. Passengers had to get out and walk part of the way. Nowadays the A592 runs south through the delightful Troutbeck ★ valley. Driven from south to north, the road gives a superb view of Ullswater ★ as it descends towards Patterdale ★ .

Lake District National Park
Created in 1951, the Lake District National Park covers 880 square miles and is the largest of the ten National Parks in England and Wales. The local planning authority, which carries out the aims of the National Park Act, is the Lake District Special Planning Board (LDSPB). This decides all applications for planning permission within the National Park. It can also buy land for public access (or if it feels that it is in the public interest) and can make bye-laws controlling the use of land or water. The meetings of the Board and its committee are usually held in the County Office Kendal, and are open to the public. I 1986/7 they spent over £2 ½ million, which just under a million came fro entrance and car parking fees. Of the res 75% came from the Government and 25° from the Cumbria County Council.

Compared to the National Trust ★ , th land owned by the LDSPB is relativel small. The largest areas are the Caldbec Fells (north of Skiddaw ★), the bed Ullswater ★ , Bassenthwaite Lake ★ an Blawith ★ and Torver ★ Commons. A well as managing its own properties, th LDSPB maintains footpaths and bridl ways and operates a Ranger service whic patrols the fells and gives guided walks. also provides a number of Informatio Centres, including the Visitor Centre Brockhole ★ , and an increasing number car parks. There are advisory services fc farmers and a daily weather forecast (Wir dermere 5151), essential for fellwalkers.

Lakeside and Haverthwaite Railway
(96,97) (SD 35-85)
Part of the Ulverston ★ to Lakeside branc line, which was closed in the mid-60s, wa reopened in 1973 by the Lakeside an Haverthwaite Railway Co. Ltd. The con pany uses steam locomotives over 3 ' miles of track between Haverthwaite, o the river Leven, and the Windermere steamer terminus at Lakeside. There ar combined rail-sail tickets and also a retur trip from Bowness ★ which goes to Lake side by steamer, Haverthwaite by train and Holker Hall ★ by bus. The lin operates five trains daily between Apr and October. Lakeside is on **Tour 9**.

A preserved locomotive with steam up

Lamplugh (89) (NY 08-20)
To the east of Lamplugh, on **Tour 1**, is th charming small tarn of Cogra Moss (se map). Turn sharp left just south of th village, signposted to Croasdale an Ennerdale Lake, and park in the car park a Felldyke. The footpath starts just past th telephone box and goes through a sma Forestry Commission plantation.

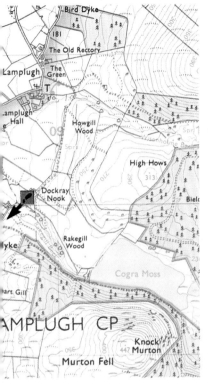

Lamplugh itself is a small hamlet. The church has gargoyles and a double bell-cote and there is an imposing gateway which leads to Lamplugh Hall.

Langdale Pikes (see Great Langdale)

Levens Hall (97) (SD 48-85)

Situated 5 miles south of Kendal ★, on the banks of the river Kent, Levens Hall is the finest Elizabethan mansion in Cumbria. The core of the house is a thirteenth-century pele tower and hall. This was acquired in the sixteenth century by the Bellingham family – who had made a fortune out of the Dissolution of the Monasteries – and transformed into an Elizabethan showpiece with magnificent oak panelling and plastered ceilings.

In the seventeenth century the Bellingham fortune was gambled away and the house was bought by a cousin, Colonel Graham. He is responsible for the furniture, which includes some Charles II walnut dining chairs said to be best in the country. Col. Graham also employed Guillaume Beaumont, a Frenchman trained under Le Notre at Versailles, to redesign the grounds. The famous topiary garden near the house dates from this period.

The park laid out by Beaumont was perhaps even more of an innovation at the time as it was designed to enhance the natural features of the landscape, with an avenue of trees following the line of the river and others planted to emphasize the depth of the gorge. The A6 now divides the house from the park but it can be visited by crossing the road. There are herds of black fallow deer and Bagot goats.

The old brewhouse contains working models of steam engines. Levens Hall is owned by the Bagot family and shut on Fridays and Saturdays. It is on **Tour 10**.

Lindale (96,97) (SD 41-80)

The iron obelisk in Lindale is a memorial to the eighteenth-century ironmaster, John Wilkinson, who worked first at Backbarrow ★ and then in Shropshire. He was known as 'Iron-Mad Wilkinson' and left instructions that his body should be buried in a cast-iron coffin in the garden of his former home in Lindale and an iron obelisk erected over the grave.

His wishes were carried out but seem to have been dogged by misfortune. The hearse stuck in a quicksand during the journey across Morecambe Bay and had to be rescued. Twenty years later the house in Lindale was sold and the new owners had the coffin moved to the church and took down the obelisk, which lay behind a hedge for over thirty years. In 1863 it was salvaged and put up in its present position. Since then it has been struck by lighting and had to be repaired. It is now rather oddly classified as an Ancient Monument.

Lindale is north of Grange-over-Sands ★ and is on **Tour 10**.

Lingholm Gardens (89,90) (NY 25-22)

On the west banks of Derwent Water ★, the Victorian mansion of Lingholm was for many years used only for summer lets. Beatrix Potter's family stayed here on several occasions and *Squirrel Nutkin* was written during one summer holiday. St Herbert's Island, opposite Derwent Bay, is said to be Owl Island.

The house is now the home of Viscount Rochdale but the large gardens are open to the public. There are wonderful azaleas and rhododendrons, both of which thrive in the acid peaty soil, and good views down the lake to Borrowdale ★. Lingholm is on **Tour 2**.

Little Langdale (90) (NY 31-03)

The valley of Little Langdale has been the major route to the west since the Romans built the Tenth Highway from Ambleside ★ to the sea. The road runs along the river Brathay, past Little Langdale Tarn, and climbs up towards Wrynose Pass ★ at its western end. Little Langdale Tarn was a watering place for the packhorse trains which went through here and is now the home of rare wild geese. At the eastern end of the tarn is Slater's Bridge, an old packhorse bridge which was used by the

Little Langdale Tarn

A traditional farmhouse

quarrymen in Tilberthwaite Fells. The bridge is at the old boundary between Westmorland and Lancashire.

Behind Fell Foot Farm, at the head of the valley, is a square terraced mound which is believed to be a Viking Thing Mount, a place where the Norse farmers met to administer justice. The farm itself was once an inn and would have been the last stopping point for the trains of packhorses before the climb to the passes ahead.

To the north of Fell Foot, a steep road runs up past Blea Tarn into Great Langdale ★ . This gives magnificent views of the Langdale Pikes and is on **Tours 6 and 8**. Little Langdale is on **Tours 1,5,6 7 and 8**.

Littletown (see Newlands Pass)

Lodore Falls (90) (NY 26-18)
At the southern end of Derwent Water ★ , the Lodore Falls are near the mouth of Watendath ★ Beck. The beck cascades through a gorge in the wooded hillside and finally plunges 40 ft down the Lodore cataract. In 1820 the poet Robert Southey, who lived at Greta Hall, Keswick ★ , wrote a poem for his children entitled *'How does the Water come down at Lodore'*. He takes 200 lines to answer the question, in what must be one of the longest examples of onomatopoeia in the English language.

'Rushing and lushing and brushing and gushing

And flapping and rapping and clapping and slapping

And curling and whirling and purling and twirling

And thumping and plumping and bumping and jumping

And dashing and flashing and splashing and clashing

And so never-ending, but always descending

Sounds and motions for ever and ever are blending,

All at one and all o'er, with a mighty uproar,

And in this way the water comes down at Lodore'

There is a car park on the B5289 about half a mile north of the falls and they can also be reached from the Lodore pier of the Keswick launch. The land is owned by the Swiss Lodore Hotel and there is an honesty box. The falls are best seen after heavy rain.

Longsleddale (90) (NY 48-05)
This long narrow valley near the eastern boundary of the National Park is now a cul de sac, like the Kentmere ★ valley which runs parallel to it. This was not always the case: in the eighteenth century the Gatescarth Pass which runs north into the Haweswater ★ valley was a busy packhorse route from Kendal ★ . The road now stops at the little hamlet of Sadgill but there is a broad track up the river Spring which is easy to follow and gives magnificent views of the dalehead (see map). It is said that the M6 planners considered this route!

Longsleddale is notable for its broadleaf woodlands and two of the oak woods are classified as of Special Scientific interest.

They are the remnants of the primeval mixed oak forest which once covered large areas of the Lake District. The bare fells which look so natural are the work of Man. Longsleddale is on **Tour 9**.

Loughrigg Tarn (see Skelwith Bridge)

Loughrigg Terrace (see Grasmere)

Loweswater (89) (NY 14-20)
The most westerly of the string of three lakes which lie in the glacial valley of Buttermere ★ , Loweswater is also the least visited. There is a pleasant, easy walk along the south-west shore of the lake through Holme Wood, where the National Trust have provided seats. The lake is a favourite haunt for water fowl and part of the shore has been fenced off to protect the nesting sites.

The footpath goes down by the telephone box, west of a small car park (see map). The fells around the lake are gentle rather than dramatic but at the western end there is a view down the lake to the massive fells of Grasmoor and Melbreak beyond. There is another marvellous view from Loweswater church, which is east of the lake. Loweswater is on **Tours 1 and 2**.

Lowther (90) (NY 53-23)
The village of Lowther is 3 miles south of Penrith ★ and just to the west of Hackthorpe, which is on **Tour 3**. There are actually two villages, one of them a model village designed by Robert Adam. To the west is Lowther Park and the ruins of Lowther Castle. The castle is a gothic mansion, built in 1802 by Robert Smirke, the designer of the British Museum. (He also restored the church in Askham ★.) It proved too expensive to run and was pulled down, only the facade remaining.

The castle was built on the site of an earlier castle which burnt down. The Lowther family were responsible for much of the industrial development of the west coast in the eighteenth century and were enormously powerful. Wordsworth's father was Sir James Lowther's agent and Wordsworth himself owed his appointment as Distributor of Stamps of Westmorland to William Lowther, the first Earl of Lonsdale. In the 1818 election, he canvassed enthusiastically in their support. Two of Lord Lonsdale's sons were standing for the Kendal ★ constituency, then a 'hotbed of dissent', and with considerable political acumen Wordsworth suggested that they change their slogan from 'Church and King' to 'King and Country' and support the repeal of the leather tax. His sonnet 'Lowther Park' is not one of his best.

Lowther Leisure Park is just off the A6, in part of the grounds of Lowther Park. There are 'over 35 attractions', including a tarzan trail, rollerball, flying turtles, a boating lake and a circus.

Mardale see Haweswater

Mirehouse (89,90) (NY 23-28)
In the nineteenth century this manor house on the eastern shore of Bassenthwaite Lake ★ was visited by many of the literary figures of the day. The house was owned by the Spedding family and the two Spedding brothers, Thomas and James, seem to have had a singular gift for friendship and hospitality. Thomas Carlyle, who was a regular visitor, wrote of his 'kind friend who lives sheltered about the rock of Skid-

St Bega's Church, near Mirehouse

The interior of St Bega's, which dates from the tenth century

daw ★ ', and on the death of Tom Spedding wrote to James that he had lost 'one of the truest hearted friends I ever had...a man of sterling probity in its gentlest shape'. Another friend was Alfred Lord Tennyson, who wrote of James:

'The wind, that beats the mountain, blows
More softly round the open wold,
And gently comes the world to those
That are cast in open mould'.

James Spedding wrote the definitive biography of Francis Bacon and apparently once said that he was not enough of a Shakespearean scholar to say that Shakespeare was not Bacon, but he felt qualified to assert that Bacon was not Shakespeare.

Mirehouse is still owned by the Spedding family but has recently been opened to the public. The house gives a vivid impression of the Spedding brothers and their friends: there are numerous portraits and the downstairs rooms are arranged as they were during their lifetime. In the dining room is the chess table at which Edward Fitzgerald (the translator of the *Rubaiyat of Omar Khayyam*) remembered 'playing chess with dear Mrs Spedding' while Tennyson read aloud his poems and James Spedding criticised them. It was during this visit (in 1835) that Tennyson worked on the *Morte D'Arthur*: the setting of the final scene is based on Bassenthwaite Lake. Fitzgerald was not working, and amused himself by making up parodies of Wordsworth, whose verse by then was at its most pedestrian. In a competition to see who could invent the weakest line in the fewest words, Fitzgerald won, with:

'A Mr Wilkinson, a clergyman'.

The portrait of Carlyle as a young man, which hangs in the library, is said to have been spotted by Carlyle on his last visit to

Mirehouse

the house. In mock surprise, he asked 'What creature is this?' and then read out the inscription, 'Your obedient servant Thomas Carlyle'. Tom Spedding remarked 'An infernal story. You were never yet anybody's obedient servant, Carlyle' Other friends were Sir Charles Lyell, whose work on fossils influenced Charles Darwin and the painter John Constable.

The house dates from the seventeenth century, with later additions, and has a magnificent setting, with Dodd Wood and Skiddaw ★ behind and Bassenthwaite Lake in front. It is on the A591 and is on **Tour 2** and **Walk 2**.

Muncaster Castle (96) (SD 10-96)

Standing on a spur of land at the foot of Eskdale ★ , Muncaster Castle has an unmatchable setting. It is surrounded by a wild garden, planted with rhododendrons, azaleas and camellias; the view from the terrace, looking up Eskdale to the Sca Fells ★ , is astonishing.

The castle itself is built of pink Eskdale granite and is flanked by two towers. One is a defensive pele tower, built in 1325, and the other was built in the 1860s by Anthony Salvin, a Victorian architect who specialized in modernising castles. The interior is a similar mixture. In the billiard room the panelling comes from timbers taken from the Fighting Temeraire, the famous battleship painted by Turner.

The castle has been lived in by the Pennington family since the thirteenth century and there are many family portraits. There is also a portrait of the seventeenth-century Muncaster fool, Thomas Skelton, who apparently gave the word 'tomfool' to the English language. The Luck of Muncaster is a shallow glass bowl, decorated with gold and enamel, which is said to have been given to the family by Henry VI. After his defeat at the battle of Hexham, in 1464

Muncaster Castle

the king fled to Muncaster Fell. He was found there by a shepherd who took him to the castle where he was sheltered by the Penningtons for nine days.

There is an aviary in the grounds (which specialises in owls) and a garden centre. The castle is closed on Mondays and is on **Tour 8.**

Muncaster Mill (96) (SD 09-97)

This eighteenth-century water mill on the river Mite is one mile upstream from Ravenglass ★ harbour, which is on **Tour 8.** There was a mill here in 1455 and it is thought that the site was probably used by the Norse settlers. The existing mill uses a millrace ¾mile long and has an 'over-shoot' water wheel 13ft in diameter. There are three pairs of millstones.

Wholemeal flour was ground here for human consumption up to the first world war and the mill produced animal feed and oatmeal until 1961. It finally closed in that year but was reopened by the Ravenglass and Eskdale Railway ★ in 1975. It is the first stop on the line. The mill is fully operational again and stone ground flour is on sale.

National Trust

The National Trust owns an astonishing 25% of the area covered by the Lake District National Park. Its role in preserving the countryside as you see it today cannot be overstated: in effect it has put a time warp on the Lake District, using its capacity as landlord to block development and maintain the traditional patterns of farming.

The Trust was founded in 1895 by Canon Rawnsley (vicar of Crosthwaite, Kendal ★), Robert Hunter (solicitor to the Post Office) and Octavia Hill (a social reformer). Of these the prime mover was Canon Rawnsley who was an energetic and enthusiastic man who had been campaigning against various threats to the Lakes for many

years. It is worth remembering that there was once a Buttermere Railway Bill. The failure to stop the flooding of Thirlmere ★ convinced him that ownership of the land was in the end the only safeguard. The first pieces of land were bought to stop building development (Brandelhow Park ★ by Derwent Water ★ and Gowbarrow Park ★ by Ullswater ★).

The National Trust is registered as a Charity and relies on public subscription, not government money. However it has on several occasions been given land which has been taken by the Treasury in lieu of death duties. (In 1979 it received over 30,000 acres which had been part of the estate of the first Lord Egremont.) The Trust also has inalienable rights over its land which are legally unique and mean that in a dispute it can appeal directly to the Houses of Parliament. Most of the land it has acquired has come through gifts. Beatrix Potter was one of the first to leave land to the National Trust in her will: she had known Canon Rawnsley since she was a child staying at High Wray ★ and spent the last thirty years of her life as a farmer in Sawrey ★ .

Near Sawrey see Sawrey

Nether Wasdale (89) (NY 12-04)

This scattered hamlet lies near the foot of Wast Water ★ and is on **Tour 1.** The depth of soil here meant that in the eighteenth century the local farmers were able to profit from the new techniques of the agricultural revolution and introduce more profitable crops, such as turnips and potatoes. This prosperity is reflected in the farm buildings which are more modern than the farms of the central dales.

The village has a small green with a maypole, put up in 1897 to celebrate Queen Victoria's jubilee. The church of St Michael and All Angels is a fifteenth-century Chapel of Ease to St Bees Priory which was enlarged in 1830. Inside there are painted texts on the walls and carved oak panelling on either side of the altar, salvaged from York Minster after a fire.

Newlands Pass (89,90) (NY 19-17)

This is the most beautiful road not driven on any of the tours and runs from Braithwaite, just west of Keswick ★ , to Buttermere village ★ . At the beginning it goes through the Newlands valley (literally new land, created in the fourteenth century by draining the Husaker tarn). The tarn itself was probably an artificial creation, caused by a Roman embankment carrying a road across the marshes at the foot of the Whinlatter Pass ★ .

The valley is lush and green and will be familiar to readers of Beatrix Potter's Mrs Tiggy-Winkle. The book was inspired by an encounter between the daughter of the vicar of Newlands and Beatrix Potter's tame and much-travelled hedgehog, Mrs Tiggy-Winkle. Many of the drawings were made near the hamlet of Littletown. The Potter family spent a series of summer holidays in rented houses on nearby Derwent Water ★ : Lingholm Gardens ★ is open to the public.

After Littletown the road starts to climb and goes through dramatic, wild country before dropping steeply down into the Buttermere ★ valley. The road was part of the Buttermere round, a Victorian excursion from Keswick which went through Borrowdale ★ and over the Honister Pass ★ to Buttermere, returning via the Newlands Pass. At the beginning to the century the cost was five shillings; a few horse-drawn wagonettes were still running up to the Second World War.

Orrest Head see Windermere town

Patterdale (90) (NY 39-15)
Lying at the southern end of Ullswater ★ , this small hamlet has a spectacular setting, surrounded on three sides by high peaks. There is a circular walk which goes up the east shore of the lake to Silver Crag (see map) and gives superb views across to the Helvellyn ★ range. Grisedale, the narrow valley which runs west from Patterdale, is one of the approaches to Helvellyn.

Patterdale is a corruption of Patrick's Dale and there is a legend that St Patrick was shipwrecked at Duddon Sands, on his way to Ireland, and came to the dale. St Patrick's Well is about a mile north of the village. The small church is decorated with local tapestries. Patterdale is on **Tour 4.**

Penrith (90) (NY 51-30)
Lying on the main route from England to Scotland, Penrith has been a market town since the Bronze Age. In the ninth and tenth centuries it was the capital of the old kingdom of Cumbria. The town suffered badly in the border wars and its role as a central refuge can still be seen in its layout: narrow roads radiate from open areas into which cattle would have been herded. The gates have gone but their names remain – Castlegate, Burrowgate, Middlegate, Sandgate and Friargate.

The hill to the north of the town is the Beacon and still has a building (the Pike) from which a warning beacon could be lit. The view from the top gives an indication of what a good lookout the hill provided. The beacon was last lit in earnest in 1745, when the Young Pretender marched on Penrith, but Sir Walter Scott saw it lit in 1804 during the Napoleonic Wars. Beacon Edge, the mile-long promenade which skirts the north of the town, also gives good views.

The **Tourist Information centre (1)** is in Robinson's School, Middlegate. The school was built in 1670 'for the educating and bringing up of poore Gerles...to Read and Seamstry worke or such other learning fitt for that sex'. In 1970 the school closed and the building now houses an exhibition about the history of Penrith and the Eden Valley. There are displays of archaeological finds, including pottery from the Roman fort at Old Penrith (NY 49-38).

To the south, in King Street, is the parish church of St Andrew (7). The church dates from the twelfth century but the nave is Georgian. The massive tower was built by the Neville family who were the lords of the manor of Penrith: Cecily Neville was the mother of both Edward IV and Richard III. The south windows in the church contain portraits now thought to be of Cecily Neville's parents. Her mother was the daughter of John of Gaunt.

In the churchyard is the Giant's Grave (3), a curious group of stones which was at one time thought to contain the bones of Owen Caesarius, King of Cumbria from AD 920-937. In fact it is a pair of Norse hogback tombstones flanked by two tenth-century crosses. The cross at the western end is probably in its original position and the rest have been grouped round it.

The churchyard is surrounded by old houses. Part of what is now the Tudor restaurant is thought to be Dame Birkett's school, where William and Dorothy Wordsworth and Mary Hutchinson (later to be William's wife) went as young children. The Queen Elizabeth Grammar School, founded in 1564, is now the Eden Craft Gallery.

Walking west through Cornmarket brings you into Great Dockray, one of the central open areas in the town. The Gloucester Arms (4) dates from 1477 and is one of oldest inns in England. The arms of Richard III (two boars rampant) hang over

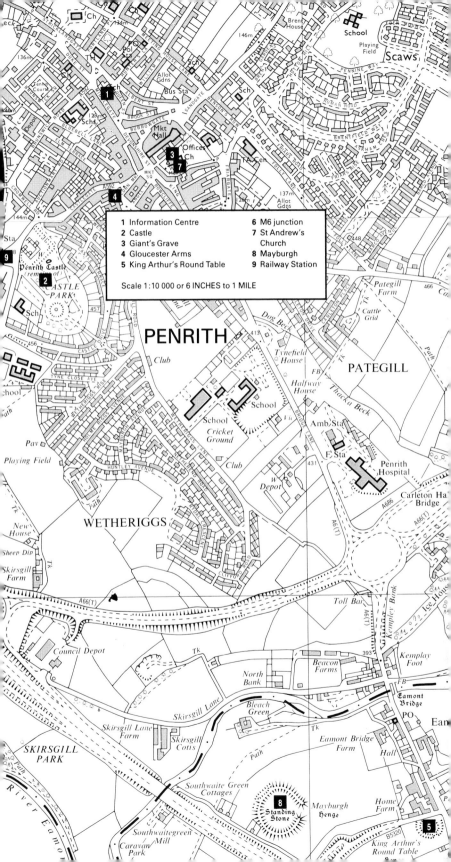

1 Information Centre
2 Castle
3 Giant's Grave
4 Gloucester Arms
5 King Arthur's Round Table

6 M6 junction
7 St Andrew's Church
8 Mayburgh
9 Railway Station

Scale 1:10 000 or 6 INCHES to 1 MILE

POOLEY BRIDGE

the entrance and he is said to have lived here at one time.

Walk up Castlegate. Near the top on the left hand side is the Penrith Steam Museum, which has a collection of massive traction engines (some of which are usually in steam) and various steam models. There are also exhibits of vintage farm machinery, a pattern shop and a working blacksmith's shop.

The ruins of Penrith Castle (2) are on the A592, opposite the railway station (9). The original defensive tower, built at the end of the fourteenth century, is still standing. The castle was later enlarged by the Neville family and used by Richard III before he became king in 1483. As Duke of Gloucester, he was Lord of the Western Marches and the Governor of Carlisle Castle. During this period a magnificent banqueting hall was added, but by 1550 the castle was already in ruins. In 1913 the council bought it from the Lancaster and Carlisle Railway Co.

Penrith is now bypassed by the M6. The main A6, which used to run through the centre of the town, leads south to Eamont Bridge. In Bridge Lane, north of the roundabout, there is a plague stone. Penrith was very badly hit by the plague, with 2,260 deaths in 1597-8. The stone is a square font and was used to wash money in vinegar on market day. It is now in the gardens of Greengarth Old People's Home.

Eamont Bridge is a medieval bridge, partly paid for by the sale of papal indulgences. There are two intriguing earthworks near here. King Arthur's Round Table (5) is a circular henge that could date from 1,000 BC. Mayburgh (8) is probably older and is a huge circular embankment of stones, 15 ft high in some places. There is a single entrance on the east and a large stone monolith near the centre. In the eighteenth century seven stones were still standing. Bronze age and stone age axes have been found here.

Penrith is the start of **Tour 3**.

Pooley Bridge (90) (NY 47-24)

This small village at the foot of Ullswater is now a tourist centre, with many hotels and guesthouses. There is an Information Centre by the car park. To the west of the river Eamont there is another large car park, at the foot of Dunmallard hill (see map). Traces of a fortified British settlement can be seen on the top and there is a pleasant walk along the river bank. The Ullswater steamers go from Pooley Bridge to Glenridding ★ , calling in at Howtown ★ , and the pier is just south of the bridge, on the B5320. Pooley Bridge can be visited on **Tours 3 and 4**.

Ravenglass (96) (SD 08-96)

The rivers of the three most westerly dales (Wasdale, Miterdale and Eskdale) meet in

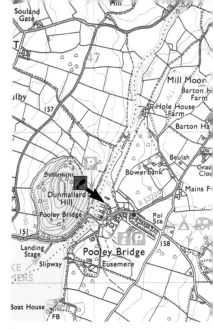

Ravenglass. Once an important port and notorious for its smugglers, the village is now almost landlocked by the sand dunes that block the mouth of the estuary. To the north they contain the largest colony of black-headed gulls in Europe. The dunes are classified as a nature reserve and can only be visited by permission.

Today the village is mainly known as the terminus of the Ravenglass and Eskdale Railway ★ . There is an Information Centre in the station. Apart from the railway line, there is a single wide street which runs along beside the estuary. Most of the fishermen's cottages are now let as holiday homes.

The Roman fort of Glanoventa was to the

Ravenglass

south of the modern village. It was linked to the inland fort at Waterhead ★ by the Tenth Highway and lasted 300 years. The only surviving ruin is the bath house, known as Walls Castle. This remarkable red sandstone building still has 12ft high walls and looks more like a barn than a Roman ruin: it is the best preserved Roman building in Northern England. It stands in a narrow strip of plantation, divided from the sea by the railway embankment, and can be reached by a footpath from the village (see map).

Muncaster Mill ★ is to the north of the village and Muncaster Castle ★ to the east. Ravenglass is on **Tour 8**.

Ravenglass and Eskdale Railway (96) (SD 11-98)

Known affectionately as t'laal Ratty, this miniature railway runs from Ravenglass ★, to Boot ★, halfway up Eskdale. The original track was a 3ft gauge, laid in 1875 to carry iron ore, but in 1915 it was replaced by a 15in gauge. This makes it the oldest narrow gauge railway in the country.

The line has had a chequered history. The original mining company failed after eleven years but the railway survived by carrying passengers and later the pink Eskdale granite from the quarries at Beckfoot. By 1960 the line was no longer viable but a Preservation Society stepped in and

Beckfoot station

bought it, for £14,000.

The 7 mile journey now takes 45 minutes and goes through an extraordinary variety of scenery. From Ravenglass the train stops at Muncaster Mill ★, Irton Road, Eskdale Green ★, Beckfoot and Dalegarth. There is a large car park at Ravenglass and a railway museum which describes the history of the line, using models, photographs and slide shows. There are twelve locomotives, five of them steam. The oldest was built in 1894.

Rosthwaite see Borrowdale

Rydal Hall (90) (NY 36-06)

The grounds of Rydal Hall contain the 'Rydal Torrent', a series of waterfalls much admired by Wordsworth who lived nearby at Rydal Mount ★. The house is mainly eighteenth-century and was built by the de Fleming family. It is now owned by the Diocese of Carlisle who use it for conferences and retreats. There is a public footpath through the park and the formal gardens are open on Wednesdays and Saturdays. These contain the Grotto, a summer house which frames the 'correct' view of the Lower Falls. There are good views across to Windermere ★.

Rydal Hall is on **Tours 5 and 6**. To reach the house, turn off the A591 as if for Rydal Mount. Admission to the formal gardens is free but donations are welcome. There is a leaflet with a guided trail.

Rydal Mount (90) (NY 36-06)

Wordsworth moved into Rydal Mount in 1813, when he was forty three, and lived there until his death at the age of eighty. During his lifetime the house was rented from Lady de Fleming, the owner of Rydal Hall ★. It is now owned by his great-great-grand-daughter and in 1970 it was opened to the public.

In 1813 Wordsworth had just been given the nominal position of Distributor of Stamps for Westmorland. The salary meant the family could afford to live in some style, employing a clerk, two maids and in due course a gardener. Wordsworth had already ceased to be the ardent revolutionary of his youth and he now became an equally passionate defender of the status quo, lamented by his former followers as the Lost Leader.

The house gives a good idea of the Wordsworths' life here, containing many of their possessions and portraits of the family and their friends. The large and beautiful garden is Wordsworth's creation. He had firm ideas about how gardens should be laid out and carried out numerous improvements; building lawns, terraces and a summerhouse. The view beyond the summerhouse 'which shows the lake of Rydal to such advantage' was shown to Queen Adelaide, the widow of

William IV, who visited them in 1840. By then Wordsworth had become a sort of national institution and in 1843, at the age of 73, he was made Poet Laureate. He lived another seven years.

Rydal Mount is reached by a steep lane to the north-east of Rydal Water ★ . The turning off the A591 is signposted and is on **Tours 5 and 6**. At the bottom of the lane is Rydal church, built in 1824 as a private chapel for Rydal Hall. Wordsworth's pew was the one in front of the pulpit.

A gate in the churchyard leads to Dora's Field, now owned by the National Trust. The land was bought by Wordsworth with the idea that he might build on it. At the time he thought he might be turned out of Rydal Mount by Lady de Fleming but he later patched up the quarrel and gave the land to his daughter, Dora. In spring the field is carpeted with daffodils.

Rydal Water (90) (NY 35-06)
The smallest of the lakes, Rydal Water lies in the same glacial valley as Grasmere ★ , bordered to the south and north by the steep sides of Loughrigg Fell and Rydal Fell. The River Rothay which connects the two lakes flows on into Windermere ★ .

The busy A591 runs along the north side of the lake and the footpath along the south shore gives the best view. Turn south off the A591 onto the Underloughrigg road (just east of Rydal) and walk up the lane to the lake. There is a 'beach' on the south shore which is used for swimming. No boats are allowed and fishing is permitted only from the shore. Rydal Water is on **Tours 5 and 6**.

Rydal Water

Sadgill see Longsleddale

Santon Bridge (89) (NY 11-01)
The Bridge Inn is now used for the Biggest Liar in the World competition. The competition is held in memory of Will Ritson, the nineteenth-century publican of the Wasdale Head Inn who first claimed the title. Wasdale was said to have the highest mountain, the deepest lake, the smallest church and the biggest liar in the world.

It is however not a lie that the river Irt which is crossed by Santon Bridge, was once famous for its pearls. These are mentioned by the Romans and as recently as the seventeenth century a local landowner was employing people to collect them. Santon Bridge is on **Tours 1 and 7**.

The Tower Bank Arms

Sawrey (96,97) (SD 37-95)
The hamlet of Near Sawrey was the home of Beatrix Potter for the last thirty years of her life and is the background to many of her books. Hill Top ★ , the first farm she owned in the village, is open to the public and in the village itself there are many

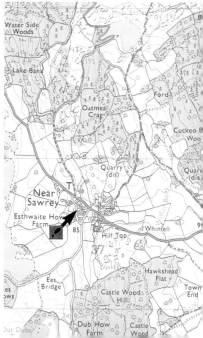

familiar scenes. The Tower Bank Arms appears in *Jemima Puddleduck* and many of the cottages in *The Pie and the Patty Pan* and *Ginger and Pickles*.

Two short walks are possible from the village centre (see map). One goes south through the lovely rolling hills that surround the village. The other goes north to Moss Eccles Tarn, which appears in *Jeremy Fisher*. The tarn still has water lilies and there are glorious views across to the Langdale Pikes.

Sawrey is between Esthwaite Water ★ and Windermere ★, on **Tour 6**.

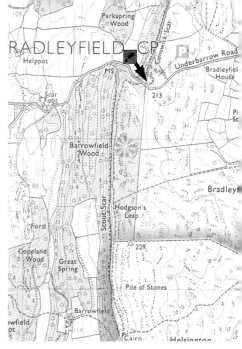

Sca Fell Pike (89) (NY 21-07)

Sca Fell Pike is the highest point of the western dome of mountains from which the lakes and dales radiate 'like spokes from the nave of a wheel', as Wordsworth (having placed his reader on a cloud between Great Gable and Scafell) first observed. It is part of a range of fells, the Sca Fell Pikes, and at 3,210ft is only slightly higher than its neighbour Sca Fell (3,162ft). To sound knowledgable you should pronounce them 'Scawfell': 'Scarfell' will immediately place you as an 'offcomer'.

The Sca Fell Pikes are the highest mountains in England and it is here that rock climbing began in the last century. The Fell and Rock Climbing Club was founded at Wasdale Head ★ in 1886 (and is passed on **Walk 9**). These are not mountains for the beginner. They can be extremely dangerous, as the graves in the church as Wasdale Head demonstrate. Even the 'easy' routes up take a long time and become difficult if the mist comes down.

Scale Force see Crummock Water

Scout Scar (97) (SD 48-92)

Three miles west of Kendal, this magnificent 700ft limestone ridge is part of the white carboniferous limestone which once covered the Lake District. Over the central dome of the high fells it has been worn away and only the outer rim survives.

The scar is on the Underbarrow and Crosthwaite road, which is on **Tour 10**. Park in the quarry on the opposite side of the road and follow the signed footpath (see map above right). The views are magnificent through 360 degrees: to the north and west the whole of the Lake District is laid out before you; to the south is the sea, and behind you lie the Yorkshire fells. The valley below is the Lyth valley, famous for its damsons which grow wild. In spring the blossom is a glorious sight.

Seathwaite, Borrowdale (89,90) (NY 23-12)

At the head of Borrowdale ★, Seathwaite holds the unenviable record of being the wettest place in England. Between 1842-

1851 a Keswick ★ clockmaker measured 140 inches of rain per year in Seathwaite, while Keswick had only 57 inches. The current average is said to be 125 inches. Rain Gauge Cottage stands on the site of the rain gauge used to measure the rainfall.

Seathwaite Fell is the site of the Wadd Mine, the source of pure graphite which led to the founding of the pencil industry in Keswick. The graphite had many other uses: casting round-shot and cannon balls, fixing blue dyes, and glazing pottery. In 1788 graphite fetched £3,300 a ton and miners were searched as they left work to try and stop smuggling. At one time there was even an armed guard on the mine. By the middle of the nineteenth century the graphite was exhausted but not before a great many fortunes had been made.

Seathwaite, Dunnerdale (96) (SD 22-96)

This is the parish of Wonderful Walker, much admired by Wordsworth who wrote

Seathwaite

a lengthy note to the Duddon Sonnets in his praise. This remarkable man lived to ninety two and was not only curate-in-charge of the small chapel but also school-master, doctor, lawyer and scribe for the surrounding district. As well as all this, he 'sold home-brewed beer, cultivated his glebe with his own hands, spun wool, made his own clothing, and worked for wages at haymaking and sheep shearing', according to John Murray's 1869 Hand-book.

The chapel was rebuilt in 1874 but there is a curious memorial on top of a stone. A brass plate explains that it was 'used as a stool for clipping sheep by the Rev Robert Walker'. Seathwaite is on the Duddon River ★ and is on **Tours 5 and 8.**

Seatoller (89,90) (NY 24-13)

This hamlet at the foot of the Honister pass ★ was built to house workers in the Honister slate quarries. The slate was transported to the west coast by packhorse trains which went round the west side of Great Gable to Wasdale Head ★ . The quarry workers apparently supplemented their income by smuggling and the route became known as Moses Trod, after a famous smuggler.

The National Park have an information centre in the village, in a converted barn, and there is a large car park which is a good base for walks in Borrowdale ★ and the surrounding fells. **Walk 10** starts from here and goes to Grange-in-Borrowdale ★. Seatoller is on **Tours 1 and 2.**

Shap Abbey (90) (NY 54-15)

Shap Abbey stands besides the river Low-ther, one mile west of the village of Shap. **Tours 3 and 4** pass close by and **Walk 4** visits the abbey. The only part of the structure which is still standing is the great west tower but the setting is magnificent, hidden in a fold of the hills.

The abbey is unique for several reasons.

Shap Abbey

It was the only abbey founded in Westmor land; the only abbey in the mountainous central core of the Lake District; the last abbey to be founded (in 1180) and the last to be dissolved (in 1540). It has been suggested that it was given a stay of execution by Henry VIII's commissioners because of the shelter it provided for travellers across the wild Shap Fells ★ .

The abbey is now maintained by English Heritage who provide a map of the layout Much of the stone was looted for Lowt-her ★ Castle.

Shap Fells (90) (NY 54-08)

The eastern boundary of the Lake District is formed by Shap Fells. Until the M6 was built, the fells were the major north-south route. They were crossed by one of the first roads in the Lake District and later by one of the first railways – a major feat achieved in only two years. In November 1745 the Jacobite army marched south across Shap (in snow) and a month later retreated north pursued by the Duke of Cumberland. They turned to fight at Clifton ★ .

It is a bleak, wind-swept place and pic-tures of lorries stranded in the snow on the A6 used to be a regular filler for newspaper editors. Nevertheless it has its admirers: John Ruskin, who later lived at Brant-wood ★ , wrote, 'Ever since I passed Shap Fells, when a child, I have had an excessive love for this kind of desolation'.

Just south of the village of Shap ★ , the road goes past the quarries that produce the famous Shap granite, used to build St Pancras Station and the Albert Memorial. Shap Fell is driven on **Tour 4.**

Sizergh Castle (97) (SD 49-87)

Owned by the Strickland family for over 700 years, the contents of Sizergh Castle are as interesting as the building. The family were strong supporters of the Stuarts and most of their wealth was con-fiscated after 1688. Since then, the castle has remained almost unchanged. In 1950 the house was given to the National Trust but the family still lives in the north wing.

The oldest part of the house is a fourteenth-century pele tower. One of the largest still in existence, it is nearly 60ft high with massive walls over 9ft thick at the base. In 1450 a Great Hall was added and a century later two wings containing workshops and kitchens were built on at rightangles, thus forming three sides of a courtyard.

At the same time the Great Hall was enlarged and modernised. The Elizabethan rooms have some of the finest panelling in the country, with several superb overman-tels – five carved before 1580. Some of the furniture was made at the same time. Although the exterior of the house was altered around 1770 ('an age when change for the sake of change was an obsession', according to the official guide) the interior is little changed since the sixteenth century. As late as the end of the nineteenth century, the kitchen was still in the north wing and the dining room the opposite side of the courtyard in the pele tower.

The house contains a large collection of Stuart portraits and relics and there is a two-handed sword dating from 1340 – the same age as the pele tower. The terraced gardens were added in the eighteenth century and there is also a rock garden, created in the 1920s, which has a noted collection of ferns and dwarf conifers. Sizergh Castle is on the A591, 3 miles south of Kendal ★ .

Skelwith Bridge (90) (NY 34-03)
One and a half miles west of Ambleside ★ , the A593 crosses the river Brathay. Just to the west of here is Skelwith Force, a fault in the rock where the bed of the Brathay slips 16ft and the whole weight of the river pours over the edge (see map). The footpath goes past the Kirkstone slate galleries. The green slate quarried locally is processed here and there is a showroom which sells finished goods.

To the north of here is Loughrigg Tarn which makes a good circular walk. It is best done clockwise. Skelwith Bridge is on **Tours 1,5,7,8 and 9.**

Skelwith Force (see Elterwater, Skelwith Bridge)

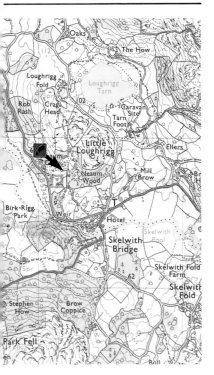

Skiddaw (89,90) (NY 26-29)
Towering over Keswick ★ is Skiddaw (3,053ft), a huge smooth lump of slate. It is the natural northern boundary of the Lake District: beyond is Back o' Skiddaw.

Skiddaw is the easiest of the large fells to climb, with a bridletrack all the way to the top. Park at Latrigg, as for **Walk 1:** the first part, up Jenkin Hill, is the steepest. There will be many other people walking up as well, but the view from the top cannot be beaten, with Scotland to the north, the Isle of Man to the west and the Lakes below you to the south.

On 21st August, 1815, Wordsworth and Southey with their families and assorted friends held a picnic and bonfire on the top of Skiddaw to celebrate victory at the battle of Waterloo. There is an extremely funny account of the occasion in the excellent book, *The Wordsworth Country.* Southey's own description will whet your appetite. 'We roasted beef and boiled plum puddings there; sung 'God save the King' round the most furious body of flaming tar barrels that I ever saw; drank a huge wooden bowl of punch; fired a cannon at every health with three times three, and rolled large balls of tow and turpentine down the steep side of the mountain. The effect was grand beyond imagination.'

Stagshaw Gardens (90) (SD 38-02)
To the south of Ambleside ★ on the A591 are the Stagshaw Gardens. They are the personal creation of the late Cuthbert Acland, a passionate gardener who was Regional Agent for the National Trust ★ for nearly thirty years. By felling trees and planting with imagination and knowledge, he transformed an area of dense scrubby woodland into a series of glades which provide shelter for numerous flowering shrubs. Like most Lakeland gardens, it is at its best in spring, but there are roses in summer and hydrangeas in early autumn.

The gardens are on the east side of the road, opposite Holme Crag, and are on **Tours 6 and 9.** Parking is limited and it is a short walk from the car park at Waterhead ★ .

Stanley Ghyll (see Boot)

Stockghyll Force (see Ambleside)

Strands (see Nether Wasdale)

Styhead Pass (see Borrowdale)

Tarn Hows (96,97) (SD 33-99)
West of Hawkshead ★ , Tarn Hows apparently gets more visitors than any of the lakes. It is a conventionally pretty 'beauty spot' and so perhaps it should not be

surprising that it is artificial – a small lake created by the Victorian owners of the Monk Coniston Estate to conform with their ideas of an ideal Arcadian landscape.

The Tarns (there were once three) are signposted off the Coniston-Hawkshead road and are on **Tour 8**. The National Trust have built two large car parks, one of which overlooks the water and is reserved for disabled drivers. In 1972 they did a survey to try and plan a management strategy for the area and found that over half the visitors stayed close to their cars, so you have been warned.

Your best strategy is probably to do **Walk 7**, which starts from Hawkshead and approaches the tarn from the north. (Only a tenth of the visitors walk all the way round.) The tarn is indeed very pretty, with wooded islands and shores and views south to Coniston Water ★ and west and north to Wetherlam and the Helvellyn ★ range.

Taylorgill Force (see Borrowdale)

Thirlmere (90) (NY 31-16)
Thirlmere lies to the north of Dunmail Raise ★ in the geological fault that runs north-south through the centre of the Lake District. It was once two smaller lakes, with a crossing between them. However in 1879 the Manchester Corporation Water Works built a dam at the north end, raising the water level by 54ft, and drowning 463 acres of farmland. Not surprisingly there had been a battle to stop them – in which John Ruskin and Thomas Carlyle were involved – and it was the failure to achieve anything which finally led to the formation of the National Trust ★ in 1895.

Time has healed most of Thirlmere's scars although the shores have been planted with conifers, giving it a curiously Swiss look. The main A591 runs up the east side but the road on the west side runs through the trees and gives good views across the lake. There is a footpath along the shore and Hause Point, halfway along, is worth climbing. Dunmail Raise lies to the south and across the lake is the smooth face of Helvellyn ★. At the southern end, Wythburn church is all that remains of the drowned village.

Thirlmere

Sailing craft and canoes can be launched from the car park at Armboth, on the west shore. **Tour 1** goes along the east shore of Thirlmere.

Torver (96,97) (SD 28-94)
This small village lies on the A593 which runs down the west side of Coniston Water ★ and is on **Tours 5 and 7**. Between the village and the lake are the Torver commons and there is a good circular walk starting from the village and going along the lake shore. This forms part of **Walk 6**. Both the Torver Commons and Blawith Common are owned by the Lake District Special Planning Board ★ – the largest single area they own apart from the Caldbeck Fells to the north of Skiddaw ★.

To the west of the village are the fells that lie between Coniston Water and Dunnerdale ★. Walna Scar and Dow Crag are in the foreground, with the Old Man of Coniston to the north. Torver church has a consecration paper signed by Archbishop Cranmer in 1538. Before then the chapel had no burial rights and the dead had to be carried to Ulverston ★. The present building is nineteenth-century.

The Old Man of Coniston from Torver

Town End (90) (NY 40-02)
This remarkable survival of a 'statesman's' house was built around 1626 and lived in for over 400 years by the same family. In the Lakes a statesman means a prosperous, educated, small landowner. The Brownes were High Constables of Kendal Ward in the seventeenth century and some members of the family went into law and medicine. But they threw nothing away, and they never modernised, with the result that Town End records a way of life that remained unchanged in the Lake District until the middle of this century.

The house is divided into two sections: a downhouse where the work of washing, baking, brewing and pickling was done; and a firehouse where the family lived. The hearth in the firehouse takes up most of the wall which partitions the house and is raised above floor level, with a smoke canopy. The same basic plan is seen in other seventeenth-century farms and is known as the 'statesman's plan'.

What makes Town End unique is the contents. The walls are panelled in dark oak and the furniture is elaborately carved in oak. There are oil paintings of notable sheep, and trophies won at local shows, and ingenious household implements. The family had kept every copy of the Westmorland Gazette since the first edition (edited by Wordsworth's disciple Thomas de Quincey) but these are now kept in the county archives.

The National Trust have owned Town End since 1947 and the house is open to the public from April to October – but only in the afternoons and not on Saturdays and Mondays. One wing has been modernised for a curator but the original house has no electric light and it shuts at dusk. The seventeenth-century barn opposite the house is also extremely interesting, with a gallery and two side wings. Town End is still farmed and the barn is in use.

Town End is on **Tours 4 and 9**. There is a car park south of the house, on the upper road.

Town End in Troutbeck

The village is really a series of hamlets and farms grouped about the wells which until recently supplied all the water. Almost all the cottages and barns date from the seventeenth and eighteenth centuries: Town End ★ , which is open to the public, was built in 1626 and there are twelve other houses in the village which predate it. The whole village is now classified as a Conservation Area.

The church lies below the village by the river (see map). Parts of it are fifteenth-century and it has a window by the pre-Raphaelite painter Edward Burne-Jones, who was apparently helped by William Morris and Ford Maddox Brown who happened to be passing on a fishing holiday. Troutbeck is on **Tours 4 and 9**.

Troutbeck (90) (NY 40-02)

Trout Beck runs down from the Kirkstone Pass ★ to Windermere ★ and gives its name to both the valley and the village which is perched along its western side. All the head of the valley belongs to Troutbeck Park Farm which was bought by Beatrix Potter in 1923. The purchase started her enthusiasm for the native breed of Herdwick sheep which lasted for the rest of her life. The farm, like the rest of her property, came to the National Trust in her will.

Ullswater (90) (NY 42-20)

Considered by many people to be the most beautiful of all the lakes, Ullswater winds its way through the landscape like 'a magnificent river', to quote Wordsworth's *Guide to the Lakes*. At the northern end it is flat and comparatively dull but at the southern end it has a tremendous dalehead with Helvellyn ★ , Fairfield, Place Fell and behind that the High Street ★ range.

The west side of the lake is the only one that can be driven. The road follows the lakeshore for most of the way and is one of the best drives in the Lake District. It goes past Gowbarrow Park, which is where Wordsworth saw golden daffodils
'Beside the lake, beneath the trees,
Fluttering and dancing in the breeze.'
These are not to be seen but the 'powerful brook which dashes amongst rocks through a deep glen' is still there. Aira Force ★ is probably the most visited waterfall in the Lakes. There is an easy path up and a car park: it is worth going further upstream where there are more falls, less visited.

Near the source of Aira Beck is Birkett Fell, renamed in honour of Lord Birkett who in 1962 argued in the Houses of Parliament against the proposal to turn Ullswater into a reservoir. In fact water is taken, but the plans were substantially modified. The pumping station is hidden underground and the idea that there should be a pipeline down Longsleddale ★ was abandoned. Both Gowbarrow Park and Glencoyne Park, to the south, were Norman deer forests.

The road is best driven from north to

Sandwick, near the south-eastern shore of Ullswater

south towards the dalehead (as on **Tour 4**). The best approach to the lake however is from the A5091 which comes down by Aira Force. As the road descends the whole lake lies below you. This is driven on **Tour 3**.

On the east side the road only runs as far as Martindale (also on **Tour 3**) and the whole of this side of the lake is wild and unspoilt. **Walk 3** starts in Martindale and visits one of the most remote valleys in Lakeland.

There are two steamers on Ullswater, Lady of the Lake and Raven. Both are about a hundred years old and are run by the Ullswater Navigation and Transit Com-pany Limited. They run between Glenridding ★ , Howtown ★ and Pooley Bridge ★ and take about an hour to go the length of the lake. A good strategy is to go to Howtown and walk along to Patterdale ★ . There is also a good circular walk from Patterdale. The country here is little changed since Wordsworth described 'a narrow track ... along the craggy side of Place-Fell, richly adorned with junipers and sprinkled over with birches'.

Ullswater is considered to be the best lake for sailing and there are two sailing schools, at Watermillock and Glenridding. Rowing and motorboats can be hired from Glenridding and Pooley Bridge and canoes from Pooley Bridge. There is a speed limit of 10 mph. Ullswater is one of the few lakes to have the schelly, a freshwater fish that looks a bit like a herring but is unrelated. Schelly used to be caught by stretching a net across the lake from Skelly Nab, the lake's narrowest point.

Ulpha (96) (SD 19-93)
This isolated village lies at the point where the road which runs down Dunnerdale from the foot of Hardknott Pass ★ is joined by the road over Birker Fell from Eskdale Green ★ . **Tours 7 and 8** go through the village and **Walk 12** starts in Ulpha and

Ullswater

Martindale

Ulpha Bobbin Mill

Ulverston

goes up into the Dunnerdale Fells to the east of the river Duddon.

'The Kirk of Ulpha', celebrated in one of Wordsworth's sonnets, is a small barn-like building dedicated to St John the Baptist. It appears on a map of Lancashire dated 1577 but is probably much older. Inside there are fragments of black and white murals. The churchyard, where Wordsworth was 'soothed by the unseen river's gentle roar', has a gravestone in memory of a man who 'perished on Birker Moor during the pelting of the pitiless storm on 1st of January 1826'.

Below the church the river is fairly wide but at Ulpha Bridge, just south of here, it runs between narrow rocks and there is a deep pool. The road south divides at the bridge. **Tour 7** crosses the bridge and takes the direct route to Duddon Bridge. The road that keeps to the west of the river also goes to Duddon Bridge but by a tortuous route which climbs up onto the fells to run past isolated farms and an old bobbin mill.

Ulverston (96,97) (SD 28-78)

Ulverston lies to the south of the National Park, on the Furness peninsula. The town appears in the Domesday book and is thought to be Saxon. In the twelfth-century it was owned by Henry I's nephew Stephen, who later became King of England, and from then on (until the Dissolution of the Monastries) it belonged to Furness Abbey.

Most of the present town dates from the eighteenth-century, when Ulverston was known as the 'London' of Furness. The town lay on the coach route from Lancaster across the Morcambe Sands and boasted a theatre – the Theatre Royal – at which Mrs Siddons once appeared. This period was also Ulverston's heyday as a trading and manufacturing centre: in 1759 a canal was cut to the Leven estuary, which brought ships almost to the centre of town, and in 1763 the Turnpike road to Kendal was built. The canal fell into disuse after the Furness railway was opened but the town remained prosperous. It is still a

manufacturing base (Glaxo Laboratories use the canal as a water tank) and there are several flourishing crafts.

The Information Centre is in County Square, next to the Town Hall, and town maps can be obtained from here. Just to the west is Market Place, with the old market cross. Ulverston has had a market charter since the thirteenth-century and there are still street markets on Thursdays and Saturdays. On Thursdays, known as L'ile Pig Day, there is a livestock auction in North Lonsdale Road, near Canal Head. At Canal Foot, the exit into the estuary, there is a charming hamlet and a pier.

Just to the south of the Market Place, in Theatre Street, is the Furness Gallery. This is a workshop where dolls houses and furniture are made. Another place to visit is Cumbria Crystal's factory in the old Cattle Market in Lightburn Street. Both places welcome visitors.

Walking north up King Street, towards the Gill car park, brings you to the Laurel and Hardy Museum which contains 'the world's largest collection of Laurel and Hardy memorabilia'. Stan Laurel was born in Ulverston. The museum is in a private house in Upper Brook Street, the first turning on the left.

Church Walk, further along on the right, leads to St Mary's Church: dating from 1111, it is sometimes called the Church of the Four Ones. Only the south door is twelfth-century but there is an interesting sixteenth-century tower, built with stones taken from Conishead Priory after the Dissolution of the Monasteries.

To the north of the town is Hoad Hill, dominated by the Hoad monument. This is an imitation of the Eddystone Lighthouse which was built as a memorial to Sir John Barrow, a famous Arctic explorer who founded the Royal Geographical Society. From the summit there is a magnificent view south over the estuary and north over the fells.

Swarthmoor Hall, south-east of the town, has many associations with the Quaker movement. The house was owned

Conishead Priory

by Judge Fell, a devout Puritan and a friend of George Fox, the founder of the Society of Friends, His wife, Margaret Fell, once obtained the release of 4,000 Friends from prison by pleading with Charles II, but was later herself imprisoned for four years. After the death of her husband, she married George Fox. The house is owned by the Society of Friends and open to the public. It is a plain seventeenth-century building but has good panelling and a unique 'box' staircase.

Conishead Priory, on the shores of Morecambe Bay, is a nineteenth-century Gothic mansion built on the site of a twelfth-century priory. Its owner went bankrupt twelve years after completing the building and subsequent owners have included a Hydropathic Hotel and the Durham Miners Welfare Committee, who used it as a convalescent home. It is currently owned by a Budddhist community called the Manjushri Institute and is open to the public.

St Olaf's Church

trains of slate from Honister ★ and wadd (graphite) from Borrowdale ★ would have made their way through the valley, crossing with imported tobacco, spirits and coal going inland to Ambleside ★ .

More recently the traffic has been made up of climbers. The Wasdale Head Hotel is closely associated with the development of rock climbing at the turn of the century; the bar has photographs of famous climbers and climbs. The tiny church of St Olaf also has many climbing links. There is an etching of Napes Needle on one of the windows above the words, 'I will lift up mine eyes unto the hills from whence cometh my strength'. And the churchyard contains many graves of climbers killed on the surrounding fells and memorials to others who died in the Himalayas.

Wasdale Head is on **Tour 7. Walk 9** starts in the car park at the head of the lake.

Wasdale Head (89,90) (NY 18-08)
The isolated hamlet of Wasdale Head is 9 miles from the nearest shop and has had electricity only since 1979. Yet the packhorse bridge in the village is a reminder that Wasdale lay on the major packhorse route to the coast and in the seventeenth and eighteenth centuries was far less isolated than many of the central dales. Pack

The packhorse bridge at Wasdale Head

Wast Water (89) (NY 16-05)
Wast Water is divided from the central Lake District by the steep passes of Wrynose ★ and Hardknott ★ . This means that

Wast Water

Ashness Bridge

it is still empty, even at the height of the season. Walkers and climbers make the journey but few motorists. This isolation reinforces the effect of the massive screes, which drop straight into the water. Facing north-west, they are dark and hostile.

The dalehead is possibly the finest of all, a flat amphitheatre walled in by Yewbarrow, Kirk Fell, Great Gable and Lingmell. Behind them are the still higher peaks of Pillar and Sca Fell Pike ★ . From the hamlet of Wasdale Head ★ the passes go up into the fells: Sty Head Pass into Borrowdale ★, linking up with passes into Great Langdale ★ , and Black Sail Pass into Ennerdale ★ , linking up with the pass to Buttermere ★ .

There is also a 'corpse track' which leads south to Boot ★ , in Eskdale: until this century the chapel at Wasdale Head had no burial rights. *'The Guardian of the Lakes'*, the excellent new history of the National Trust, gives a story about this track which sums up the whole atmosphere of Wast Water. The story goes that as the procession of mourners made their way over the fell, carrying the coffin of a young man strapped to a horse, the mist came down. When it cleared, the horse had gone. After searching in vain, the mourners returned to the village and soon after the mother of the dead man died from grief. The procession set out again, and again the mist came down. When it lifted, the horse was there – but carrying the body of the young man, not the mother.

Two walks around Wastwater are described in **Walk 9**, both starting from the car park at the head of lake. One explores the head of the valley and the other climbs Illgill Head, the highest point of the screes. The walk along the road by the lake goes past small, rocky bays. Do not be tempted to paddle: a short distance out the floor of the lake drops sheer to the bottom – at 258 ft, the deepest lake in England.

Watendlath (89,90) (NY 27-16)
This remote moorland hamlet of stone farms is set beside a large tarn in a hanging valley east of Borrowdale ★ . It was the meeting place for several ancient tracks; coming from Thirlmere ★ (to the east), Keswick ★ (from the north), Great Langdale ★ (from the south, via Stake Pass) and Rosthwaite ★ from the west.

Only in the 1930s was a road built to Watendlath. This runs up the Watendlath Beck, branching off the B5289 near the head of Derwent Water ★ . It offers two superb views. The first is at Ashness Bridge,a packhorse bridge which is immediately familiar from calendars and jigsaw puzzles, and the second is at Surprise View. Opposite the car park the ground drops away to give a birdseye view of Derwent Water. The road is singletrack, with rather few passing places, and best avoided in the summer. The old track from Rosthwaite is still the shortest route and there is also a signposted path from the Lodore Falls ★ .

Waterhead (90) (NY 37-03)
South of Ambleside ★ a group of hotels and houses has grown up around the head of Windermere ★ , many of them built to cater for the Victorian tourists. The Windermere steamers have a pier here and boats go to Bowness ★ and then on to Lakeside, at the foot of the lake, where they connect with the Lakeside and Haverthwaite Railway ★ . There are also launches to Bowness and Brockhole ★ and cruises around the head of the lake. There is a National Park Information Centre in the car park and a 'beach', from which small craft can be launched and hired.

Just inland from Borrans Park, at the mouth of the river Brathay, is the site of the Roman fort of Galava. The stones have long ago been plundered: Borrans is the Norse word for a heap of stones and even these are gone now. The layout can be seen from the surrounding fells.

Built in AD 79, the fort protected the link between Ravenglass ★ , on the coast, and the fort near Brougham Castle ★ which lay on the vital routes to the north and York. The road ran across the Hardknott ★ and Wrynose ★ passes, through Little Langdale ★ to Windermere, and then on up through the Troutbeck ★ valley and across the spectacular ridge of High Street ★ – an extraordinary feat of engineering. The fort was attacked at least once and there is a gravestone, now in the Museum of Natural History and Archaeology at Kendal ★ , which reads, 'To the Good God of the Underworld: Flavius Romanus, Record Clerk. Lived for 35 years. Killed in the fort by the enemy'.

Just south of Waterhead on the A591 are the Stagshaw Gardens. Waterhead is on **Tours 6 and 9.**

Whinlatter Pass (89,90) (NY 19-24)

This is the easiest east-west pass in the Lake District and also the dullest. It runs from Braithwaite, west of Keswick ★ , to Lorton Vale, south of Cockermouth ★ . The pass formed part of the 1761 turnpike road from Kendal ★ to Cockermouth which went via Ambleside ★ and the Dunmail Raise ★ to Keswick, and then on to Cockermouth. The Romans had a road through here too, starting from their fort at Papcastle, outside Cockermouth. It seems likely that it connected up with the road which can be traced running south-west from their fort at Old Penrith on the main north-south route. This goes through Greystoke ★ . Father West, the scholarly Jesuit priest who wrote the first guide book to the Lakes (in 1778), thought the two roads must have met at a fort at Keswick but no evidence has yet been found.

There is a good view of Bassenthwaite Lake ★ just before the road enters Whinlatter Forest. The Forestry Commission have an information centre here, with films and slide shows, and there are forest trails.

Whinlatter Pass

Windermere (90,96,97) (SD 38-94)

Windermere is the largest lake in England and also the busiest. Hotels and houses line its eastern shore and in summer the water is crowded with boats of every variety. Despite this, Windermere remains beautiful. There are good views of the lake from Queen Adelaide's Hill, north of Bowness ★ , and from Gummers How ★ , at the foot of the lake. However the best view of all, according to Wordsworth's *Guide to the Lakes*, is from the lake itself.

'None of the other Lakes unfold so many fresh beauties to him who sails upon them. This is owing to its greater size, to the islands, and to its having two vales at the head, with their accompanying mountains of nearly equal dignity. Nor can the grandeur of these two terminations be seen at once from any other point, except from the bosom of the lake.'

There are three ways of seeing the lake from a boat. The first is to take one of the Windermere steamers which ply up and down the lake from Lakeside in the south to Waterhead ★ in the north, calling in at Bowness ★ . A one-way trip takes about 1½ hours. The second way is to take one of the cruises which visit the islands or the head of the lake. These go from Bowness or Waterhead and take about the same length of time.

The third way is to join the crowds of other small craft on the lake. Motor boats and rowing boats can be hired from the Bowness Bay Boating Company, Bowness, and rowing boats from Fell Foot Park, at the foot of the lake. Sailing dinghies can be hired from Windermere Lake Holidays Afloat, Shepherd's Boatyard, Bowness and Performance Marine, Windermere Marina. There is no speed limit on Windermere and the main hazard is water skiers.

On top of all this, there is the Windermere ferry, which crosses the lake from Ferry Nab to Ferry House and takes 7 minutes. The ferry runs just to the south of Belle Isle ★ , the largest and the only inhabited island on the lake. There has been a ferry on this spot for about 500 years.

The only good walks around Windermere are on the western shore. The land to the north of the ferry is owned by the National Trust and it is possible to walk along the lakeshore as far as Wray Castle. There are also some lovely walks on Claife Heights, the long wooded fell which stretches northwards from the ferry. At Red Nab, south of High Wray ★ , there is a car park. This is visited on **Tour 5. Tour 9** drives the west coast south of the ferry.

The eastern shore gives a very good idea of what the Lakes might be if the National Trust had never been formed. Almost all this land was built on in the nineteenth century and the lakeshore forms the gardens of these houses or the hotels that have succeeded them. A recent development is the Windermere Marina, a time-share complex. At the southern end of the

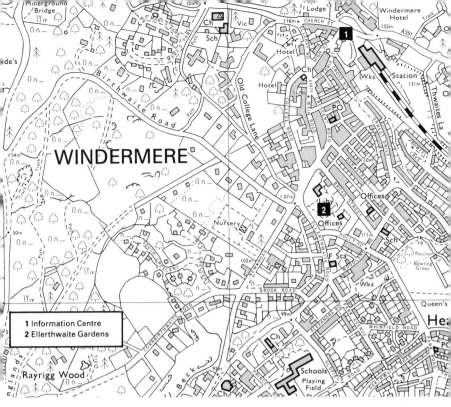

1 Information Centre
2 Ellerthwaite Gardens

SCALE 1:10 000 or 6 INCHES to 1 MILE

lake is the Fell Foot Park. This covers what were once the grounds of a large house; it was opened in 1972 by the National Trust to provide an open area for picnicking, sailing, fishing, swimming: in short a 'family day out'. Access is free and there is an information centre. There is also public access to the lake from Millerground, north of Bowness, and Cockshott Point, north of Ferry Nab.

Windermere town (96,97) (SD 41-98)
In 1847 a railway branch line was built from Oxenholme (outside Kendal ★) to the little village of Braithwaite, one mile from Bowness ★ . The line had been bitterly fought by Wordsworth and others, who feared the 'Advance of the Ten Thousand', and to some extent their predictions were correct. The station, which was called Windermere, created a new town which rapidly engulfed Bowness. Hotels and boarding houses sprang up and by the end of the century the Windermere Express was able to deliver tired Manchester businessmen to their country retreats in just over 2 hours.

The site of the original station has been sold by British Rail and is now a supermarket. The new station, built in the 1980s, is next to the Information Centre (1). On the opposite side of the A591 is the footpath to Orrest Head, a famous viewpoint from which all the central lakeland fells can be seen. There is a viewfinder at the summit which identifies the various peaks.

Ellerthwaite Gardens (2) are behind the Library, a large house built in the 1850s which was donated to the Town Council by the Groves family. The gardens belonged to the house; there is a large lawn with rhododendrons. Beside the house is a magnificent Californian redwood tree, nearly 200ft high.

Tour 4 starts from Windermere town and **Tour 6** goes along the A591.

Wordsworth (see Grasmere, Rydal, Hawkshead, Cockermouth)

Wray Castle (see High Wray)

Wrynose Pass (89,90) (NY 27-02)
This notoriously steep, narrow road runs between Little Langdale ★ and Hardknott Pass ★ and is on **Tours 1,5,7 and 8**. At the summit (1,281 ft) is the Three Shires Stone, which marks the meeting point of the old boundaries between Lancashire, Westmorland and Cumberland. From here the road drops down to Wrynose Bottom and Cockley Beck, where the Dunnerdale ★ road branches off to the south.

Up to the last war, the road over the Wrynose and Hardknott passes was still a track, unsuitable for cars. There were seven water-splashes on Wrynose Bottom. During the war the roads were used as practice routes for army vehicles. This did so much damage that the roads had to be completely remade.

89

Tour 1
Eight lakes and three mountain passes

90 miles. This long tour takes in some of the most spectacular scenery in Lakeland. It can include eight lakes – Derwent Water, Buttermere, Crummock Water, Loweswater, Ennerdale Water, Wast Water, Rydal Water and artificial Thirlmere. The tour will take you over three high passes, Honister, Wrynose and incomparable Hardknott – and close to some of the most famous fells in the Lake District. Cyclists would be better restricting themselves to the A to K section.

Leave Keswick ★ town centre on the B5289 to Borrowdale ★. The road climbs gently and then drops down through woods by the side of Derwent Water ★.

The road follows the River Derwent down into Rosthwaite. The Borrowdale Fells, ahead as you enter the village, are like monstrous animal shapes (see **Walk 10**). Go through Rosthwaite, taking care as the road is very narrow.

Ignore any side turnings and keep on to Seathwaite ★. At the next signpost you go left for Seathwaite village, and straight on for our route to the Honister Pass on the B5289. Almost immediately the road climbs steeply beside a deep chasm. The route passes a green slate quarry on the left and then begins to descend. After crossing the bridge at the bottom you will soon see the tranquil waters of Buttermere ★. **Walk 11** begins at the head of the lake. Follow the road through Buttermere village, keeping on the B5289 towards Cockermouth ★. At the top of the rise Crummock Water ★ comes into sight through the trees.

At the T-junction, **(A)**, turn left to Loweswater ★. The road descends a 1-in-6 hill and crosses a stream before entering Loweswater. Go straight on. The peak to the left is Mellbreak. Follow the sign to Ennerdale ★, straight ahead.

Soon you will see Loweswater. Drive along the lakeside. There are beautiful views back along Loweswater from the car park at the far end of the lake. There is also a suggested short walk here.

The road climbs for some time and, at the top, bends sharply to the left at **(B)**. Follow it round to Lamplugh ★. Turn left at the T-junction. The church of St Michael's, Lamplugh is on your right and

a Hall to the left. There is a suggested short walk near here.

Do not turn left to Ennerdale Water ★, go straight on.

At **(C)** there is a junction with the A5086 – turn left. Follow the main road for less than ½ mile and turn left at the signpost to Kirkland and Ennerdale Bridge. At the crossroads in Kirkland keep straight on. After the village, the fells open up before you and down to the left you will see Ennerdale Water. Enter Ennerdale at **(D)** and go left at the first junction following the sign to Ennerdale Water. For the suggested stroll, turn right at the green sign and go down through the trees to the car park. If you do not have time even for a stroll, still make the detour, but instead of turning right at the Forestry Commission sign go straight on to the lake.

To continue the tour, retrace your route to Ennerdale Bridge. Just before the gate, take time to read the stone plaque on the old house by the side of the road. Go over the bridge and straight on, and at **(E)** go left where it is signposted to Calder Bridge ★ and Gosforth. Crossing a cattle grid you will enter moorland, passing a stone circle to the left of the road.

Passing over two cattle grids, the road winds down a 20% hill. Follow the signs to Calder Bridge, joining the A595 at **(F)** and turning left. Pass through the village of New Mill and take the first, unmarked, turning on the left at **(G)** just before an inn on the left.

Where the road forks, keep right, passing through a farmyard. At the bottom of a steep, narrow hill, you will come to a junction – turn left, following the sign to Nether Wasdale ★ and Wasdale Head ★.

Do not turn left at the signpost to Nether Wasdale, keep straight on towards Wasdale Head. Go over a cattle grid. The road descends through bracken and a maze of drystone walls at the bottom. Suddenly you will be confronted with the most dramatic view in Lakeland.

There is a place to park at **(H)**. From here follow the sign to Wasdale and Santon Bridge ★. At the next signpost you can go straight on into Nether Wasdale ¼ mile ahead, but our route goes left towards Santon Bridge.

At the T-junction, go left over the bridge. When you reach the T-junction in Santon Bridge go left at **(J)** and then turn right to Irton ★. Go past Irton House School on the right and at the next junction go left at **(K)** following the sign to Eskdale Green ★. At the next junction go right – this is Eskdale Green where there is a suggested short walk.

Turn left at the next junction, signposted to Boot ★ and Langdale ★ via Hardknott Pass ★ . After winding through a succession of small farms, you will see the village of Boot signposted to the left – go straight on.

After crossing the second bridge, you will go over a cattle grid and begin the ascent to Hardknott. In winter conditions do not attempt this route. Going down is as potentially dangerous as coming up, and drivers should use extreme caution.

Go through the gate at the bottom (remembering to close it behind you) over the bridge and turn left towards Wrynose ★ . After reaching the highest point and beginning the descent from Wrynose there are splendid views ahead.

At the bottom go straight on over the cattle grid, following the signs for Coniston ★ and Ambleside ★ . At the T-junction turn right. Pass over a bridge and you will come to another T-junction, go left here towards Ambleside on the A593.

Pass through Skelwith Bridge ★ , at (L), in the direction of Ambleside. Soon you will see a minor road indicated to the left. This is (M), go left here. The road climbs up: ignore the turning to the right following the signs straight on to Grasmere ★ .

At (N) you will pass a turning to the left to Chapel Stile , go straight on. At the 25% incline – where you will catch your first glimpse of Rydal Water ★ below. Follow the road down into Grasmere. Go through the village (P) past the church on your right, until you reach the T-junction with the A591. Turn left here at (R).

After a little over 4 miles you pass Thirlmere ★ down to the left of the road.

At (S) the A591 bends left towards Keswick ★ : there is a fork to the right to Threlkeld and Penrith ★ . Go right here. Follow the B5322 to St John's in the Vale. The road runs along by St John's Beck for a time in a valley dominated by the jostling peaks on either side.

You will pass a signpost to St John's in the Vale Church and Keswick. Less than 2 miles further on, at (T), turn left onto the A66. Threlkeld is to the right and north of the road. To the left is the sign to Castlerigg Stone Circle ★ . As you follow the A66 down into Keswick you will see the huge mass of Skiddaw ★ to your right.

Leave the A66 following the Keswick sign. Traffic merges at the bottom of the hill and the road enters the town completing the tour.

Scale 1:250 000 or ¼ INCH to 1 MILE

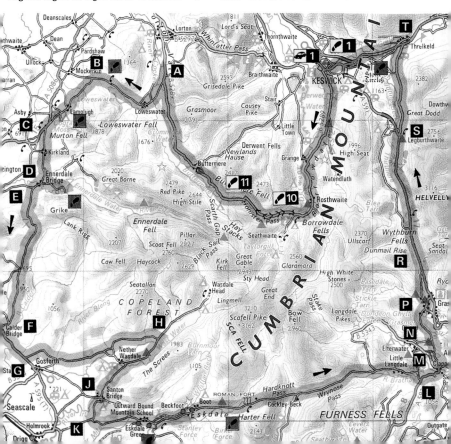

Tour 2
Cockermouth and north-west Lakeland

54 miles. This tour includes a visit to quiet Loweswater, which means 'leafy lake'; Derwent Water, with some of the most famous views in Lakeland; as well as the twin lakes of Buttermere and Crummock Water which, although very close, have a quite different temperament which has always intrigued visitors. The route goes through the glaciated valley of Honister Pass and includes a trip to Mirehouse with its associations with the poet Tennyson. Honister is a long punishing haul, but otherwise cyclists should not find the going too difficult.

Leave Cockermouth ★ centre on the B5289. The road makes a long climb up out of the town. You will see the outline of the high fells in the distance ahead. Our route passes under the A66 and soon there is a panorama of Lakeland scenery. At the crossroads go straight on.

At **(A)** keep on the B5289 following the signpost to the right towards Low Lorton, Loweswater ★ and Buttermere ★ . Our route goes through the village of Lorton past a castellated Victorian Gothic house on the right. Do not turn left or right but keep straight on, following the signpost to Buttermere. Ignore the turning to Hodge Beck. At the next junction, **(B)**, go straight on if you are making the detour to see Loweswater where there is a suggested short walk. The road descends a 1-in-6 hill and crosses a stream before entering the village of Loweswater. Go straight on following the sign to Ennerdale ★ . Soon you will see Loweswater to the left of the road. Half way along the lakeside road, through a break in the pines, you can look up to Darling Fell. From the car park at the far end of the lake there are magnificent views back along Loweswater.

Retrace your route to continue the tour, turning right at **(B)** towards Buttermere. Rising up steeply above the road to the left are Whiteside and, further on, Grasmoor Fells. After crossing a cattle grid you will catch your first sight of Crummock Water ★ . Above the lake to the right is hump-backed Mellbreak. This is the best view of Crummock, which is a very beautiful lake although generally thought to be somehow less friendly than

Buttermere. The slopes of both Buttermere and Crummock are clad with bracken: its russet autumn and winter colours suit Crummock, while Buttermere is more beautiful when the bracken is vivid green in spring and early summer. People have always compared Crummock and Buttermere: perhaps the difference in mood between the two is the difference between spring and autumn.

Go through Buttermere village where **Walk 1** begins. Our route climbs up the hill, past the little redstone church on the left, to a crossroads. Go straight on, following the signpost to the Honister Pass ★ . At the end of Buttermere, as you begin to climb up towards the Pass, you will see Fleetwood Pike to the left: to the right is the jagged outline of Hay Stacks. While driving through Honister Pass it is impossible to forget that you are following the route of a glacier. All around are scattered the large and small boulders which were left when the ice melted. When they were frozen into the glacier, these rocks were the teeth which gouged out the U-shape of the valley bottom under the massive weight of the ice.

At the top of the Pass, to the right, is the man-made detritus of a green slate quarry. After crossing a cattle grid on the descent from Honister, the road once again drops steeply. Although the road over Honister is wider than some of the other passes, extreme caution must still be exercised by drivers. None of the passes in Lakeland should be attempted in wintry conditions.

Our route enters Rosthwaite ★ and continues up Borrowdale ★ where **Walk 12** begins. After Rosthwaite the road follows the River Derwent. At the greenstone bridge over the Derwent at **(C)** go left to Grange ★ . The houses, the church and even the gravestones are green.

Our route follows the beautiful west bank of Derwent Water. Its higher reaches provide some of the very best views of the lake: there is a suggested short walk here. Go round a sharp hairpin bend towards the end of the lakeside road and drop down to Keswick ★ . You will pass over a cattle grid. Keep following the signposts to Keswick. As it winds down, the road is bordered on the right by a long stretch of beech hedge. At the T-junction, **(D)**, turn right onto the A66 and soon afterwards turn right again at the signpost to Keswick on the B5289.

Look out for a church on the left of the road at **(E)** and go left here following the signpost to Penrith ★ , Carlisle and the M6. At the large roundabout which is **(F)**

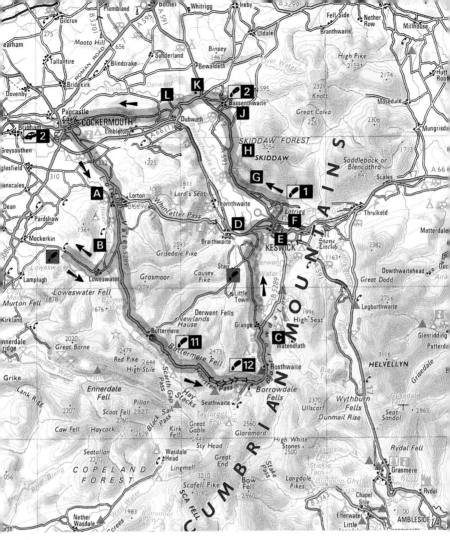

Scale 1:250 000 or ¼ INCH to 1 MILE

take the second turning signposted to Carlisle on the A591 and Mirehouse ★. Immediately, turn right onto the minor road signposted to Ormathwaite. The road climbs up in the shadow of Skiddaw ★: the public footpath to Skiddaw is signposted to the right at the top of the hill. Ignore side turnings and keep straight on. Down to the left you will see the lush fields at the southern end of Bassenthwaite Lake. The road finally drops down through woods to rejoin the A591 at (G). Go right here. Soon you will see Bassenthwaite Lake ★ to the left, and a plantation of great trees marks Mirehouse.

At (H) there is the possibility of taking a detour down to the left on the minor road which leads to the church, rejoining the A591 further on. Whether making the optional detour, or continuing on the main road, look out for (J) – the turning to Bassenthwaite ★ village. Go right here. Follow the road up through the avenue of trees which cross the green, turning left when you see a large yew tree ahead of you. Cross over a bridge and bear round with the road to the left. At the T-junction with the A591 go right and then immediately left at (K). This is the B5291 signposted to Bassenthwaite Lake and Cockermouth. To the left of the road you will see the head of Bassenthwaite.

Our route goes over a bridge at (L) and then turns right where it is signposted to Higham Hall and Embleton. The road goes through a fine avenue of trees. Follow the signs for Cockermouth. At the next junction go right. Go through the village of Embleton still heading for Cockermouth. Our route follows the ridge above the main road and is a pleasant alternative way of returning to Cockermouth to complete the tour.

Tour 3
Ullswater, Aira Force and Broughton Castle

57 miles. Ullswater has been described as the most 'complete' of all the lakes. This tour, with its optional detour to Martindale, explores the beautiful countryside around Ullswater. In addition to well-visited centres like Pooley Bridge. The tour also explores little villages seldom visited by tourists. There is also a visit to the spectacular waterfall of Aira Force and the interesting ancient monuments of Shap Abbey and Brougham Castle.

Leave Penrith ★ centre, following the signs to Keswick and the A66. This will take you past the ruins of the castle and the railway station. At the large roundabout over the A6 take the third exit signposted to Keswick ★ and Ullswater ★ . At the next roundabout turn left to Ullswater

on the A592 at **(A)**. As the road drop: down there are fine views of the fell: ahead. At the bottom you will see Dale main House ★ to your right, after cross ing a bridge the road follows the Rive Eamont on the left.

Look out for a signpost to the right to Dacre ★ . Turn right here at **(B)**. Climb up the hill, ignoring the deadend to the left After descending a 1-in-8 hill you wil cross a bridge and see a castle up to the right of the road. This is Dacre. Turn left a **(C)**, the signpost to Sparket and Thack thwaite. Recross the river, do not turn lef at the next sign, go straight on. When you reach some crossroads go straight on. To the left you will see the dome-shape o Little Mell Fell. The road drops dowr crossing a narrow V-shaped valley. At the top end of the curve turn left to Matter dale End. Ahead of you now is Great Mel Fell.

At **(D)**, the T-junction, turn left following the signs to Matterdale End. Entering the village there are fine views ahead. At the T-junction in Matterdale **(E)** turn left ontc the A5091. Go straight on, entering Dock-

Scale 1:250 000 or ¼ INCH to 1 MILE

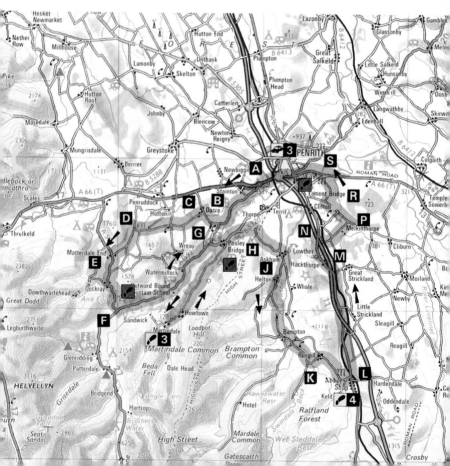

ray. Continue through the village towards Ullswater. The road begins a long descent here, with spectacular views of the lake and the fells beyond.

At the bottom, turn left to Pooley Bridge ★ on the A592 at **(F)**. Aira Force ★ car park is immediately on your left (there is a suggested stroll here). Our route now follows the magnificent lakeside of Ullswater. Pass through the village of Watermillock. After about 6 miles you will come to a junction with the Penrith road at **(G)**. Keep on your road bearing right into Pooley Bridge.

There is a suggested short walk in Pooley Bridge and an optional detour to Martindale. Carry straight on and ignore the next paragraph if you do not wish to make this 10 mile round trip.

Going over the bridge and through the village turn right at the church, following the sign to Martindale. At the T-junction go right. Up to the left of the road is Barton Fell. You will come to a place where there are Scots pines growing by the lakeside – Hallin Fell, with its obelisk, is directly ahead. Cross a cattle grid, climbing up an unfenced road through the bracken. Parking is forbidden on the steep bends, but passengers should look back at the magnificent views over Ullswater. Go past the church of St Peter Martindale on the left (**Walk 3** starts here) and where the road forks go left. Soon you will come to the Old Church of St Martin. Retrace your route to Pooley Bridge to continue the tour. When you come to the crossroads do not turn back into Pooley Bridge. Go straight on, rejoining the B5320 turning right towards Penrith.

At **(H)** turn right at the signpost to Celleron and Askham ★ . Go straight on at the top of the hill following the sign to Askham. At the next junction **(J)** turn right. Go through Askham following the signs to Bampton ★ . Pass through the villages of Helton and Butterwick.

In the village of Bampton go left towards Bampton Grange and Shap ★ . Turn left at the next junction. Go over the bridge passing St Patrick's Church on the right. Go straight on, following the sign for Shap. You will pass the sign to Rosgill on the right at **(K)**: go straight on.

At the bend in the road you will pass a sign to Shap Abbey to the right. Continue on towards the village where you will turn left at the sign to Penrith and the A6. Join the main road with care at **(L)**. **Walk 4** begins in Shap.

The road crosses and recrosses the railway, and some miles further on goes under the M6 Motorway. You will pass the stone gatehouse to Hackthorpe Hall on the left before again crossing the M6. Our route passes through the village of Hackthorpe ★ and the road to Lowther ★ (½ a mile to the left) at **(M)**.

Immediately after crossing the M6 once again, turn right to Melkinthorpe at **(N)**. Go under the railway bridge and follow the straight, undulating road past the sign to Melkinthorpe village, until you reach a T-junction. Turn left, following the sign to Penrith at **(P)**.

Pass through Clifton Dykes ★ and as the road climbs the hill follow the signpost on the right to Brougham ★ at **(R)**. After driving through a great avenue of oaks and beeches you will see the ruins of Brougham Castle. Go straight on over the crossroads. There is a suggested short walk at Brougham.

To complete the tour go on and join the A66 turning left to Penrith.

The Ullswater Steamer

Tour 4
Ullswater, Windermere and the highest road in the Lake District

71 miles. This tour includes a worthwhile detour to Kentmere where there is a suggested stroll, and then follows the Shap route north. This was the road Bonny Prince Charlie took in hope and in retreat. Later the tour includes a visit to Pooley Bridge, and continues along the magnificent lakeside road by Ullswater before going over the Kirkstone Pass and dropping down to Windermere. Apart from the incomparable Ullswater stretch, this route is not suitable for cyclists.

Leave Windermere ★ centre on the A591 signposted to Kendal ★, climbing up out of the town past the railway station. After about 1½ miles of pleasant rolling country you pass through the village of Ings★. Continue on the main road to the larger village of Staveley. Turn left here at the signpost to Kentmere ★ (**A**), following the narrow street between houses and past the Wesleyan Chapel on the right.

At first the road follows the river, with rocky outcrops above and to the left. At a fork in the road, turn right over the bridge following the signs to Kentmere.

At the next fork in the road go left. Soon you will see the church across the valley to your left. Go over the bridge and follow the road round and up towards the church. It is inadvisable to take your car any further than this point as there is no parking further up the track. There is a suggested stroll here.

Retrace your route to return to Staveley. Instead of re-entering the village, turn left over the bridge by the weir (if you reach the War Memorial on the right, you have come too far).

Follow the signs to Burneside. Drive with great care, as there are several blind corners where the road rises. Keep straight on, do not fork left.

In a wood of large trees you come to a T-junction. Turn right here. This stretch of the road has been planted with oaks. At the next fork go left. You will come to a T-junction – turn left.

Turn left again almost immediately, following the sign to Longsleddale ★ at (**B**). At the next unmarked fork, at an oak tree, go right. It is a very narrow, steep lane

which drops away quickly. Do not fork left half way down, keep straight on. Pass over a bridge. The road winds up into Garth Row. Go left at the crossroads and climb up the hill to join the A6. Turn left towards Shap ★ at (**C**).

As the road climbs, the High Street range comes into view on your left and shortly afterwards the high Shap fells ahead of you. As the road descends again, it passes the Shap quarries on your left and on your right you can see the M6 in the middle distance. The country becomes flatter and more open and the road runs alongside the London to Glasgow railway and comes into Shap.

As the road leaves the village (**D**), turn left just past the Bulls' Head to Bampton and Haweswater. For **Walk 4**, bear left shortly afterwards to Keld ★ and Thornship. The tour carries straight on. At the next left turn, it is worth making a short detour to see the ruins of Shap Abbey ★.

To continue the tour, go straight on. The road at this point is signposted to Rosgill. Where the road bears round to the left into Rosgill (**E**), go straight ahead, signposted to Bampton ★ and Haweswater ★. Just before you enter the village of Bampton Grange (**F**), turn sharp right to Knipe and Whale. This soon becomes an unfenced road which runs across the edge of Knipe Moor, with the river Lowther below you on the left. At the telephone box, turn right through a gate, signposted to Whale and Lowther. Go through another gate and back onto a fenced road. Cross over the river Lowther and bear right at the junction, signposted to Askham ★, Lowther ★ and Penrith ★.

Follow the road into Askham, a charming eighteenth-century village which is worth exploring. To continue the tour, go through the village, ignoring a signpost to the right to Penrith and Ullswater ★, and just outside the village at (**G**) turn left to Celleron. This is a narrow road with passing places. As the road descends, there is a view across the hills west of Ullswater. At the T-junction (**H**), turn left onto the B5320 to come into Pooley Bridge ★.

Pooley Bridge, at the foot of Ullswater, is a busy tourist village with an information centre. To continue, cross the bridge and turn left down the A592 (**J**). The Pooley Bridge pier for the Ullswater steamers is just after the bridge. The road now runs down the west side of Ullswater ★, following the lake shore for most of the way. Go through the hamlet of Watermillock and past the Outward Bound school to come to Gowbarrow

Park, on your right.

At the far end of Gowbarrow Park, just before the A5091 comes in from the right, there is a National Trust car park for Aira Force ★ , a spectacular waterfall. The road then follows the water's edge past the Glencoyne estate (also National Trust) to Glenridding ★ , a former mining village.

Just past Glenridding, at the head of the lake, is the village of Patterdale ★ . There is a car park just before the road bends left at the head of the lake. From Patterdale, there is a superb walk up the east side of the lake. The road now starts to climb towards Kirkstone Pass ★ , the highest road in the Lake District. Before you reach the pass, the road bears left round the foot of Brothers Water ★ , a large tarn. As the road bears sharply right again to go past the tarn, there is a minor road straight ahead to Hartsop ★ .

The A592 now goes straight ahead into the dramatic cleft of Kirkstone Pass. At the head of the pass is an old coaching inn and a view of Windermere ★ in the distance. The unsignposted road on the right just past the inn leads down into Ambleside ★ and is known as 'The Struggle'. Do not take this but follow the main road as it bears left into the Trout-beck valley. To your left there are fine views of the hills across the valley. The next road on the right, signposted to Ambleside, is just by the Mortal Inn pub which has a famous pub sign. Turn right here **(K)** and follow the road through the lovely little village of Troutbeck ★.

At the far end of the village is Town-end★, a yeoman's house built in 1626 and lived in by the same family for the next three centuries. If the house is open fork right just past the house to park in the National Trust car park. If not, fork left and follow the road down to the A591. Turn left at **(L)** into Troutbeck Bridge ★ – following the main road back into Windermere to complete the tour.

Scale 1:250 000 or ¼ INCH to 1 MILE

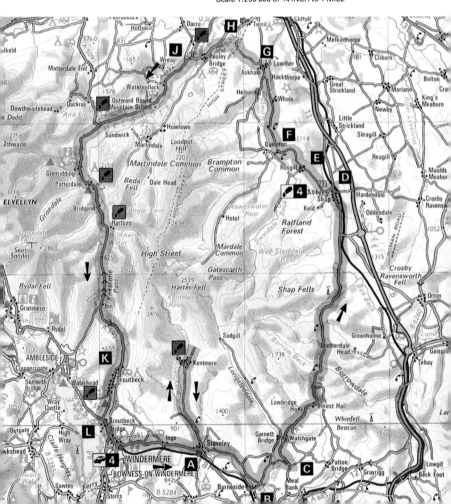

Tour 5
Coniston, the Duddon Valley and Wordsworth's home

59 miles. This tour includes a wide variety of elements. The places visited include medieval Hawkshead, the slate village of Coniston and Grasmere village where William Wordsworth lived in Dove Cottage. The route takes in the attractive western lakeside road by Coniston Water before crossing the moors and following the valley of the River Duddon. After crossing Wrynose Pass, with its fine views, the tour passes by Rydal Water – smallest of all the lakes. Cyclists should avoid Wrynose Pass, but the other sections do not present too many problems.

Leave Ambleside ★ on the A593 Coniston ★ road. Pass through Clappersgate and turn left on to the B5286 to Hawkshead ★ at (A). Recross the river and bear round to the right. Look out for a sign to the left to Wray Castle. Go left here at (B). You will see the outline of the castle across the fields to the left. Climb up the hill past the castle and turn left at the sign 'to the ferry' at (C). The road is unsuitable for motorcars after about a mile, but it is worth it for the splendid views across Windermere ★.

Retrace your route along the track through the woods, and turn left at the junction with the grass island in the centre at (C). You will see Esthwaite Water ★ down to your right. An interesting stone drinking trough is passed on the left bearing the date 1891 and the inscription 'In memory of happy days'. Continue along the upper road after the trough, ignoring all the turnings on the right until the road itself bends sharply and the signpost indicates Hawkshead. Follow the signs into Hawkshead, and turn right into the village at the T-junction at (D). This will take you over an iron bridge. Turn right at the signpost to Hawkshead village where there is a suggested stroll and the beginning of **Walk 7**. Leave Hawkshead following the signs to Coniston. Turning left just outside the village at the signpost to Coniston and Brantwood ★. Our route passes the road to Tarn Hows ★ on the right – always worth a detour. Keep straight on to Coniston, ignoring the sign to 'East of Lake'. You will catch glimpses of Coniston Water ★ over the drystone wall to the left of the road.

The road winds down through mixed woods until it is level with the lake. Brantwood House ★ is signposted to the left, but keep on the main road and enter the town. You may see the mute swans who live at this end of Coniston Water. Go through Coniston and at (E), the junction with the A593, go left. It is signposted to Broughton ★ and Ulverston ★.

Follow this road until you reach the village Torver ★. Across the water are the densely-wooded eastern banks of Coniston. In Torver turn left on the A5084 signposted to Greenodd ★ at (F). **Walk 6** begins in Torver.

The road descends to a bridge over the river and then follows the west bank of Coniston. Along this stretch are some of the best views of Coniston Water. The road then veers aways from the lakeside and passes through the village of Water Yeat. Go straight on and enter Blawith ★, where **Walk 8** begins.

On entering the village of Lowick, turn right at the signpost to Gawthwaite at (G). The road climbs up gently, past the Church of St Luke of Lowick on the right. Ignore turnings to the left and right, and keep straight on.

At the crossroads go right to Workington on the A5092. Go through Gawthwaite, climbing up onto the moors. At the highest point, at (H) take the turning to the right signposted to Woodland.

You will see spectacular views to the left and ahead of you. It is not a pretty landscape, but it has a rugged beauty: summer or winter, whether the carpet of bracken is vivid green or rust red.

At the T-junction, turn right and go over a cattle grid at (J). Go past the little church of St John's Woodland, and bear left at the fork in the road. At the next fork, follow the sign left to Broughton. You will join the A593 at (K): go left.

Take the second turning on the right, signposted to Broughton Mills. Keep left at the fork in the road at (L), drop down and go over a bridge. Turn right here to Seathwaite ★ and Duddon Valley ★. Our route goes up through a gate (remember to close it behind you). There are spoil heaps of slate to the left and the right of the road. As you come over the brow there are fine views to the right and straight ahead.

Go on, passing over a cattle-grid and winding down a steep, unfenced road. Taking care not to alarm the sheep, go over another cattle grid. At the bottom of the valley the road follows the river for some time. When you reach the next junction at (M) go right to Seathwaite and

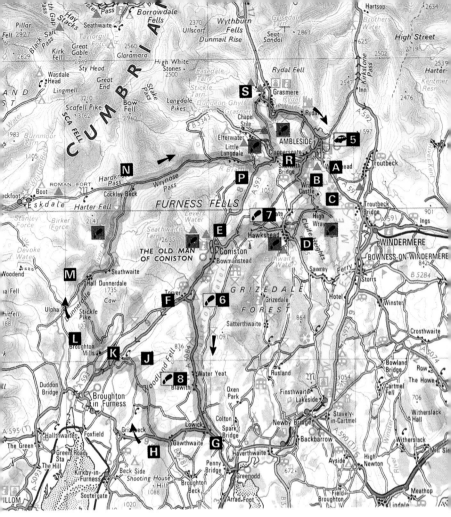

Scale 1:250 000 or ¼ INCH to 1 MILE

Wrynose ★ . You will pass a little green-stone church on the right.

As you go up through the trees, there is an attractive stream to the left. When you reach the fork go left, signposted to Langdale ★ via Wrynose Pass. Trees soften an otherwise gaunt landscape, thick with bracken. Our route passes through Dunnerdale Forest, which is a good place to have a stroll.

When you reach Cockley Bridge, over the beck which feeds the River Duddon, at **(N)** go straight on. The route traverses Wrynose Bottom, and goes up through Wrynose Breast, past Wrynose Breast. The fell to the left is Little Stand.

Wrynose Pass is the route of the Roman road which continues over Hardknott. Legions from the warmer part of the Empire must have found this a bleak place in winter. The pass was a daring piece of civil engineering which must have taken its toll of the indigenous population in the Roman labour gangs.

Descending from Wrynose, Lingmoor Fell dominates the skyline to the left. At the next junction turn right and go over the cattle grid. Keep straight on, following the signs to Coniston. Pass a row of cottages with unusual gateposts and down a 1-in-4 hill. When you reach the T-junction, go right at **(P)** towards Ambleside and Coniston. At the next T-junction which is the A593, turn left. Stay on the road to Ambleside until, at the top of a rise , you see a minor road signposted to the left. A few yards further on the road itself appears 'width restriction 6 ft 6 ins' – go left here at **(R)**.

Climb up between some houses. Do not bear right, keep straight on following the signs to Grasmere ★ . Cyclists are advised to dismount at the 25% hill which gives you your first glimpse of Rydal Water ★ and Grasmere below. Follow the road down into Grasmere village, turning right at **(S)** onto the A591 to return to Ambleside and complete the tour.

Tour 6
Grizedale Forest, Coniston and Little Langdale

60 miles. This tour crosses Windermere by the Hawkshead Ferry and winds down through heavily wooded countryside to the bottom of Coniston Water. Following the beautiful lakeside road past Brantwood, the house where John Ruskin chose to spend his last years, we then have an opportunity to see the Langdale Pikes and one of the best views in Lakeland. The tour returns via Wordsworth's Grasmere and Rydal Water and ends with a circuit of the interesting and little-visited area beyond Ings. Apart from the steep parts around Langdale, which is worth the effort, this tour should present few problems for cyclists.

From Windermere ★ centre drive down through the town to Bowness ★ and take the Hawkshead ★ ferry which is clearly signposted to the right off the lakeside road.

Coming off the ferry, follow the road round and up the hill bearing left to Sawrey ★ – first going through Far Sawrey then Near Sawrey. There is a suggested short walk here. Turn left in Near Sawrey at the sign to 'Lakeside' at **(A)**.

The road drops down. Take the right fork signposted to Hawkshead. This takes you over a bridge and around the southern end of Esthwaite Water ★ . At **(B)**,

Scale 1:250 000 or ¼ INCH to 1 MILE

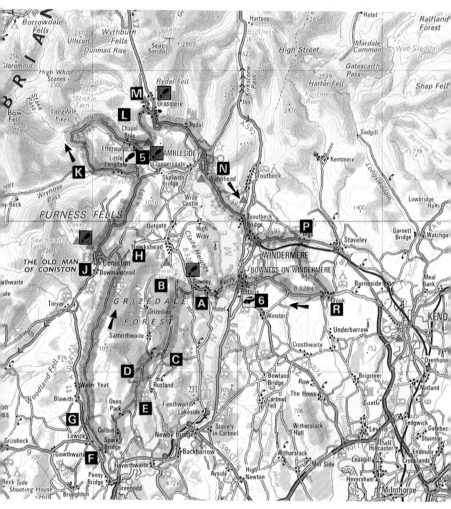

the T-junction, go left.

The road goes through pastureland, conifer plantations and deciduous woods. Soon after passing some impressively tall pines on the left you will go through Graythwaite village. After the road from Cunsey merges from the left, look out for a turning on the right signposted to Rusland and Satterthwaite. Here, at (C), turn right.

The road goes through massive stone gateposts, and gradually drops down through dense conifers. When the road forks, go left. The road becomes increasingly narrow and passes through several farmyards. At the next junction turn left. Shortly afterwards, at (D), you enter Rusland.

In Rusland, turn right where it is signposted to Oxen Park and Ulverston ★ . You will pass Rusland Hall on the left. At the next junction bear left.

Below Rusland Church, at the next junction, turn left again. Do not take any of the turnings to the right – keep straight on. When you reach the T-junction at (E) turn left.

Follow the road, ignoring the sign to Bouth: after rising for a time the road enters Oxen Park. Go straight on following the sign to Greenodd ★ and Ulverston. Keep right at the next junction.

When you reach a crossroads, turn right to Spark Bridge. As you enter Spark Bridge village, turn right before the bridge at (F). Follow the road to (G) where you go right at the sign indicating 'East of Lake'.

At the next bridge, turn right. Soon you will see Coniston Water ★ to the left of the road. The peak of the Old Man of Coniston becomes visible on the far side, as the road goes through mixed woodland. At the northern end of the lakeside road you will pass Brantwood ★ , John Ruskin's house.

At the head of the lake, follow the sign to the left to Coniston ★ . At the T-junction at (H) turn left to Coniston village. Go over the bridge, past the church on the left and at the T-junction (J) turn right to Ambleside ★ on the A593 (there is a suggested short walk in Coniston).

The road passes through pleasant woodland and pasture with especially fine views glimpsed to the left. Look out for a minor road to the left – it is not signposted but you will see a 'Give Way' sign. Turn left here. Almost immediately there is a blue sign indicating a width restriction of 6 ft 6 ins after 600 yards. Follow this road down from the A593 (if you find yourself in Skelwith Bridge ★

you will have missed the turning!).

As the road winds down you will catch glimpses of the Langdale Pikes ahead and to your right. The road crosses a bridge at the bottom. Immediately afterwards, turn left to Little Langdale ★ . The road climbs steeply. After about ½ mile there are fine views to the left.

Go through the village of Little Langdale. Where the road forks at (K) go straight on to Blea Tarn and Wrynose ★ . Down to the left of the road is Little Langdale Tarn.

After crossing a cattle grid, go right. The colour, scale and form of the landscape are a perfect example of Lakeland scenery. Ahead the skyline is dominated by the saw tooth outline of the Langdale Pikes. Down to the left is Blea Tarn.

Cross a cattle grid. Shortly afterwards you will see one of the finest views in the Lake District. Ignore the turning to the left over the bridge and go straight on. The road bends and zig-zags for about 2½ miles.

At the crossroads after the village at (L) you can go right to see Elterwater ★ (see **Walk 5**) or follow our route left here to Grasmere ★ . Continuing the tour, climb up through a steep curve past the Youth Hostel Association. Go left at the next junction. At the next hill cyclists are warned to dismount because of the 25% gradient. At the bottom go right in Grasmere following the sign to Ambleside. Rejoin the A591 at (M).

From Grasmere you pass through Rydal ★ . The road then enters Ambleside. Go through the town following the signs to Windermere and Kendal ★ on the A591. Pass through Waterhead ★ at (N) continuing on the A591. You pass the National Parks Visitors Centre at Brock Hole ★ on the right.

Go through Troutbeck Bridge ★ . At the mini roundabout go straight on. Unless visiting Windermere, keep on the main road passing the station on your right.

The road climbs to the village of Ings ★ . Turn right here and right again up the gated road (remembering to close it behind you). Go under the railway and pass through three more gates before coming to a T-junction. Turn left here towards Crook ★ . It is interesting terrain with rock breaking through the thin covering of turf everywhere.

At the next junction go right (or left to visit Crook). Continuing the tour, pass the Windermere Golf Club on the left and 2 miles further on turn left at the bottom and then immediately right to re-enter Bowness and complete the tour.

Tour 7
A Roman pass, the deepest lake and Tarn Hows

66 miles. This tour takes the road constructed by the Romans over the steep passes of Wrynose and Hardknott. After following Eskdale there is a visit to Wast Water to see some of the most dramatic scenery in Lakeland. After striking down across moorland to Broughton in Furness, we return past Coniston and visit beautiful Tarn Hows. Cyclists should use their Landranger maps to plan a route avoiding the (A-B) section over the high passes. Otherwise the terrain does not present too many difficult stretches.

Leave the centre of Ambleside ★ , following the signposts to Coniston ★ and the A593. Pass over a hump-backed bridge and through Clappersgate. Do not turn off to Hawkshead ★ ; continue on the A593, leaving Windermere ★ behind you to the left. Keep on the main road, ignoring the turnings to Grasmere ★ and Langdale. Follow the A593 in the direction of Coniston. The route passes through Skelwith Bridge ★ and as it rises the Langdale Pikes become visible over to the right and a plantation of conifers straight ahead. Turn right here, at **(A)**, where there is a blue sign indicating 'width limit '6 ft 6 ins, 600 yards ahead'. This is the road to Little Langdale ★ .

Wind down the hill and cross two bridges. After the second, turn left to Little Langdale and Wrynose ★ . The views to the left and ahead, become increasingly impressive as the road climbs. Ignore the side turning to the left to Tilberthwaite, and follow the road round to the right.

At the next junction go left towards Blea Tarn and Wrynose. You will see Little Langdale Tarn down to the left of the road. After crossing the cattle grid, go left. This is the road to Wrynose and Hardknott ★ Passes. There are severe bends, and gradients of 1-in-3. Do not attempt this route in wintry conditions.

Passing through a farmyard, the sawtooth skyline of the Langdale Pikes is visible ahead. The higher you climb, the more majestic the scenery becomes. Find a suitable and safe place and stop to admire the splendid views behind you. From the summit, the road, stream and drystone wall disappear into the distance

like uncoiling ribbons. The rounded boulders of all sizes – which are strewn across the valley in all directions – are a reminder of the glaciation of this area.

When you reach the bridge at the bottom, turn right following the sign to Eskdale via Hardknott Pass. Immediately over the bridge is a gate – remember to close it behind you. Drive with extreme caution, even in good weather conditions: in addition to the gradient there are blind bends. From the top there are wonderful views of the bracken-covered fells and the green pastureland far below.

At the bottom cross a cattle grid and a hump-backed bridge and keep straight on. Cross another bridge, continuing on past the Woolpack Inn. The undulating road down Eskdale is a welcome rest for both car and driver. Go straight on where the village of Boot ★ is signposted to the right.

Go right at the next junction at **(B)**, to enter Eskdale Green ★ . A bridge takes you over the narrow gauge railway. Out of Eskdale Green take the left fork towards Holmbrook. Descending a 1-in-6 hill you may glimpse the coast in the distance.

At the next junction, at **(C)**, turn right to Santon Bridge ★ and Wasdale. Go left at the next junction at **(D)**, and then immediately right towards Wasdale. Follow the road up past Nether Wasdale ★ , keeping to the right and following the signs to Wasdale Head ★ .

After winding through hillocky country, set with large oaks, you will suddenly come upon Wast Water ★ . Follow the road by the side of the lake, looking across the deepest water in Lakeland to the awesome screes on the other side. Pass the road coming in from your left and continue to the dead-end of Wasdale Head where **Walk 9** begins.

To continue the tour, retrace your route through Santon Bridge to Eskdale Green. In Eskdale Green go past the Mountain Rescue Post on the left and back over the railway bridge. Instead of returning to Hardknott Pass, go straight on to Ulpha ★ and Broughton ★ at **(B)**.

Cross a bridge over a river, going straight on towards Ulpha at **(E)**. The road becomes unfenced with a landscape of bracken and shattered rock on either side. Stop at a safe place to enjoy the views to the left.

Ignore all side turnings, keeping straight on towards Ulpha. After crossing a cattle grid, the road begins to descend. Ahead is a marvellous patchwork quilt of drystone walls on the fellside, just before you drop down into the woods. At the T-junction at **(F)**, go right to Broughton past Ulpha Post Office and the little church on the left.

The road follows the river, lined with great pines. Go round to the left here, over the bridge, and on to another unfenced road. **Walk 12** begins in Ulpha.

As the road drops down a 1-in-5 hill you will see the estuary of the River Duddon ahead, if the light is right. At **(G)**, a T-junction, turn left to Broughton. At **(H)**, take the turning left into Broughton (there is a suggested short walk near here).

Follow the road down into Broughton, climbing up again to the centre, where there is a stone obelisk, turning left onto the A593 signposted to Torver ★ and Coniston.

The road climbs slowly with views of the fells to the left. At the signpost near the top of the hill, keep right towards Coniston on the A593. From the high point, find a safe place to stop and look back towards the coast.

At the next signpost go on towards Coniston. You will pass another sign by a farm – keep on to Coniston. About 3 miles further on you enter Torver where **Walk 6** begins. As you leave Torver on the Coniston road you will pass over a bridge.

Before entering Coniston the lake becomes visible down to the right. Ahead are the high fells. Coming into Coniston from this direction you realise how the Old Man of Coniston dominates the village.

At **(J)** take the B5285 towards Hawkshead, going over the bridge and to the right, past the church. Keep on the road as it goes round to the left at the head of Coniston Water, signposted to Hawkshead, Windermere and Tarn Hows ★.

Go past the exit from Tarn Hows at **(K)** (this is a no-entry). Soon afterwards, Tarn Hows is signposted to the left at **(L)**, turn here and follow the signs to Tarn Hows.

The single track road with passing places takes you up to a perfect example of Lakeland scenery. Purists have complained that the hand of Man is too evident in the beautiful views – but the same can be said of much of Lakeland. There is a car park for the disabled at the top and another lower down.

Descending, you will reach **(K)** again. Turn left, and this time go straight on at **(L)** following the sign to Ambleside. Ignore the signs to Hawkshead and the fork to the right, keeping straight on towards Ambleside. At the next junction at **(M)** go straight on.

When you reach the brow of the hill you will see the town and Windermere ahead of you. At the next junction go left, cross over the bridge and right towards Ambleside. Recross the river and turn left into the town to complete the tour.

Scale 1:250 000 or ¼ INCH to 1 MILE

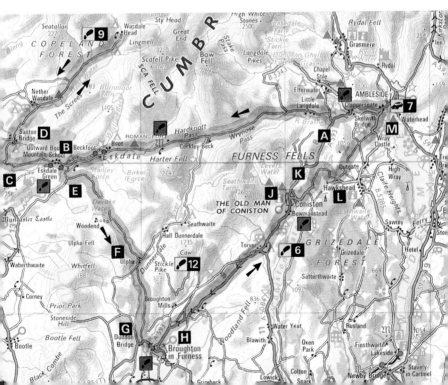

Tour 8
Tarn Hows, the coast at Ravenglass and Ruskin's home

71 miles. This tour first explores the man-made landscape of Tarn Hows before taking-in the more dramatic scenery around the Langdale Pikes and over Wrynose Pass. There is also a visit to Muncaster Castle and the ancient settlement of Ravenglass on the coast, before returning across moorland to Conison Water. The lakeside road which completes the tour passes John Ruskin's home, Brantwood, which is well worth visiting. A brief energetic climb to see Tarn How might be worthwhile, otherwise unsuitable for cyclists. The east side of Coniston Water can be seen as part of Tour 6.

From the centre of Coniston ★ take the B5285 signposted to Hawkshead ★ , passing over a bridge leaving the town. Soon you will see Coniston Water on your right. Do not follow the road around the head of the lake – continue on the main road signposted to Hawkshead, Windermere ★ and Tarn Hows ★ at **(A)**.

The road climbs slowly, turning and twisting through mixed woodland. You will pass a grey stone drinking trough on the right. Go past the exit from Tarn Hows (a no-entry) at **(B)**. Soon afterwards Tarn Hows is signposted to the left. Turn here at **(C)**. Turn left again at the next junction, still following the signs to Tarn Hows.

You are now on a single track road with passing places. The view from the summit is a perfect example of the scale and variety of Lakeland scenery, although purists complain that the hand of Man is too much in evidence.

Rejoining the road at the bottom, turn left at the T-junction. Re-pass the drinking trough and again take the signpost to Tarn Hows. If you enter the small village of Hawkshead Hill you will have gone too far. This time do not take the second signpost to Tarn Hows, but continue straight on following the sign to Ambleside ★ . You will pass a hotel on the left.

Ignore signs to the right to Hawkshead and continue in the direction of Ambleside. At the next crossroads **(D)**, turn left at the Drunken Duck Inn towards Skelwith Bridge ★ . Where the road forks, go left. Then right at the next fork down a narrow lane which drops away steeply. At the bottom, where a road joins from the right, you will see the sign to Skelwith. Continue straight on.

Join the A593 Ambleside road. Cross over the bridge ahead of you and turn left onto the B5343 signposted to Elterwater ★ at **(E)**. There is a suggested stroll in Skelwith Bridge. You will catch glimpses of Elterwater down through the trees to the left. At the point where you pass over a cattle grid there are superb views of the mountains ahead.

Unless you intend to do **Walk 5** which begins in Elterwater, do not turn off the main road to the village on the left. After about half a mile you will pass through Chapel Stile. Go straight on, following the signposts to Great Langdale ★ . The mountains dominate the road increasingly and there are impressive views on all sides.

You will come to a sharp bend to the left. Pass over a small bridge and begin a steep climb – this route should not be attempted in winter conditions. After the road descends again pass through a gate remembering to close it behind you. You then descend a 1-in-4 incline.

At the bottom, do not cross the cattle grid – follow the sign to the right to Wrynose Pass ★ at **(F)**. Some of the gradients on Wrynose are 1-in-3: extreme caution should be exercised. Your car is unlikely to make many steeper climbs than this.

From the summit of Wrynose the road diminishes into the distance like an uncoiling ribbon. Be as careful going down again as you were coming up. Do not go over the bridge to Hardnott Pass – go straight on over the cattle grid following the sign to Broughton ★ via Duddon Valley at **(G)**. You will pass Dunnerdale Forest to the right and further on will pass over Seathwaite ★ Bridge. (There is a suggested short walk in this area). Go right after the bridge towards Broughton. Where the road forks to the right, keep right.

Go through Hall Dunnerdale and take the right road at **(H)** signposted to Broughton and Whitehaven. In the tiny hamlet of Ulpha ★ turn right at the signpost to Eskdale and Whitehaven at **(J)**. Ascend a 1-in-4 hill (**Walk 12** begins in Ulpha).

Go over the bridge (constructed in 1895). As the road climbs there are good views of Ulpha Fell to the left and the higher peaks far away to the right. At the signpost, keep straight on.

The road descends through wide expanses of bracken, with a shattered cliff

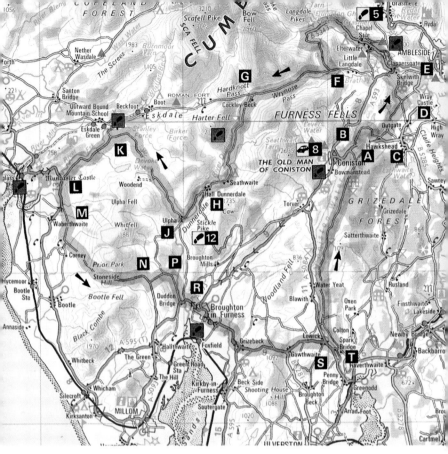

face to the left. You may catch a brief glimpse of cooling towers at Sellafield far ahead on the coast. At the bottom keep a sharp look out for a minor, anonymous road to the left, where you will turn at **(K)**. (If you find yourself at the King George IV Inn, you have missed your turning).

When you come to the T-junction with the A595, turn right to Ravenglass ★ and Muncaster Castle at **(L)**. The road climbs up past rhododendrons on the right: the car park to Muncaster Castle is another ½ mile further on.

Continue towards Ravenglass. Where the A595 curves right to Workington, go straight on to Ravenglass. After passing under two bridges you will see the estuary ahead.

Leaving Ravenglass return up the hill to the A595 and turn right. Go back past Muncaster Castle and straight on at **(L)**. Keep on the A 595 as far as Waberthwaite★ . Turn left just before the sign announcing the village, at the sign to Broughton in Furness ★ at **(M)**. Do not turn off to Corney at the next signpost, but continue on to Broughton.

There are fine views crossing this moorland. At the next signpost do not go

Scale 1:250 000 or ¼ INCH to 1 MILE

to Millom, go on to Broughton at **(N)**. Cross a cattle grid where a road merges from the left at **(P)**.

At the T-junction with the A595 turn left towards Barrow. Immediately the route bends to the left and crosses Duddon Bridge ★ . A mile further on is Broughton itself, signposted to the left. Unless you are visiting Broughton (where there is a suggested short walk) continue on the main road at **(R)**.

At Grizebeck keep straight on, do not follow the A 595 to Barrow. From this point on our road becomes A5092. Rising up the hill go through the tiny hamlet of Beanthwaite. You will pass a slate quarry on the right of the road. Do not turn to Ulverston ★ , go straight on.

At the sign to Spark Bridge turn left at **(S)**. Go straight into Spark Bridge, crossing over the river, and turn immediately left signposted to Coniston 'East of Lake' at **(T)**. When you reach another bridge turn right. Soon Coniston Water becomes visible to the left of the road.

The road passes through beautiful woods by the lakeside.

At the head of the lake follow the signs down into Coniston to complete the tour.

Tour 9

Sadgill, Troutbeck, Newby Bridge and the Ferry across Windermere

68 miles. This tour follows the beginning of the notorious Shap route, before offering a detour from Garnett Bridge up to Sadgill where there are beautiful views. After attractive Troutbeck and Ambleside, it goes down through Grizedale Forest to Newby Bridge, returning to Kendal via the Hawkshead ferry across Windermere. Apart from the long climb out of Kendal at the beginning, this tour does not present too many difficulties for active cyclists.

Leave Kendal ★ at the town centre following the signs for Penrith ★ and the A6, which will take you past Kendal railway station. Soon the suburbs of Kendal and

Scale 1:250 000 or ¼ INCH to 1 MILE

the industrial estate are left behind, and the low hills on either side of the road are criss-crossed with drystone walls. This is the beginning of the long climb to Shap ★ so dreaded by lorry drivers in bad weather before the building of the M6: if it is a fine day you may see glimpses of Shap Fell in the distance ahead. A little over two miles outside Kendal you will see a signpost to Meal Bank on the right. Our route takes the third turning to the left off the A6 after this, signposted to Longsleddale. This minor road winds down to a bridge over the River Sprint. Turn right at **(A)** here if you are going to take the detour up to Sadgill ★ . If not, ignore the next paragraph.

The detour should not take more than 10 minutes each way. There is a suggested stroll at Sadgill, but even if you do not leave your car the scenery is beautiful. There are several interesting buildings and the beetling, lichen-encrusted drystone walls tower over the single-track road, particularly towards the end. The little bridge at Sadgill itself is another interesting feature. Take care on this detour – the passing places are very

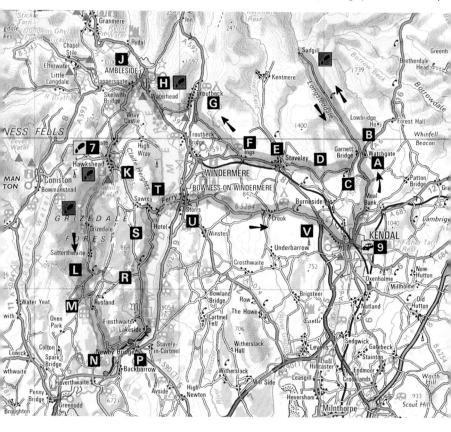

necessary and there are many blind corners and hills.

To continue the main tour, cross over the bridge at **(B)** in Garnett Bridge. After about ¾ mile, turn right at **(C)**. The road is not signposted but it leads to Staveley. The town of Kendal is visible down to the left.

When you reach the T-junction at **(D)** turn right to Staveley. Our route takes us along by the still River Kent until we can cross it at Barley Bridge. Turn immediately left towards the village, continuing on past the War Memorial until you reach the T-junction with the A591 at **(E)**. With great care, join the main road turning right. Very soon you will enter the village of Ings ★ . Turn right here at **(F)** where it is signposted to Troutbeck ★ .

Ignore turnings to the left and right and carry straight on. There are fine views of the high fells ahead in the distance. When you reach the fork in the road, go right. At the T-junction with the A592, turn right. Immediately after passing over a small bridge turn left to the village of Troutbeck. There is a suggested short walk near the village.

Climb up the hill and turn left at the Post Office which faces you at a T-junction at **(G)**. After leaving Troutbeck take the right fork signposted to Waterhead ★ – do not go left to Windermere ★ . However, you may catch glimpses of the lake through the gaps in the drystone wall on the left.

When the road begins to descend a steep hill the lake is clearly visible ahead. At **(H)**, the intersection with the A591, turn right towards Ambleside ★ . There are beautiful views across the lake to the left.

If not visiting Ambleside itself, bear left just before the town where it is signposted to Keswick ★ , Coniston ★ and Langdale. There is also a sign to the steamer pier. The road bends, following the head of the lake. Look out for a signpost to the left to Coniston, Hawkshead ★ and Langdale – turn left along this road. Almost immediately turn left again over a small stone bridge. You will now enter the village of Clappersgate at **(J)**.

From Clappersgate take the B5286 to the left in the direction of Hawkshead. The road winds and undulates through pleasantly-wooded country. Pass through the village of Outgate and continue to Hawkshead. There is a suggested stroll in Hawkshead, but if you are not visiting the village on this occasion, follow the sign for Grizedale and Newby Bridge ★ at **(K)**. There is a T-junction on the road which bypasses the centre. Turn right here and

immediately left.

After a bend in the road there is a sign to Grizedale to the right: follow this. Climbing steeply through several curves you will enter the beginning of Grizedale Forest ★ . The road passes through pastureland and pockets of deciduous trees as well as the ubiquitous conifers. There is a suggested short walk in the forest.

Pass through the settlement of Satterthwaite ★ and eventually you will come to a T-junction. Turn right at **(L)** close to Force Forge. Follow the road down the hill until you reach a sign to Rusland Hall. Turn left here at **(M)** and left again at the T-junction. Follow the road up the hill bearing right to Rusland Cross ★ .

When you reach the point where Rusland Church rises above you on a hillock to the left of the road, go right over Lim Bridge towards Newby Bridge ★ . Our route curves to the left at the gatehouse just before a T-junction. Turn right here. The road passes through a beech wood.

Take the next turning on the left to Finsthwaite and Newby Bridge. At the T-junction turn left, and at the next T-junction turn left again. Immediately after that, turn right to Newby Bridge and Lakeside at **(N)**.

After passing over the railway bridge at Newby Bridge Halt, you will soon catch sight of the weir below Newby Bridge at **(P)**. Unless visiting Newby Bridge, turn left at the T-junction towards Lakeside.

Follow the road by the side of Windermere ★ . You will pass the Stott Park Bobbin Mill Museum on your left. This is well-worth a visit. Continue through the village of Graythwaite, with its amazing topiary on the left, following the signs for the Hawkshead ferry.

Turn right at the telephone box at **(R)** for a more pleasant route to the ferry which takes you through pine woods. Pass through Cunsey at **(S)** and follow the sign to 'Windermere by Ferry'. At the top of the rise there is another sign to the ferry. Drop down here and turn right at the T-junction at Far Sawrey **(T)** to the ferry.

From the ferry you can see Belle Isle ★ to your left. On reaching the far side, climb the hill and turn right at the T-junction **(U)**. Immediately afterwards, bear left, following the sign to Kendal. At the next T-junction turn left and then right onto the B5284 also signposted to Crook ★ . Pass through Crook.

At the junction at **(V)**, a large roundabout, take the A5284 to Kendal, completing the tour.

Tour 10
Morecambe Bay and Gummer's How

69 miles. This tour visits the delightful village of Kirkby Lonsdale, before skirting the sands of Morecambe Bay to pass through Cartmel with its ancient Priory. After Newby Bridge there is a climb up to Gummer's How with its spectacular views before dropping down again into Kendal. The climb up to Gummer's How is very well worthwhile, and the only section which should give any problems to cyclists.

Leave Kendal ★ on the A65 signposted at first to Skipton. After crossing the bridge, the road follows the river out of the town: stay in the left lane. Soon you will see the signpost to Oxenholme on the B6254. Go left here at **(A)**, still following the river. You will pass the newly-built South Lakeland Leisure Centre on your left. Follow the signs to Oxenholme on the B6254. The road takes you over the railway at Oxenholme Station: do not enter the village, stay on the main road. Ignore roads to the right and left following the signposts to Kirkby Lonsdale ★ . The road passes through rolling pastureland where hedges are as numerous as drystone walls. Pass through the village of Old Hutton: the road goes under the M6 Motorway at this point. Continue in the direction of Old Town. You will pass and a shallow lake to your right. Entering Old Town, there are fine views of the hills beyond. Continue through the village.

Two trees almost touching over the road mark the beginning of Kirkby Lonsdale. Make your way carefully through the charming centre of the village until you reach the junction with the A65. Turn left here, and then immediately right to Whittingdon at **(B)**.

When you see the tower of Whittingdon Church ahead, prepare to turn right where it is signposted to Hutton Roof at **(C)**. Go up past the church and Whittingdon Hall on your left. Follow the road round to the right towards Burton West, passing a sawmill on the left.

Do not turn right at the sign to Burton and Holme, keep straight on. In Burton you will reach a T-junction. Turn left here and immediately right, signposted to Yealand. The road soon passes over the M6, a canal and the railway.

When you reach the junction with the A6 go straight on to Yealand, Redmayne.

At **(D)**, turn right to Arnside ★ . Keep a sharp lookout for the sign to Arnside on your right – it is easy to miss!

The road goes through pleasant woodland. Turn right at the signpost to Arnside and Milnthorpe. Just before Arnside you will reach a level-crossing at **(E)**. Pass over this, and just before the station turn right to Milnthorpe. This takes you back under the railway.

Our route passes through Sandside with its gap-toothed drystone wall to the left of the road. A sudden sharp bend reveals a wonderful view of the estuary of the River Gilpin. Continue along the road by the sands in the direction of Milnthorpe, passing over a hump-backed bridge. At the traffic lights in Milnthorpe at **(F)** turn left towards Heversham and Leasgill.

Do not turn off to Heversham and Leasgill, keeping straight on to Levens ★ . Just past Levens Hall at **(G)**, turn left along the A590. Fork left immediately, following the sign to Barrow. There are sections of dual carriageway on the A590. Soon you will see the first sign to Grange ★ . At the large roundabout **(H)** take the turning to Lindale ★ and Grange.

Pass through Lindale and turn left on the B5277 to Grange. Up above the road to the right are large hotels built to take advantage of the sands and the magnificent views to the south. After passing through Grange-over-Sands, where there is a suggested stroll, look out for a small white sign indicating Cartmel ★ to the right. Our route goes right here at **(J)**.

After about 2 miles you enter Cartmel. Turn left at the T-junction towards Cark at **(K)**. Unless visiting Cartmel Priory to the right go straight on towards Cark. Just after the sign announcing that you are in 'Cark-in-Cartmel' take the turning to the right to Holker ★ and Ulverston ★ at **(L)**. Rejoin the B5278 , turning right again. You will pass Holker Hall on your left.

Follow the road to Haverthwaite. On entering the village you will pass over a river bridge: turn right almost immediately at **(M)** towards Newby Bridge. At the top of the hill there is a junction with the A590 to Kendal and Lancaster with Newby Bridge also indicated. Turn right.

Continue along the A590 for some miles until reaching Newby Bridge. In Newby Bridge turn left onto the A592 in the direction of Windermere ★ at **(N)**.

Do not take the first minor road on the right to Stavely Church, or the second to Stavely-in-Cartmel, but the third at **(P)** which is signposted to Kendal and Bowness ★ .

Newby Bridge

The road rises very steeply, and there are splendid views to the left – both below and up towards Gummers Howe★. The road dips briefly, then climbs again, with breathtaking views. The road soon begins to descend. After a steep hairpin bend you will come to a junction by an inn. Turn right here following the signs for Kendal. Unless planning a walk do not take the turning to the right to the church and Cartmel Fell ★ .

Go straight on until you reach Bowland Bridge at **(R)**. From here follows the signs to Crosthwaite and Kendal. After a steep climb you reach a T-junction. Turn right here. When the road bends to the right, take care to go straight on towards Crosthwaite. At **(S)** continue through Crosthwaite following the Kendal sign.

You will pass through the village of Underbarrow at **(T)**. After Underbarrow the road twists and climbs steeply – at the high point there are fine views with Kendal spread out below.

Our route continues down a 1-in-7 hill, passing over the main A591. You will descend steeply into the town of Kendal itself to complete the tour.

Scale 1:250 000 or ¼ INCH to 1 MILE

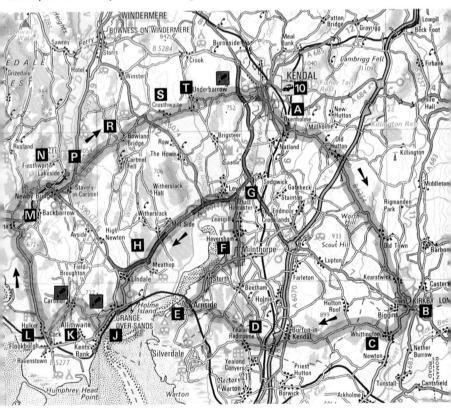

Walk 1
Latrigg and Glenderaterra Valley

Latrigg is the smooth, grassy hill at the foot of Skiddaw. It was one of the 'viewing stations' described in the first guide book for the Lakes (published in 1778) and it is easy to see why. It is only 1,203 ft, high, but on a clear day all the principal Lakeland fells can be seen from its summit. The walk described here starts by climbing Latrigg and then goes on up the steep-sided Glenderaterra valley which separates Skiddaw from Blencathra. This leads into some of most remote moorland in the Lake District. Allow 4 hours for the round walk and 5 hours if the extension to Skiddaw House is included.

Latrigg lies just north of **Keswick** (89,90) (NY 26-23) which is on **Tours 1 and 2**. Turn off the A66 onto the A591 which runs up the east side of Bassenthwaite and almost immediately turn right down an unclassified road. Go through the village of Ormathwaite and as the road bears round to the left into Applethwaite, turn right up Gale Road. Where the road ends there is a car park.

Leave the car park by the signed public bridleway which is near to a plantation and goes downhill – not the one going to Skiddaw. The path soon levels out and runs beside the plantation for a time. Fork left onto a slowly rising, broad grass track. Views of Bassenthwaite Lake and the Grisedale Fells soon open up, with Skiddaw in the foreground. The easy path zig-zags up the slopes of Mallen Dodd and gradually makes its way to the highest point of Latrigg, whose summit is unmarked by any cairn **(A)**.

On a clear day all the principal fells can be seen from this point, although the actual summit of the nearest one, Skiddaw, is hidden from view. Grisedale, Causey Pike, the Buttermere Fells, Pillar, Great Gable, the Scafells, Bowfell, Helvellyn and Blencathra are all there to be recognised and enjoyed. To the east of Blencathra you should be able to see Cross Fell, the highest of the Pennines, in the distance.

It is worth remembering that although the views from Latrigg are enjoyed by thousands every year, it was not always so. In the last century the closure and barricading of the footpath over Latrigg was one reason for the formation of the Keswick & District Footpath Preservation Association, which came into being in 1856. As a result of its efforts, the path over Latrigg was eventually reopened.

Continue along the summit ridge, cross the stile and take the slowly descending grass path which follows the fenceline on the left to join a cart-track at the plantation. Turn right along the track, pass through a gate and slowly descend to a stile where three tracks meet **(B)**.

From the stile take the middle of the three tracks and then turn left along a path signed Blencathra, Derwent Folds. The path descends through woodland to a footbridge over Glenderaterra Beck and then climbs an ancient stony lane to the farmhouse at Derwent Folds. Here turn right along the tarred road to a stile where the road turns sharp right **(C)**.

Cross the field to a kissing gate and follow the clear, uphill path through similar gates to the Blencathra Centre **(D)**. This is a conversion by the Lake District National Park Authority of the old Blencathra Hospital (Sanatorium) into self-catering holiday cottages and hostel-type accommodation.

Make your way through the buildings, turning left up a signed footpath to meet the road near where it ends. Turn left again and follow the track round into the steep-sided Glenderaterra valley. This is a wild, almost treeless valley and a striking contrast to the short, green turf of Latrigg. The track contours along the eastern side of the valley for about one mile, after which it descends slightly to cross Roughten Gill by a bridge of stones and then crosses the two streams of the main beck by two wooden footbridges. Cross the adjacent wall by a ladder stile and follow the path alongside a wall and up the slope of the west side of the valley. At **(E)** the wall bends away to the right.

To visit Skiddaw House **(F)**, follow the main track round to the right above the wall, turning left in about ½ mile to cross Salehow Beck. Skiddaw House is a shepherd's cottage which was converted and opened as a simple hostel in July 1987. The detour will add 2 miles to your walk.

To return down the Glenderaterra valley, at **(E)** turn off the main path onto a lesser one near some ruined buildings. Care is needed when crossing some rocky outcrops at Lonscale Crags especially if the rocks are wet. Otherwise it is a broad, high-level track walked with ease The path crosses the secluded gill of Whit Beck and brings you back to the car park.

Scale 1:25 000 or 2½ INCHES to 1 MILE

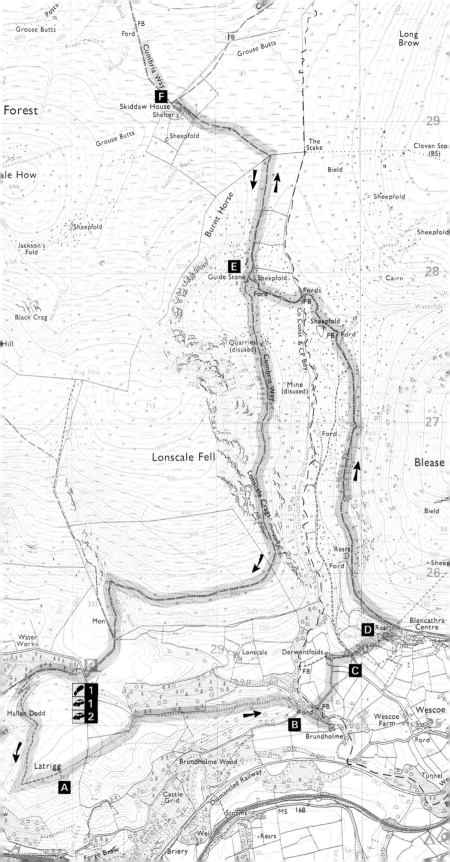

Walk 2
Bassenthwaite, St Bega's church and Mirehouse

Bassenthwaite Lake is dominated by the massive bulk of Skiddaw, the mountain 'rooted in a lake'. Although close to Keswick and Cockermouth, the lake is still peaceful: motor boats are banned and there are many waterfowl. Two walks are described here, both starting in Bassenthwaite village and visiting an attractive headland on the lake shore. The shorter walk (allow 2 ½ hours) returns to the village by a green lane whilst the longer one (about 4 ½ hours) goes on to visit a pre-Norman church on the lake shore and a manor house where many writers, including Tennyson, stayed. The return route goes through a forestry plantation and an open fell side on the flanks of Skiddaw.

Bassenthwaite (89,90) (NY 23-32) is on **Tour 2**. It is reached by a turning off the A591 which runs down the east side of the lake.

Park in the village. From the village green, take the road diagonally opposite the telephone box. This leads past a playground sign. Where the road turns sharply right, turn left through a gate and then left again at a waymarked stile just before the third power pole. Cross the next field and turn right along the road. When you reach the main road, take the narrow lane on the opposite side, a little to the right, and go alongside the caravan park until you reach a stile with a sign 'To the Lake'. The path closely follows Hall Beck. Where it is joined by Chapel Beck, cross the footbridge and continue along the trod.

Turn left through the kissing gate, pass a 'waymarked' tree and cross a stone bridge to a gate. Cross the next bridge, noting the direction of the waymark. Walk to the top of the field, keeping the wood on your right, and up to the house. Go through the gateway, turn right past a garden and left out of the drive. At **(A)** turn right along the wooded track at the edge of a caravan park which leads to the lake.

When you near the shore, turn left to follow the many signs and stiles around Scarness Bay. This section of the walk is part of the Allerdale Ramble – a 55-mile walk running from Seathwaite in central

Lakeland to the Solway Coast. On a fine day you will see sailing boats and canoes on the lake, as well as optimistic windsurfers. There are many water birds and you may see a cormorant winging low over the water. Rounding the headland you come to Bowness Bay, a complete contrast to its better-known namesake. From here there is a magnificent view of Ullock Pike, one of the flanks of Skiddaw. Near the buildings of Broadness Farm, cross a stile to follow a path through tall reeds to the road **(B)**.

For the shorter walk, turn left along the road and then right along a green lane after you pass the drive to Broadness Farm. Ignoring any turns to the right, pass through Mire Side and along its track to the road. Turn right along the Bassenthwaite road for about ⅓ mile, cross the main road and soon afterwards turn left through a gate into a field. Cross the field to a stile near the corner and then walk along the side of the hedge to the road. Cross the road and retrace your steps to the village.

For the longer walk, turn right along the road at **(B)** and right again down a path where the road bends left. From the corner of the wood, head towards a gate near the tall tree. Cross the lane to the kissing gate and go over the field to an iron gate and then to a stile near a small, wooden gate. Cross a small bridge and follow the trod and stiles to St Bega's Church **(C)**. St Bega, the daughter of an Irish chieftain, gave her name to St Bee's Head where she landed after fleeing to England rather than marry the Norseman her father had chosen. The oldest parts of the church are thought to be tenth-century or earlier.

From the church, walk back to the wood and then follow the stream to the right towards Mirehouse, home of the Spedding family and now open to the public. Tennyson was at Cambridge with one of the Speddings and he and many other writers, including Edward Fitzgerald who translated the Rubaiyat of Omar Khayam, stayed at Mirehouse. The romantic position of St Bega's church is said to have inspired Tennyson's description of the death of King Arthur.

Turn right along the track past the house and right again by the fine old dovecote to reach the road. Here turn left and cross over to the Dodd Wood car park **(D)**. There is an excellent coffee shop in the Old Saw Mill, where you can also obtain tickets for Mirehouse. Dodd Wood forms part of the Forestry Commission's Thornthwaite Forest.

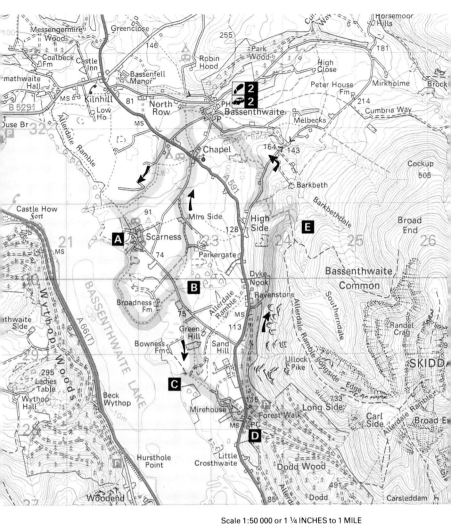

Scale 1:50 000 or 1 ¼ INCHES to 1 MILE

Above the cafe, follow the markers to the forest road. Turn left along the road and then take the narrower, upward track on the right. Continue straight on at a junction, climbing steadily, to reach a more open stretch affording fine views over Bassenthwaite Lake and the headland you have just walked around. After crossing Sandbeds Gill, the track descends to a place where four tracks meet. Take the right hand track.

After about 300 yards, take a narrower path on the right which climbs steeply to a stile. Stay near to the forest fence on the left for a steep section which levels out as the forest ends. Ignore all paths off to the right, using a trod near the fell wall. Looking to your left you will see wonderful examples of Old English field patterns. Stay with the wall as it curves to the right

and follow it until it ends at a wooden stile overlooking the hidden valley of Southerndale (E).

Cross this stile and follow the track as it meanders downhill, crossing two more stiles. Turn right along the road, pass by High Side House and in a few minutes walking you will reach a passing place and stile on the left. Go over this stile and turn half right to come to a combined bridge and stile. Cross this and turn left on a track. Where the track leaves the field, turn right and go over two more stiles, keeping the fence on your left. A third stile puts a hedge on your right and leads down to a further stile above Chapel Beck. Over this stile, bear left to a footbridge. One more field brings you to a minor road leading back to Bassenthwaite village.

Walk 3
Martindale and Boredale

The road along the eastern shore of Ulls-water serves one of the most remote parts of the Lake District, with wild red deer sharing the fells with the native sheep. Two walks are described, both starting at the top of Martindale Hause, the winding pass between Howtown and Martindale. The shorter walk follows the lower slopes of Hallin Fell to the lake, returning via Bridge End. Allow 1 ½ hours. The longer walk, which will take about 3 hours, uses the same route around Hallin Fell but continues on to Scalehow Force and returns through Boredale. The climb to the top of Hallin Fell, an option for both walks, offers magnificent views of Ullswater and the surrounding fells.

Martindale (90) (NY 43-19) is on **Tour 3** and is reached by a narrow winding road which runs from Pooley Bridge down the east side of Ullswater.

Park in the car park opposite St Peter's Church. A wide, grassy path leads directly from the car park to the summit of Hallin Fell (1,271 ft) **(A)**. The climb involves just over 500 ft of ascent, and descent is best by the same path.

Walk back along the road for 200 yards to join a grassy path on the left. Follow

Boredale

the well-used track around the lower slopes of Hallin Fell towards the lake. There are good views towards Pooley Bridge and the lower reaches of the lake. As the path enters the wood, there is an excellent resting place and viewpoint at Kailpot Crag **(B)**.

Continue through the woods to reach the hamlet of Sandwick (pronounced Sannick) at **(C)**. For the shorter walk follow the road to cross the bridge with white railings at Bridge End and walk up a short road before entering a gateway on the left. A second bridge with a stile on the right leads into a short riverside path giving access to a field. Cross the field diagonally up a slight incline towards a cottage on the right. The path continues through the yard at the rear of the cottage and into the lane beyond. Leave the lane here and take the grassy path alongside the wire fence until you reach steps leading to a wicket gate on the left. Cross two fields using the waymarked stiles to come out onto the open fell and so back to the car park.

For the longer walk, follow the route around Hallin Fell as far as Sandwick. At Sandwick take the Patterdale footpath at Townend Cottage **(C)** and follow the wall until you reach a barn on the right. Cross the stream and follow the wide, grassy path straight ahead up a steepish slope with Scalehow Force on the right. The path wends its way under rocky outcrops, giving good views of the lake, and past a waterfall. It then bears left towards a depression between High Dodd on the left and Place Fell on the right and

reaches the ruins of an old quarry. Continue along the track until a walled enclosure is reached at **(D)**.

Ignore the path ahead which leads to Place Fell and turn sharp left in a north-easterly direction towards the valley floor. Boredale was visited by Wordsworth in 1805, who described it as 'smooth and bare, a long, narrow, deep cradle-shaped glen, lying so sheltered that one would be pleased to see it planted by human hands'. The valley, and its neighbour Bannerdale, are still virtually deserted and one of the few places in the Lake District almost unchanged since Wordsworth's time.

Descend to the clapper bridge over Boredale Beck and into a lane which joins a road. Cross the metalled road into the green lane opposite and climb the steepish path over the ridge into the Martindale Valley, descending towards Winter

Crag Farm and the Old Church of St Martin beyond **(E)**. There has been a church on this site for over 700 years and remnants of the original church are visible protruding on the south side of the building. The font is reputed to be a Roman altar, brought down from the nearby High Street range. When the church fell into disrepair, the new church of St Peter was built – but St Martin's was later repaired and is used on some Sundays in the summer. It is claimed that the massive yew tree in the north-east corner of the churchyard is 'not less than 700 years old'.

After leaving the church, follow the road for about 250 yards and then bear right through a gateway. and take the path which crosses in front of a cottage, bearing right along the grassy path alongside a wall. Turn left to return to the car park.

Scale 1:25 000 or 2½INCHES to 1 MILE

Walk 4
Shap Abbey and Keld Chapel

The village of Shap sprawls along the A6, once a major north-south link but now bypassed by the M6 and an empty 'ghost' road. To the south and west lie the bleak Shap Fells but this walk follows field paths through the sheltered valley of the river Lowther. The walk starts in the hamlet of Keld, where there is a rare pre-Reformation chapel, and goes past the ruins of Shap Abbey. These lie by a wooded stretch of the river, hidden from the outside world by the fold of the hills. Allow 2 ½ hours for the full walk and about 1 hour if the section to Rosgill is omitted.

Scale 1:25 000 or 2¼ INCHES to 1 MILE

Shap (90) (NY 56-15) is on **Tour 4**. Going north, turn left out of the village up an unclassified road signposted to Shap Abbey. Turn left off this road, to Keld, and park where the road ends at a cattle grid.

Walk back along the road, passing the chapel on your right. Keld is a small hamlet which was probably built by Shap Abbey to house tenants employed in milling. The chapel may also have been an offshoot of the abbey. It was built at the end of the fifteenth century and is one of the very few rural church buildings which survive from that period. The chapel is now owned by the National Trust and there is a notice on the door telling you where to get hold of the key.

Continue along the road until you come to a large house on the left, just past the turning to Thornslip on the right. Turn left at **(A)** through a narrow gap stile on the

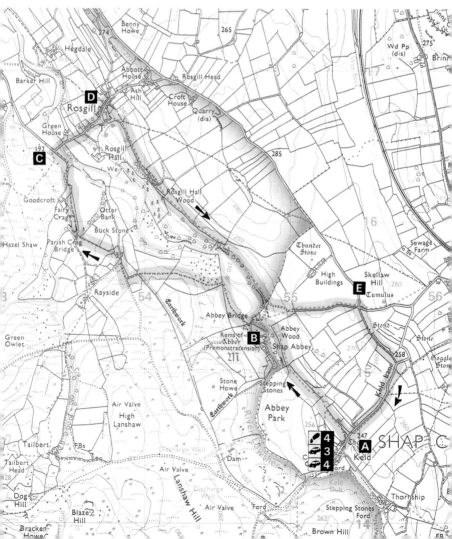

The starry saxifrage grows on wet rocks, cliff ledges and around seeping groundwater, even at high altitudes

right of the gateway. Follow the wall on your right to the corner, crossing a wire fence across your path by a wooden stile. At the corner, carry on in the same direction until you reach another wall corner . Now follow the wall on your left until you come to a stone step stile. Cross over the stile and bear right parallel with the wall. Go over a stile to the left of a gate and follow the wall and fencing on your left. Below and to your left are the ruins of Shap Abbey. Cross another stile and bear left down the field to a concrete track leading down to the river.

Cross the river by the old pedestrian bridge at **(B)**, to the right of the broad road bridge (not shown on the map). This brings you to the abbey. Shap Abbey was the last Norman monastery to be founded in the Lake District.

Walk back towards the bridge. To continue the walk to Rosgill, look out for a high ladder stile on your left, above the field gate as you approach the old bridge. Go up the steep slope to cross the stile into a field. Cross the field and go over another stile. Then follow the wall to a stile, cross and go over a very wet patch to turn right onto a metalled road.

After a short distance turn right off the road at a Coast to Coast signpost and then left over a stile and past a corrugated iron barn. Go over a stile into a field and down a bank to the charming packhorse bridge over Swindale Beck, with the rather odd name of Parish Crag Bridge.

Cross the bridge and follow a post and wire fence until you come to a stone stile. Cross and continue to a ladder stile. Bear right here and go through an iron gate into the field beside the river. Follow the track to a gate leading onto the road **(C)**.

Turn right and cross the river by Lowther Bridge. Walk up to the village of Rosgill. About 112 paces beyond the telephone box, turn right at **(D)**, alongside the house named Fell View. Cross two small fields into a larger field and leave by a field gate in the bottom right corner. From here it is almost a straight line back across the fields, following the wall on your right. About halfway along are some farm buildings near Rosgill Hall Wood. Pass to the left of these and turn right beyond the buildings and then left to regain your original direction. At the next wall, take the left hand of the two gates.

Go through two gates to come out by a house at a bend in the road. Turn left up the road until you come to a cattle grid. Cross the stile on the left into a field and continue in the same direction, following the road on your right. Near the road junction, go over a boulder stile in the wall on the left and turn right onto the road.

At the junction, take the path on the right between the walls. Where the track joins a road, turn right and walk back

The eggar moth is found on moorlands where its larvae feed on heather, bramble and other shrubby plants

towards Keld. Cross over a stile in the wall on your left, signposted to Shap, and immediately turn right (away from Shap) along a path which runs parallel with the road. Follow the wall, crossing another stile, until you can see the corner at the end of the wall. Go over a stile on your right into the road and turn left into the village.

To shorten the walk, the section to Rosgill can be omitted by returning across Abbey Bridge after seeing the abbey. Where the road up the hill turns right, the return route from Rosgill comes in from the left.

Walk 5
Elterwater, Lingmoor Fell and Great Langdale

The village of Elterwater is a cluster of houses at the edge of a large, open common surrounded by high peaks. East of the village lies the lake of the same name but the two walks described here go west, into the valley of Great Langdale. The longer walk (allow 5 hours) climbs Lingmoor Fell, the mass of high ground which separates Great Langdale from Little Langdale. The highest point of the fell is Brown Howe (1,530 ft) and on a day of high cloud this is a magnificent viewpoint for the Langdale Pikes. The shorter walk uses the lower slopes of Lingmoor and the river bank and will take about 1 ½ hours.

Elterwater (90) (NY 32-04) is on **Tours 6 and 8**. It lies just to the south of the B5343 which runs from Skelwith Bridge up Great Langdale.

Park in the car park in the centre of the village and cross over Elterwater Bridge. Follow the road as it curves round to the left and a little way beyond the Youth Hostel fork right onto the unsigned road. At the next junction **(A)** the two walks diverge.

For the longer walk, continue uphill on the rougher road, signposted as unsuitable for motors. (For the shorter walk, read the last paragraph now.) After ½ mile, and before you reach Dale End Farm, the fenceline on the left changes to a continuous wall **(B)**. Turn right here onto the open fellside and follow a permitted path which climbs to a ladder stile and then slants upwards to cross a second ladder stile. Here the path turns right and zig-zags more steeply up the hillside, soon rewarding you with good views to the south of Little Langdale, with its tarn, and Wetherlam standing guard over the Greenburn valley. It becomes obvious as you climb up that you are walking on a carefully engineered path. It was constructed many years ago to provide easier access for workers in the quarries higher up the fell.

Do not be misled by the cairn perched invitingly on a rocky knoll to the left. This is not the summit of Lingmoor – just a pleasant spot to rest and take in the surroundings, with Elterwater and Windermere now in view. Follow any of the paths that lead uphill towards the higher wall and turn left along a trod which keeps the wall more or less in sight, soon reaching the ridge of the fell. As you walk along to the highest point, Great Langdale comes into view on the right with Chapel Stile sited near to the quarry spoil heaps. The summit of Lingmoor boasts a large cairn **(C)** which is reached by a stile over the fence.

After admiring the grandeur of the Langdale Pikes, progress along the ridge. As the ridge begins to descend, the path stays close to the wall on the left. A small tarn can be seen below, named after the fell. After a short, rocky section, cross the wall by a wooden stile and head towards the sheer rock face of Side Pike. At its foot, a fence comes up from the left. Cross the stile and turn downhill with the fenceline. As you approach another stile lower down, turn right to contour through the bracken a little way above the Blea Tarn road.

Pass by a stone memorial seat **(D)** and continue alongside the wall bordering the road. The road soon turns left but the path continues downhill towards the wood. Do not go into the wood but turn right along the edge of it and follow a permitted path to pass just above the

National Trust's Great Langdale camp site. The line of the path is obvious as it crosses numerous fields and ladderstiles to pass close to Side House Farm.

After passing the farm, go through a gap in the wall and over another stile and immediately fork right uphill. Follow the path to Oak Howe, on the far side of a rocky knoll. Near the barn, the shorter walk comes in from the right. Turn left here and follow the lane to the river.

At the footbridge (E), do not cross the bridge but turn right. The river curves away to the left here in a broad loop. Follow the wall and fence across the loop to rejoin the river. Behind you there are magnificent views of the Langdale Pikes and on your right, beyond the flat fields, the craggy slopes of Lingmoor.

Walk along the bank, going through several gates, until you come to a stone bridge. Great Langdale Beck is rather canal-like in this section. Much work has been done on it to try and prevent the serious flooding which has inundated the dale many times. Over 31 inches of rain fell in almost as many days in 1967 and caused devastation in the valley.

Cross the stone bridge (built in 1818) and walk up a lane, bearing right into a green lane which runs between walls. Go through a narrow gate and follow the footpath signs through Thrang Farm, bearing right again into a lane which leaves the village school on your left. This runs beside a wall and comes out onto the main road. Turn right, past the Wainwrights Inn, and then right again over a metal footbridge.

Turn left and follow the river bank downstream past the weir, with the old quarry spoil heaps on your right. The timeshare lodges on the opposite side of the river are built on the site of a gunpowder factory. The manufacture of gunpowder was a major Lakeland industry and the Elterwater mill, opened in 1824, only closed in 1930.

Where the path joins a road, turn left. The road comes down by Elterwater bridge. Turn left and cross the bridge to return to the car park.

For the shorter walk, turn right at (A) and follow the tarred road through woodland for about 1 mile. Beyond Baysbrown Farm, keep to the main track ignoring first a right and then a left fork. After about ½ mile the track leaves the woodland and soon Oak Howe comes into view away to the right. Pass in front of the house to rejoin the longer walk just before the footbridge at (E).

Scale 1:25 000 or 2½ INCHES to 1 MILE

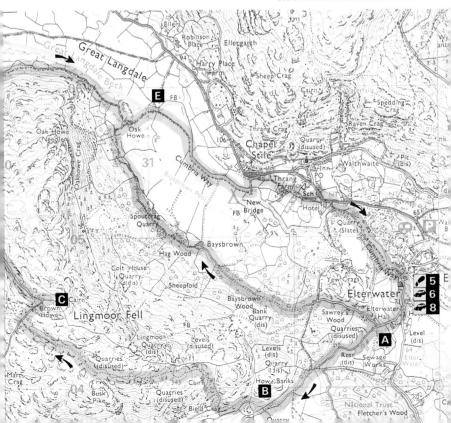

Walk 6
Torver, Little Arrow Moor and Coniston Water

Coniston Water is Arthur Ransome country and many parts of the lake look familiar to anyone who knows the Swallows and Amazons books. Both the walks described here start at the little village of Torver, some 3 miles south of Coniston, and follow a lake shore path. The longer walk also takes in Little Arrow Moor, with fine views of the Coniston Old Man range, and visits a water-filled quarry with its own waterfall. Allow 4 hours for the longer walk and 2 hours for the shorter.

Torver (96,97) (SD 28-94) is on **Tours 5 and 7**. It is a small village at the junction of the A593 and the A5084.

Park in a lay-by on the right hand side of the road to Greenodd (**A**). For the longer walk, head for the row of terraced houses and pass between Railway Cottages and Wilson Cottages. (For the short walk, read the last paragraph now.) Follow the walled lane, turning right at the first junction. After a short distance a narrow tar macadam road is reached, signposted as the bridleway to Walna Scar. The road soon becomes a stony track between walls and passes a small quarry on the left. Eventually the huge bulk of Coniston Old Man appears ahead, with the spectacular Dow Crag to the left.

Head for the spoil heaps of the disused quarry, crossing a bridge and going through a gate and across a small paddock. A slate-built cairn points the way to Walna Scar. Follow the rough path between the spoil heaps as far as the huge water filled hole which was Banishead Quarry (**B**). The water level is maintained by a beck which cascades into the quarry, leaving by a tunnel which was carved out to remove the quarried slate.

Retrace your steps to the slate cairn and take the path to Little Arrow. Cross a footbridge and go through a gate and over a ladder stile. With Torver Beck on your right, follow the obvious path across Little Arrow Intake, eventually passing between some houses to join the main road at the hamlet of Little Arrow (**C**).

Turn left along the road and after 400 yards leave it at a footpath sign on the right. Go through two gates, crossing the track of the now dismantled Foxfield-Coniston railway line into a large field.

Follow the faint path diagonally across the field, passing between two hummocks, to reach Hoathwaite Beck. Cross the stream and go through the gate ahead and along the path to Hoathwaite Farm. Go between the farm buildings and past the sheep pens, leaving the farmyard by a wooden gate.

Keep to the fence on your left until you reach a wooden stile. Cross the stile and continue until you reach a wire fence enclosing a plantation. Then turn right and keep the fence on your left until you come to a stone gap stile. Go straight ahead and through an avenue of trees to a gate at Brackenbarrow Farm onto a narrow lane (**D**).

Follow the well-worn track to the left, which is signposted to the lake shore. Passing between the ruins of Grass Guards, the path drops down through the woods to meet the Coniston Water lakeside path. The large white house on the opposite side of the lake is Brantwood, once the home of John Ruskin.

Turn right along the lake shore. A speed restriction limits the traffic on the lake to sailing boats, with a few slow motorboats. The exception is the majestic steam yacht 'Gondola', first launched in 1859 as the 'perfect combination of Venetian gondola and English steam yacht' and still a magnificent way to see the lake. After nearly eighty years the Gondola was taken out of service and became first a houseboat and then a wreck until the National Trust came to the rescue. Restored to her former glory by Vicker's shipyard at Barrow-in-Furness, she was relaunched in 1980.

The path follows the lake shore for about 1 ½ miles. Peel Island, familiar to readers of Swallows and Amazons as Wild Cat Island, is to the south. The woods round the lake have been extensively coppiced, the thick poles going to the bobbin mills and the thin poles to the charcoal burners.

Where the path meets a wall, it leaves the lake. Cross a stile beside a gate to reach the road near Sunny Bank and then cross the road to the stile opposite and drop down to the stream. Cross the stream by a footbridge and follow the grassy, rising path until a beck appears on the left. Do not cross the beck but carry on uphill to arrive at a small dam at the end of Torver Tarn (**E**). This is a natural tarn apart from the 3 ft dam, built to increase the water supply to a former bobbin mill at Sunny Bank.

Take the path which runs alongside the tarn and carry on, with the tarn down on

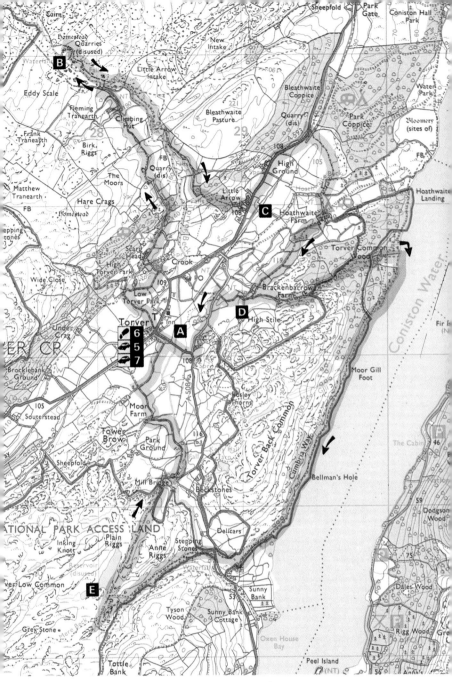

your left, until the path drops down to a gate in the corner. Go through the gate and into a lane which leads to the buildings at Mill Bridge. Do not cross the bridge but take the bridleway on the left to Torver. Leave the narrow lane and follow the raised track, with a hawthorn hedge on the left, until you reach a stile. Cross the stile and take the road to the right which takes you back to the start.

For the shorter walk, leave the lay-by **(A)** and walk away from the T-junction along the A5084 towards Greenodd. After 300 yards, a narrow road leads off to the left. Follow this road for ¼ mile and then take the rough track on the right. After a few minutes a sign indicates the way to the lake shore. The remainder of the walk follows the same route as the longer walk, starting from **(D)**.

Walk 7
Hawkshead, Tarn Hows and Black Crag

Hawkshead grew up as a medieval market town, supplying Kendal with wool, and the clutter of courtyards and narrow alleyways still gives the village a medieval flavour not found anywhere else in the Lakes. Two walks are described from Hawkshead to Tarn Hows, probably the most visited spot in the Lake District and

a spectacular example of Man 'improving' on nature. Both go through rolling hills and woodland and the longer walk also gives the option of climbing Black Crag (1,056 ft), a superb viewpoint for much of southern Lakeland. Allow 2 ½ hours for the shorter walk and 3 hours for the longer. The ascent of Black Crag will add another hour.

Hawkshead (96,97) (SD 35-98) is on **Tours 5 and 9**. It lies on the B5285 road which connects Coniston to the Bowness ferry. The road bypasses the central Conservation Area and there is a large National Trust car park outside the village.

Scale 1:25 000 or 2½ INCHES to 1 MILE

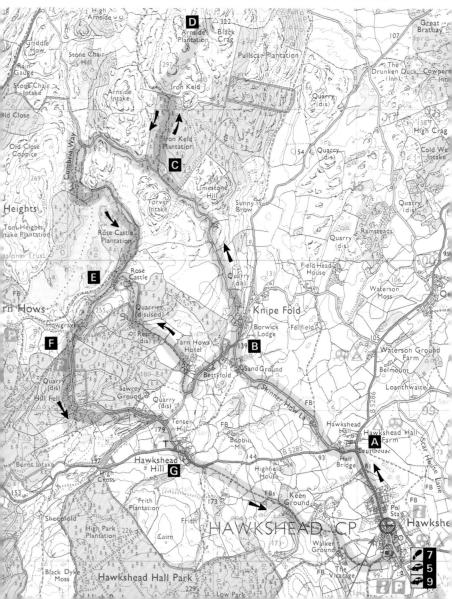

From the car park, walk into the village and turn right. In summer the tourists almost overwhelm the buildings but it is worth taking time to look at the white-washed houses in the former Market Square, the old Market House or Shambles and the overhanging timber-framed houses. The National Trust has opened a Beatrix Potter exhibition, with a collection of original drawings, in the eighteenth-century Solicitors Office where her husband William Heelis worked.

Walk north along the road through Hawkshead to the road junction at (A). From here you can see the fifteenth-century Courthouse which is the only surviving building of Hawkshead manor, held by the monks of Furness Abbey for more than 300 years.

Turn left at (A) and go past the Saw Mill. After about 200 yards bear right up Skinner How Lane to the road junction at (B). Here the two walks diverge. (For the short walk, read the last paragraph now.)

For the longer walk, take the inclined road (unsuitable for motors) opposite Borwick Lodge gates. This was once an old packhorse route. Views open up of hills and lakes to the right. If visibility and other conditions justify the climb of Black Crag, turn right at the second entry into the coniferous Iron Keld Plantation, beneath a crag (C). Climb the stony track through the woods to emerge in about ten minutes at a stile. After about 35 yards, turn right up the fell by an old stone wall and follow a permitted footpath to the summit (D). To the east are the Pennines, to the north Blencathra (over 15 miles away), to the west Bowfell and The Crinkles and to the south Coniston Water.

Return to (C) by the same route and continue along the stony road, with Tarn Hows visible on your left. After about ten minutes, turn left across a ladder stile and continue for about 300 yards until the water comes into view again. Turn left and walk round the head of the Tarns, going through a kissing gate. Where the path forks ahead on the east side of the Tarn, bear left up the incline. Soon after this the shorter walk comes in from the left at (E).

The natural beauty of Tarn Hows is in fact a nineteenth-century creation. The lake was formed by building a dam where there had once been a small mill, thus converting three shallow pools into one, and the lake shore and islands were planted with trees to create an 'ideal' landscape. In 1930 the National Trust acquired the land and have carried on the work of improvement. Trees cut down during the war were not replanted when it was felt the view was enhanced and paths have been created and repaired to try and minimise the erosion caused by so many visitors. The Tarns are probably seen at their best in winter.

Continue along the terrace path to emerge on to the road by a seat at (F). Then bear left and use the waymarked path through the trees, to the right of the road to Hawkshead Hill. This is a permitted path. After about ⅔ mile, leave the wood by a ladder stile and bear left past the yellow waymarks to emerge onto the road. Then follow the Hawkshead signposts. Ahead of you are the wooded Claife Heights.

At (G) there is a modest Baptist Chapel on the left of the road, dating from 1678 and rebuilt in 1876. After 200 yards, turn right to follow the left hand of two Public Footpath signs through the fields. Go through two kissing gates with a small wood in betweeen. Turn right in the middle of a large field, following the Hawkshead waymark, to reach a minor road near the gates of Walker Ground. Turn left along the road and then right to follow a field path to Hawkshead Church.

This fifteenth-century church occupies a commanding position on the hillside above Hawkshead and is on a grand scale. Wordsworth, who was educated at Hawkshead, called it 'the snow-white church upon a hill' but that was before it was restored and its rough-cast rendering removed. Inside, the broad nave has low, wide painted arches and partly painted columns.

Keep right of the church down to the former Grammar School, founded in 1585 and now a museum. Wordsworth was a pupil from 1779 to 1787 and his first known attempt at poetry was in honour of the school's bicentenary.

For the shorter walk, turn left at (B) and walk along the road for ¼ mile, passing a large house (Bettyfold) on the left. Turn right at the Public Footpath sign by a cattle grid and go through a kissing gate into the drive which runs through a group of houses behind the Tarn Hows Hotel. Walk up the walled lane and along the path to the right of some larch trees. Go through a metal gate and over a forestry track, almost immediately turning right over a stile. Follow the rising path diagonally left through the pasture, keeping to the right of the former gatekeeper's humble cottage (grandly known as Rose Castle) and at Tarn Hows rejoin the longer walk (E).

Walk 8
Blawith, Beacon Tarn and the Beacon

Blawith Common is owned by the Lake District Special Planning Board, who try here to reconcile the different priorities of conservationists, farmers and walkers. The terrain offers great variety, with bracken, heather or bilberry carpeting the ground and outcrops of rock giving additional interest. Both walks start in the hamlet of Blawith and visit Beacon Tarn. The longer goes on to climb the Beacon, a magnificent viewpoint overlooking the panorama of Morecambe Bay and the Duddon estuary to the south and the central Lakeland fells to the north. Allow 3 hours for the longer walk and 2 for the shorter.

Blawith (96,97) (SD 28-88) is on **Tour 5**. It is a small hamlet on the A5084, one mile from the southern tip of Coniston Water.

Both walks start at the church **(A)**. The present Victorian building replaces a sixteenth-century church, the ruins of which can be seen on the opposite side of the road. The story goes that in 1792 a local bishop ordered the parishioners of Blawith to enlarge the church and buy a bell. To raise the money they had to sell a piece of common grazing land.

> *Blawith poor people*
> *An auld church and new steeple,*
> *As poor as hell*
> *They had to sell*
> *A bit of fell*
> *To buy a bell*
> *Blawith poor people.*

Go down the minor road opposite the front of the new church and after 100 yards bear right at the junction. Shortly after you pass Houkler Hall (a farm on the left of the road not to be confused with the more famous Holker Hall a few miles away) a surfaced track leads off to the right. Do not take this but carry on for another 50 yards to leave the road by a grassy track leading off to the right. When this reaches a wall, go over a stile with stone steps and continue, keeping a wall on the right, to another stone step stile beside a beck. Cross this and go over the field diagonally, making towards some white buildings. Cross yet another stone step stile and head for the white gate leading to the buildings of Appletree Holme **(B)**.

Go through the gate and turn right between the buildings. Cross a cattle grid and turn left down another narrow track. After a few yards, leave the surfaced track and take the rising grassy path on the left. When a wall appears on the right, follow it as far as a gate alongside a large tree. Go through the gate and straight on, with the buildings of Cockenskell to your right. Cockenskell is believed to have been one of the farms owned by the abbots of Furness Abbey. The abbey, sited on the once isolated peninsula between Morecambe Bay and Duddon Sands, was one of the richest Cistercian abbeys in England before the Dissolution of the Monasteries, second only to Fountains Abbey.

Pass between walls to a gate and drop down to a beck. Cross the beck by the bridge and go over the stile. Go up a rising path, keeping the beck and a wall on the left. Where the wall veers away to the left, go straight ahead to the top of the rise. Beacon Tarn now appears dead ahead, with Walna Scar, Dow Crag and

Ring ouzels are summer visitors. They nest on rocky hillsides, eating snails and insects, and berries in the autumn before returning to the Mediterranean

Coniston Old Man in the background. The small hill on the left is Wool Knot. Drop down to the tarn for a well-earned rest **(C)**. At this point you need to choose whether or not to make a circuit of the tarn plus a climb to the top of the Beacon (836 ft).

For the longer walk, follow the obvious path round the west (left hand) side of the tarn to reach rather wet ground at the tip of the tarn, where a path leads forward up a rise. Leave this path to find a sharply climbing path on the right which meanders to the summit of the Beacon **(D)**. Bonfires lit on the top of landmarks such as this were an effective way of passing messages over a long distance, warning of Scottish raids across the border. The flat top of the Beacon is one of the finest viewpoints in the district. To the west is Black Combe, a famous landmark for sailors; to the north the Coniston mountain range; beyond and further east the Helvellyn and High Street ranges and turning clockwise the full length of Coniston Water and then Morecambe Bay and the Duddon estuary.

Use one of the several paths to drop down to the path running above the tarn on the opposite side to your approach. On arriving back near the point where you commenced the circuit of Beacon Tarn **(C)**, cross the beck flowing out of it.

To return to Blawith, follow the well-worn path downhill and cross the stream by a footbridge. The path goes across a pleasant stretch of open fell and then runs first between walls, with a wood on the right, and then beside a wall on the right.

At Greenholme Farm **(E)** leave the track and turn right between the farm buildings, taking care (as always) not to impose on the farmer's goodwill. After a few yards, go through a gate and cross a small grassy area to a slate slab bridge over Greenholme Beck. Another gate ahead leads to a stone stile. Continue in the same direction, with a wall to the right, until another wall appears ahead. Veer left here and follow this wall as far as a gate leading to a grassy lane. This takes you between the buildings of Picthall. Follow the narrow road until you come to the main road. Turn right to arrive back at Blawith church.

Scale 1:50 000 or 1¼ INCHES to 1 MILE

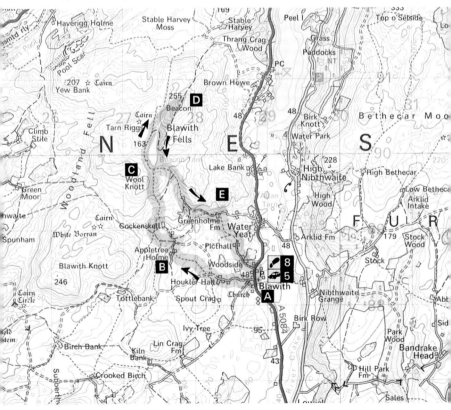

Walk 9
Wasdale and Ilgill Head

Wasdale is said to have the deepest lake, the highest mountain, the smallest church and the biggest liar in the whole of England. The lake is the 250 ft deep Wast Water, the mountain is the 3,210 ft Scafell Pike, the church is St Olaf's and the liar was Will Ritson, publican of the Wasdale Head Hotel in the last century. Two walks are described here. The shorter has very little climbing, explores Wasdale Head and is an excellent introduction to the dale. The longer walk climbs Illgill Head, at 1,983 ft the highest point of the formidable Wast Water Screes, but the route up is an easy gradient on grass. Allow 2 hours for the shorter walk and 4 hours for the longer.

Wasdale Head (89,90) (NY 18-08) is on **Tour 7**. Both walks start at the the head of the lake, before you reach the village. Follow the road up the north-west shore of Wast Water and turn right, soon after you cross a cattle grid, along a lane signed Wasdale Head Hall Farm and National Trust Wasdale Camp Site. Then fork right for the Trust's free car park.

For the shorter walk, carry on along the road and cross the bridge over Lingmell Gill at (A). Then take the track alongside the gill. The size of the boulders give some indication of the force of the winter storms that sweep them down the fell-sides. Pass to the left of Brackenclose, home of the Fell and Rock Climbing Club founded at Wasdale Head in 1886. Re-cross the gill by a footbridge and walk up the gently climbing path to a kissing gate. Keep alongside the gill to the next fence-line or wall (B). Above you are the crags of Scafell Pike.

Do not go through the gate but turn about, cross a wet patch and leave the gill

on a gently rising path through bracken. This goes across the fellside, with the path already walked below you on your left. You are now looking out to sea and on clear days the southern half of the Isle of Man is visible.

Cross a broad, grass path and continue along the face of the fell (Lingmell), now starting to descend. Ahead is Kirk Fell above the hamlet of Wasdale Head. Pass through a kissing gate in the wall. Great Gable (2,949 ft) now comes into view alongside Kirk Fell. This magnificent mountain, set in the notch of the fells, is the official emblem of the National Park.

Descend to a footbridge and cross the field to·meet the road. The piles of stones were collected together after floods washed them onto the fields. Turn right and then fork right across the green. You are now on a track to Burnthwaite which is also the start of Sty Head Pass. St Olaf's Church, a little way along, is worth a visit. It is used by climbers and the graveyard contains memorials to climbers killed in climbing accidents both in the Lakes and abroad.

Continue up the stony lane, noticing even bigger heaps of stones cleared from the fields. Pass between the buildings at Burnthwaite (**C**) and through a gate behind the farm. Turn left on a grassy track which soon runs between walls. Follow the course of a small stream, crossing and recrossing it by numerous foot-bridges, until the path joins a stony track. Turn left along the track to bypass a farm and reach a charming packhorse bridge. Before crossing the bridge you may want to stop off in Wasdale Head. The Wasdale Head Inn, now famous for its mountain-eering connections, still has a Ritson's Bar in memory of the tall stories of Will Ritson.

To return, cross the bridge and turn left to follow the river to the road at Down in the Dale Bridge. The car park is ½ mile along the road to the right.

The climb of Illgill Head also starts by crossing the bridge over Lingmell Gill. Continue a short way up the side of the gill and in front of Brackenclose turn right alongside the wall, signed Eskdale, and gradually climb up along a track which becomes rougher and stonier as height is gained. Hollow Gill and Groove Gill are crossed by adjacent footbridges. This is a good place to stop and appreciate Wasdale Head and the field patterns of the upper dale.

After the plantation ends a cairn marks the crossing of the next stream. The path divides here (**D**). Take the right fork (not

Mountain ringlet butterflies are found in Scotland and the Lake District but nowhere else in England

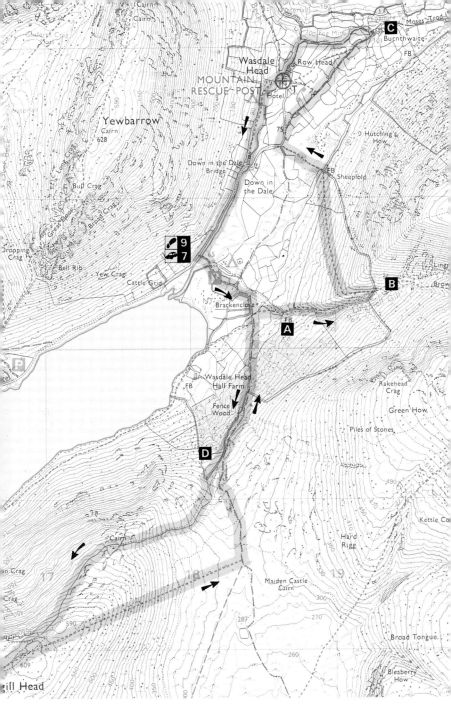

the cairned route) and follow the wall which has been on the right so far. This is ruinous from now on but leads almost to the summit of Illgill Head and should be your guide.

Two cairns mark the summit area: the further more westerly one, surrounded by grass, is generally accepted as the summit. Walk a few yards to the rim of the crags for a dramatic view of Wast Water. The screes fall sheer to the bottom of the lake, 200 ft below sea level. Return to the more easterly cairn amongst its scattering of stones (E) and follow the cairned track downhill to (D), from where the outward route is followed back.

Scale 1:25 000 or 2½ INCHES to 1 MILE

Walk 10
Borrowdale and the river Derwent

Steep wooded hillsides backed by high crags and higher fells make Borrowdale one of the most beautiful dales. Two walks are described starting from the hamlet of Seatoller, built to house workers from the nearby Honister slate quarries. The green Honister slate was carried to the coast by strings of packhorses who followed an extraordinary route, known as Moses's Trod, which went across the side of Great Gable to Wasdale. Both walks go through the lovely woodland and riverside scenery which lies near the head of the valley. The longer should take about 3 ½ hours and the shorter 1 – 2 hours.

Seatoller (89,90) (NY 24-13) is on **Tours 1 and 2** and lies on the B5289 near the foot of the Honister Pass.

Park in the Seatoller car park. From the car park, turn right into the village. On the right is the Seatoller Barn Information Centre, with a small collection of old farm machinery outside. Inside is an exhibition of Lakeland farming and climate. Continue uphill on the Honister road. When the road turns sharp left, go through a gap in the roadside wall and climb up to a small gate. The path climbs steeply uphill and then levels out before reaching a broad track, one of the old toll roads. Cross over this to a large cairn of stones and go through a small gate in the fell wall.

Turn right alongside the wall. At Scaleclose Gill, which is crossed by a footbridge, there is a good view of Rosthwaite and the upper Borrowdale valley. Cross another gill and continue until you come to a stile and small gate in a fenceline across the path **(A)**. This is just before Tongue Gill.(For the long walk, miss out the next paragraph.)

For the short walk, do not cross the stile but turn right and make for a gate in the wall below. Walk downhill to the right of the gill to reach the River Derwent at **(B)**. Turn right along the river bank to Longthwaite Farm and go through the white gate into the grounds of Longthwaite Youth Hostel **(C)**, purpose-built in Canadian red cedar wood. Continue alongside the river which is particularly beautiful in this section. After a short rocky scramble, ending at a fenceline, turn right through a gate (not obvious) and go along a path just inside the wood. The path bears right through a gate behind the guest house and then turns left to Seatoller.

For the longer walk, cross the stile at **(A)** and then the footbridge over Tongue Gill, which has its source high up on the slopes of High Spy. Stay with the main track and at the highest point of the pass you will be rewarded with magnificent views of Derwent Water, with Skiddaw as a backdrop. The track you are following was formerly the road out from Rigghead Quarry, high on the fellside where Tongue Gill comes tumbling down.

Castle Crag **(D)** dominates the immediate scene to the right. This impressive pyramid-shaped crag was once an Early English fort. In more recent times quarrying has been carried on there and much evidence of this is to be found on its eastern slopes. In 1920 Castle Crag was given to the National Trust in memory of the men of Borrowdale killed in the 1914-18 war. If you wish to climb to its summit, go through a gap in the wall soon after you start to descend the narrow ravine. It is a short, steep climb over rough ground, the descent being made by the same route.

Continuing the walk, follow the stony track downhill and pass through a gate into the wood. Cross the stream and walk alongside it to reach the River Derwent at **(E)**. Recross the stream and follow the obvious track to where it forks. Bear left to Hollows Farm and go through the yard to a kissing gate. Follow the track until it turns, opposite a white gate marked 'Private'. Turn right here through the farm gate and climb the knoll, known as Peace How. At the top there is a stone seat commemorating Canon Rawnsley's gift of the surrounding land to the National Trust in 1917. The view is magnificent, with Grange village below and Derwent Water to the left.

Go downhill and through the gate to the road. Turn right into Grange-in-Borrowdale, a small hamlet with a beautiful position on the river Derwent. To leave the village, turn right down the bridleway by Grange Cafe. This soon widens out into a pleasant leafy lane. At the junction, take the left fork and retrace your steps back to the river **(E)**.

After recrossing the bridge over the side stream, take the path on the left signed Rosthwaite. It follows the river for a short way and then curves to the right. follow the gravel track until it becomes a small stony path. Turn right beside a wall for a few yards, cross through a gap and continue along the rough track to a T-junction of paths. Here turn left, following the yellow waymark through the mounds of quarry waste. In a nearby cave made by the quarry workings a gentleman by the name of Millican Dalton used to spend his summer months. He was a mountaineer and a familiar figure in the neighbourhood between the two world wars. He died in 1947 aged 80.

After passing through a gap stile, the path meanders through the rocky woodland to the sound of the unseen river. Once out of the wood, the track rejoins the river to pass by the picturesque stone packhorse bridge and cross two wooden footbridges. The signed path to Seatoller rejoins the shorter walk at **(B)**.

Scale 1:25 000 or 2½INCHES to 1 MILE

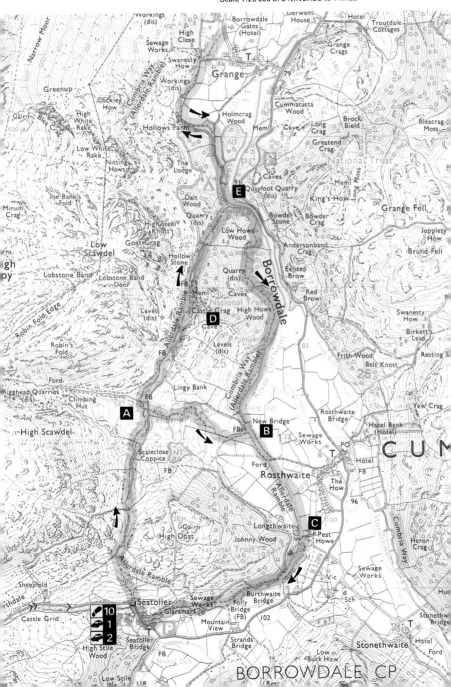

Walk 11
Buttermere and Hay Stacks

Buttermere is set in a remote valley, enclosed by fells. High crags run along its western shore and the steep ridge of Fleetwith Pike dominates its head. Two contrasting walks are described here, each of about 4 miles. The first climbs Hay Stacks, the undulating, knobbly skyline just west of Fleetwith Pike and will take about 4 hours. This is a rough, mountain walk which should not be undertaken without boots and suitable clothing. The summit area offers magnificent views but can be confusing in mist and it is important to choose a day with a high cloud base. The second walk is an easy circuit of the lake, one of the few which has a path running all round it. A short section is not shown on the map because of space but the path is well-used and easy to follow. Allow 2 hours.

Buttermere (89,90) (NY 17-17) is on **Tours 1 and 2**. The B5289 runs the length of the lake and the village lies at the foot, between Buttermere and Crummock Water. Both walks start at the head of the lake, so do not park in the village but in the car park opposite Gatesgarth Farm.

From the car park, cross the road and take the signed footpath to Scarth Gap, just before the bridge. Go past the farm buildings and then bear left through a gate to follow a track across the head of the lake. On your right is a wall and fence. Cross the bridge and go through the gate (**A**).

For the climb of Hay Stacks, go up the steep path ahead of you to reach a gently climbing path running across the hillside. Turn left here to walk up Scarth Gap Pass, the lowest possible route between Buttermere and Ennerdale. Much of this lower section has had to be repaired because of massive erosion by thousands of feet. As you climb up the pass, Hay Stacks is on your left with the lower slopes of High Crag on the right. Cross a stile, pass through a gap in a wall and continue up to the top of the pass where there is a large cairn (**B**). Ahead can be seen the tops of the plantations in Ennerdale, although the dale itself is not visible from here.

There are three possible routes up Hay Stacks. One is a thin, steep path straight up the hillside which includes some rock scrambling. Another (probably the one most used) is a broader path slanting across to the right which, after about 200 yards, turns left up steep, loose scree with a short rock scramble at the top. The third, and recommended, route starts along the slanting path but, instead of turning up the scree, crosses just below it and continues on a narrow trod through the heather and bilberry. This path does not climb very much at first. It comes near to the remains of an old fenceline, which it then crosses and follows uphill.

Continue upwards and when the summit cairn at (**C**) comes into view, a little way to the left, follow one of the many trods towards it. Ennerdale Water, Crummock Water and Buttermere are all in view and Pillar, Kirk Fell and Great Gable are seen to advantage with Scafell Pike framed between Kirk Fell and Gable.

After appreciating the view from the rocky summit, turn your back on Scarth Gap and make across the undulating ground to Innominate Tarn (**D**), a most attractive tarn with numerous bilberry-covered rock islands. Various paths converge on the left of the tarn. Now the rocky path descends a little and crosses above a cleft with dramatic views down to Buttermere and Crummock Water. Soon the stream issuing from Blackbeck Tarn is crossed. The tarn itself is not seen from the path as it is at a higher level, a few yards to the right. Climb a short scree slope and then bear right with the cairns.

Continue on a broad path for some way until it starts to descend slightly. Where the path divides, there is a cairn on a large slab of rock (**E**). Dubs Quarry and a small climbing hut can be seen to the right across the valley. Take the left fork, which initially descends quite steeply over rough ground but then meanders interestingly downhill. Do not attempt to cross to the other side of the main stream, Warnscale Beck, as there is no easy crossing here.

As your path (cairned in parts) zig-zags its way down to the flat area of Warnscale Bottom, there are impressive views of the crags and gullies of Hay Stacks. On reaching the valley floor, the path becomes a carpet of short turf. Cross Warnscale Beck by a flat bridge to join the old quarry road. This brings you out onto the road near Gatesgarth Farm.

For the walk around the lake, go through the gate at (**A**) and then turn right to follow the lakeside path. Cross Comb Beck and go through first Burtness Wood and then Old Burtness Wood. At the foot of Sourmilk Gill, which falls almost perpendicularly down the steep hillside from the unseen Bleaberry Tarn, turn right. Cross the footbridge and follow the path across the flat land which separates Buttermere and Crummock Water, bearing left at a stile and then right. The track comes out in Buttermere by the Fish Hotel.

Turn right out of the village and almost immediately turn right again at Wilkinsyke Farm. Cross the farmyard and turn right and then left to reach the lake shore. The path now follows the shore, sometimes going through patches of woodland and at others along more rocky stretches. At one point it goes through a manmade tunnel, built where the rock face plunges down to the water.

Near the head of the lake, the path comes out onto the Honister road. Follow the road back to the car park.

Scale 1:25 000 or 2½ INCHES to 1 MILE

Walk 12
A circuit of the Dunnerdale Fells from Ulpha

Dunnerdale, the valley of the river Duddon, is a dale of great variety with an attractive rugged skyline. Wordsworth called it the 'most romantic of all our vales' and wrote a sequence of sonnets in its praise. Two walks are described starting from Ulpha, a small isolated village in the lower part of the dale. Both give fine views of the fells and the Duddon Estuary and the option of climbing Stickle Pike (1,231 ft). Allow 2 ¼ hours for the shorter walk and about 4 hours for the longer.

Ulpha (96) (SD 19-93) is on **Tours 7 and 8**. It lies at the point where the winding hilly road which runs down through Dunnerdale from the Wrynose Pass divides,

one fork crossing the river and continuing to Duddon Bridge and the other meandering along the slopes of the western fells.

Park near the village school, just south of the bridge over the river Duddon, and walk up the tar macadam side road. When the road ends at Birks, take to the open fell. Climb steadily uphill, soon leaving the wood on the left. Do not be misled by various sheep tracks you will meet: although this is a bridleway there is no obvious path on the ground. Soon you will see ahead of you a pyramid-shaped mountain: this is Caw (1,735 ft). The much bigger but similarly shaped mountain further away on the left side of the valley is Harter Fell (2,129 ft). After a while you will also see Stickle Pike (1,231 ft) nearby on your right. When you cross a rather wet, flattish area free of bracken around Hollow Moss Beck, you should be about 300 yards above the fell wall on the left and on the right you may notice a small, stone, circular sheepfold. Keep making towards Caw.

Scale 1:50 000 or 1 ¼ INCHES to 1 MILE

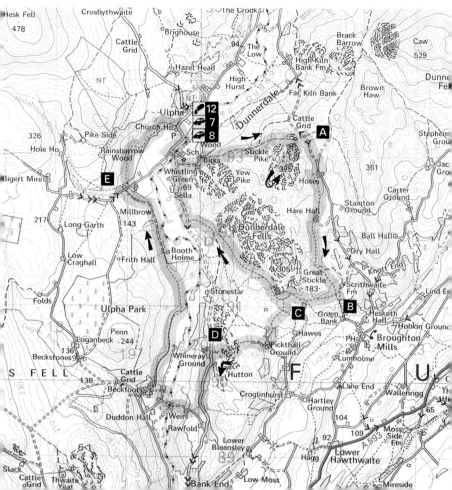

The Church of St John, Ulpha

About 300 yards above the cattle grid, you meet the fell road at (A). Turn right and follow the road to its summit. If you want, you can go to the top of Stickle Pike which is a good viewpoint. There is a well defined path and the 400 ft climb will take about 25 minutes.

To continue the walk, go on down the road for about 400 yards and then turn right up a signed path by a gate in the road. Follow the wall up for a short way, turning left with it, and continue downhill past Hare Hall, a white farmhouse. At the stream (Red Moss Beck) bear left and go through a gate into a grass lane with crumbling walls. Behind you Stickle Pike now looks like a high, rugged mountain.

At the end of the lane, bear right through the gateless exit and go across and down a field to reach another walled, grassy lane at (B). Turn right along this lane and then bear right uphill just before a barn. Go through the gate at the top and turn left to keep just above the wall. Great Stickle (1,001 ft) is now prominent on your right. Follow a well defined track through the bracken for about 300 yards until you come to a gate on the left leading into a walled track (C). The choice of the longer or shorter walk is at this point. (For the longer walk, miss out the next paragraph.)

For the shorter walk, do not go through the gate at (C) but continue on above the wall. After a steepish climb you will notice a large square boulder on your right. Ignore the path forking right uphill and continue on level ground. The houses around Ulpha can now be seen. Follow the path down to the road and turn right to return to the starting point. There is a long history of iron making in this area and just above the road near Cinderhill Beck there was an ancient bloomery, where iron was smelted.

For the longer walk, go through the gate on the left at (C) into the walled track. At the next gate, where the track seems to end, turn sharp left. You will soon pick up the track again as a built-up grass track leading to Pickthall Ground. Go left by the front of the house and through a gate on the right between outbuildings. Climb upwards on a good track which soon follows a line of electricity poles. When the poles swing away downhill, find a gap stile in the wall below and take the path down to the Duddon road, meeting it at Whineray Ground (D). Many of the farms in this area are 'grounds'.

Turn left along the road for ⅓ mile and about 200 yards before the next farm (Rawfold) turn right at a small gated stile. Go down by the wall and through a gap stile to a gate by a small barn. The stony drive crosses the river Duddon and goes up to a house. Turn right over a stile and then left as the signposts direct.

At the barns, turn sharp right and follow the track ahead. You will be in woodland most of the time: much of it has been coppiced, the timber being used to make bobbins, charcoal, poles etc. There are numerous large nests of wood ants by the path and you may see roe deer.

At (E) you reach a narrow road. Up to about 1910 the house by the road was an old bobbin mill with a water wheel at the front. The nearby square tower was used to dry the timber and originally had a further 30 ft of brickwork on it. Behind the tower are the remains of the pipe line that brought water to power the mill.

Cross over the bridge, inscribed 'Bobbin Mill Bridge', and immediately turn left onto another good track through woodland. The path comes into Ulpha by the Post Office. Turn right and go past the church to arrive back at the starting point.

CONVENTIONAL SIGNS
1:250 000 or 1 INCH to 4 MILES

ROADS
Not necessarily rights of way

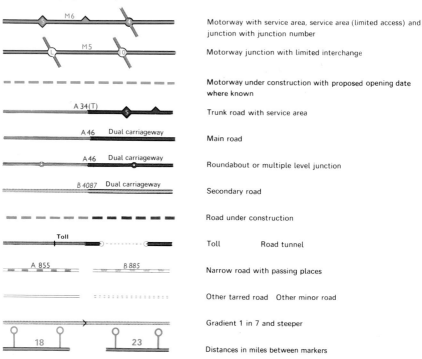

Motorway with service area, service area (limited access) and junction with junction number

Motorway junction with limited interchange

Motorway under construction with proposed opening date where known

Trunk road with service area

Main road

Roundabout or multiple level junction

Secondary road

Road under construction

Toll   Road tunnel

Narrow road with passing places

Other tarred road   Other minor road

Gradient 1 in 7 and steeper

Distances in miles between markers

The representation of a road is no evidence of the existence of a right of way

PRIMARY ROUTES

These form a national network of recommended through routes which complement the motorway system.
Selected places of major traffic importance are known as Primary Route Destinations and are shown thus KENDAL
Distances and directions to such destinations are repeated on traffic signs which, on primary routes, have a green
background or, on motorways, have a blue background.
To continue on a primary route through or past a place which has appeared as a destination on previous signs, follow
the directions to the next primary destination shown on the green-backed signs.

RAILWAYS

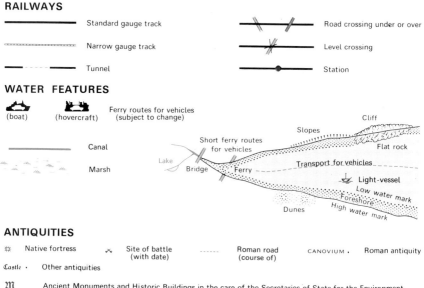

Standard gauge track

Narrow gauge track

Tunnel

Road crossing under or over

Level crossing

Station

WATER FEATURES

(boat)   (hovercraft)   Ferry routes for vehicles
(subject to change)

Canal

Marsh

Lake

Bridge   Ferry

Short ferry routes
for vehicles

Cliff

Slopes

Flat rock

Transport for vehicles

Light-vessel

Low water mark

Foreshore

Dunes   High water mark

ANTIQUITIES

Native fortress   Site of battle   Roman road   CANOVIVM .   Roman antiquity
(with date)   (course of)

Castle .   Other antiquities

ꝳ   Ancient Monuments and Historic Buildings in the care of the Secretaries of State for the Environment,
for Scotland and for Wales and that are open to the public.

BOUNDARIES

+ — + — + — + — National

— — — — — — { County, Region or Islands Area

GENERAL FEATURES

Buildings

Wood

Lighthouse (in use)

Lighthouse (disused)

Windmill

Radio or TV mast

▲ Youth hostel

⊕ Civil aerodrome { with Customs facilities

✦ without Customs facilities

Ⓗ Heliport

☏ Public telephone

☏ Motoring organisation telephone

+ Intersection, latitude & longitude at 30' intervals (not shown where it confuses important detail)

TOURIST INFORMATION

✝ Abbey, Cathedral, Priory

🐟 Aquarium

Å Camp site

🚐 Caravan site

🏰 Castle

Cave

Country park

Craft centre

✿ Garden

⚑ Golf course or links

🏛 Historic house

ℹ Information centre

Motor racing

🖼 Museum

Nature or forest trail

🦆 Nature reserve

☆ Other tourist feature

✕ Picnic site

Preserved railway

🏇 Racecourse

Skiing

Viewpoint

Wildlife park

🐘 Zoo

WALKS, CYCLE & MOTOR TOURS
Applicable to all scales

Start point of walk

Route of walk

Featured walk

 Start point of tour

➜ Route of tour

Featured tour

Start point of mini-walk

FOLLOW THE COUNTRY CODE
Enjoy the countryside and respect its life and work

Guard against all risk of fire

Fasten all gates

Keep your dogs under close control

Keep to public paths across farmland

Leave livestock, crops and machinery alone

Use gates and stiles to cross fences, hedges and walls

Take your litter home

Help to keep all water clean

Protect wildlife, plants and trees

Take special care on country roads

Make no unnecessary noise

CONVENTIONAL SIGNS
1:25 000 or 2½ INCHES to 1 MILE

ROADS AND PATHS

Not necessarily rights of way

M I or A 6(M)	M I or A 6(M)	Motorway
A 31 (T)	A 31(T)	Trunk road
A 35	A 35	Main road
B 3074	B 3074	Secondary road
A 35	A 35	Dual carriageway

Narrow roads with passing places are annotated

Road generally more than 4m wide

Road generally less than 4m wide

Other road, drive or track

Unfenced roads and tracks are shown by pecked lines

.... Path

PUBLIC RIGHTS OF WAY

Public rights of way may not be evident on the ground

Public paths { Footpath / Bridleway

+ + + + + Byway open to all traffic

- + - + - Road used as a public path

The indication of a towpath in this book does not necessarily imply a public right of way

The representation of any other road, track or path is no evidence of the existence of a right of way

RAILWAYS

═══	Multiple track } Standard gauge
──	Single track
—+—+—	Narrow gauge
	Siding
	Cutting
	Embankment
	Tunnel
	Road over & under
	Level crossing; station

DANGER AREA

MOD ranges in the area
Danger!
Observe warning notices

BOUNDARIES

— · — · — County (England and Wales)

— — — District

—◦—◦—◦— London Borough

·············· Civil Parish (England)* Community (Wales)

— — — — Constituency (County, Borough, Burgh or European Assembly)

Coincident boundaries are shown by the first appropriate symbol

*For Ordnance Survey purposes County Boundary is deemed to be the limit of the parish structure whether or not a parish area adjoins

SYMBOLS

Church or chapel — with tower / with spire / without tower or spire

▨ △ Glasshouse; youth hostel

Bus or coach station

Lighthouse; lightship; beacon

△ Triangulation station

Triangulation point on — church or chapel / lighthouse, beacon / building; chimney

Electricity transmission line
pylon   pole

VILLA — Roman antiquity (AD 43 to AD 420)

Castle — Other antiquities

Site of antiquity

1066 — Site of battle (with date)

Gravel pit

Sand pit

Chalk pit, clay pit or quarry

Refuse or slag heap

Sloping wall

Water   Mud

Sand; sand & shingle

National Park or Forest Park Boundary

NT — National Trust always open

NT — National Trust opening restricted

FC — Forestry Commission

VEGETATION
Limits of vegetation are defined by positioning of the symbols but may be delineated also by pecks or dots

Coniferous trees

Non-coniferous trees

Coppice

Orchard

Scrub

Bracken, rough grassland

In some areas bracken (∩) and rough grassland (·····) are shown separately

Heath

Shown collectively as rough grassland on some sheets

Reeds

Marsh

Saltings

HEIGHTS AND ROCK FEATURES

50 · Determined by — ground survey
285 · — air survey

Surface heights are to the nearest metre above mean sea level. Heights shown close to a triangulation pillar refer to the station height at ground level and not necessarily to the summit

Vertical face

Loose rock   Boulders   Outcrop   Scree

75
60
50

Contours are at 5 metres vertical interval

ABBREVIATIONS
1:25 000 or 2½ INCHES to 1 MILE also 1:10 000/1:10 560 or 6 INCHES to 1 MILE

BP,BS	Boundary Post or Stone	P	Post Office	A,R	Telephone, AA or RAC
CH	Club House	Pol Sta	Police Station	TH	Town Hall
F V	Ferry Foot or Vehicle	PC	Public Convenience	Twr	Tower
FB	Foot Bridge	PH	Public House	W	Well
HO	House	Sch	School	Wd Pp	Wind Pump
MP,MS	Mile Post or Stone	Spr	Spring		
Mon	Monument	T	Telephone, public		

Abbreviations applicable only to 1:10 000/1:10 560 or 6 INCHES to 1 MILE

Ch	Church	GP	Guide Post	TCB	Telephone Call Box
F Sta	Fire Station	P	Pole or Post	TCP	Telephone Call Post
Fn	Fountain	S	Stone	Y	Youth Hostel

Maps and Mapping

Most early maps of the area covered by this guide were published on a county basis, and if you wish to follow their development in detail R. V. Tooley's *Maps and Map Makers* will be found most useful. The first significant county maps were produced by Christopher Saxton in the 1570s, the whole of England and Wales being covered in only six years. Although he did not cover the whole country, John Norden, working at the end of the sixteenth century, was the first map-maker to show roads. In 1611-12, John Speed, making use of Saxton and Norden's pioneer work, produced his 'Theatre of the Empire of Great Britaine', adding excellent town plans, battle scenes, and magnificent coats of arms. The next great English map-maker was John Ogilby, and in 1675 he published Britannia, Volume I, in which all the roads of England and Wales were engraved on a scale of one inch to the mile, in a massive series of strip maps. From this time onwards, no map was published without roads, and throughout the eighteenth century, steady progress was made in accuracy, if not always in the beauty of presentation.

The first Ordnance Survey maps came about as a result of Bonnie Prince Charlie's Jacobite rebellion of 1745. It was, however, in 1791, following the successful completion of the military survey of Scotland by General Roy that the Ordnance Survey was formally established. The threat of invasion by Napoleon in the early nineteenth century spurred on the demand for accurate and detailed mapping for military purposes, and to meet this need the first Ordnance Survey one-inch map, covering part of Essex, was published in 1805 in a single colour. This was the first numbered sheet in the First Series of one-inch maps.

Over the next seventy years the one-inch map was extended to cover the whole of Great Britain. Reprints of some of these First Series maps incorporating various later nineteenth century amendments, have been published by David & Charles. The reprinted sheets covering most of our area are Numbers 7, 8, 11, 12 and 15.

The Ordnance Survey's one-inch maps evolved through a number of 'Series' and 'Editions', to the Seventh Series which was replaced in 1974 by the metric 1:50 000 scale Landranger Series. Between the First Series one-inch and the current Landranger maps many changes in style, format, content and purpose have taken place. Colour, for example, first appeared with the timid use of light brown for hill shading on the 1889 one-inch sheets. By 1892 as many as five colours were being used for this scale and at one stage the Seventh Series was being printed in no less than ten colours. Recent developments in 'process printing' – a technique in which four basic colours produce almost any required tint – are now used to produce Ordnance Survey Landranger and other map series. Through the years the one-inch Series has gradually turned away from its military origins and has developed to meet a wider user demand. The modern detailed full colour Landranger maps at 1:50 000 scale incorporate Rights of Way and Tourist Information and are much used for both leisure and business purposes. To compare the old and new approach to changing demand, see the two map extracts of Keswick on the following pages.

Modern Ordnance Survey Maps of the Area

The Lake District is covered by Ordnance Survey 1:50 000 scale (1¼ inches to 1 mile) Landranger map sheets 89, 90, 91, 96 and 97. These all purpose maps are packed full of information to help you explore the area. Viewpoints, picnic sites, places of interest, caravan and camping sites are shown as are public rights of way information such as footpaths and bridleways. For a single map covering the area Ordnance Survey also publishes a Tourist Map of the Lake District at 1 inch to 1 mile scale.

To examine the Lake District in more detail and especially if you are planning walks, Ordnance Survey Outdoor Leisure Maps at 1:25 000 scale (2½ inches to 1 mile) are ideal. Four Outdoor Leisure Maps cover the main Lake District National Park area as follows:-

Sheet 4 – NW Area showing Ennerdale and Derwent

Sheet 5 – NE Area showing Ullswater and Haweswater

Sheet 6 – SW Area showing Wast Water and Coniston

Sheet 7 – SE Area showing Windermere and Kendal

These Outdoor Leisure Maps are now also available together in an attractive boxed set. Standard series Pathfinder maps also at 1:25 000 scale cover the remainder of the Lake District area.

To look at the area surrounding the Lake District, the Ordnance Survey Routemaster Sheet 5 (Northern England) at 1 inch to 4 miles scale will prove most useful. An alternative will be found in the form of the OS Motoring Atlas of Great Britain at the larger scale of 1 inch to 3 miles.

To place the area in a historical context the following Ordnance Survey Historical Maps and Guides will also be useful: 'Ancient Britain' and 'Roman Britain'.

Ordnance Survey maps are available from official agents and most booksellers and newsagents. The local agent is:

Westmorland Gazette,
22 Strickland Gate,
Kendal.
Telephone: 0539 20555

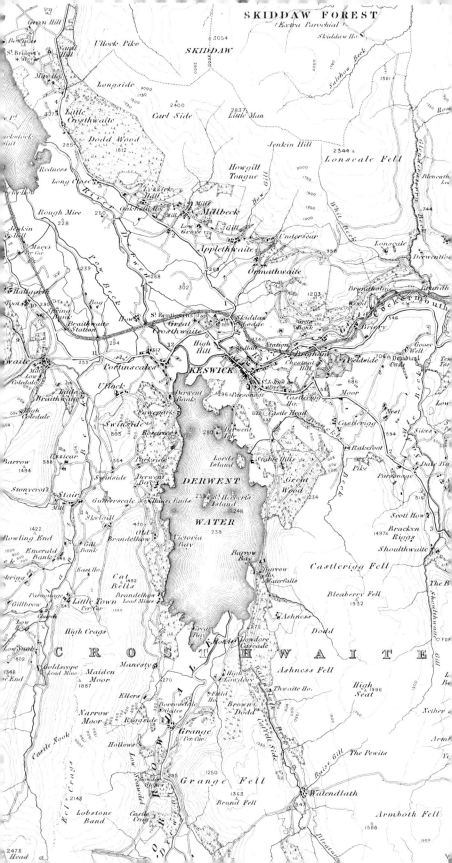

◄

Early One Inch Map. This is an extract from the 1866 edition of the Ordnance Survey One-inch map. It shows Keswick to be an important town with its own railway station and at the confluence of a number of main roads.

These early One-inch maps were remarkable for the amount of detail and the number of names which they carried. The portrayal of the region's mountains and dales was ingeniously executed by finely-drawn contours, their heights clearly labelled in imperial feet.

►

Modern 1 : 50 000 Landranger Map. This extract shows the same area around Keswick and is taken from the modern 1 : 50 000 Landranger map (sheet 89) the metric successor to the old One-inch. Colour is now used to distinguish woods and water and to show at a glance the different classes of roads. The addition of tourist symbols and information illustrates just one of many uses made of modern Ordnance Survey maps.

The countryside has changed cosiderably in the years between the two maps. Keswick has lost its railway. The course of the track is still shown however on the map.

Index

INDEX